D0812618

WILLIAM F. MAAG LIBRARY
YOUNGSTOWN STATE UNIVERSITY

Communicating Naturally in a Second Language

Communicating Naturally in a Second Language

Theory and practice in language teaching

Wilga M. Rivers

Harvard University

WITHDRAWN

Cambridge University Press

Cambridge
London   New York   New Rochelle
Melbourne   Sydney

Published by the Press Syndicate of the University of Cambridge
The Pitt Building, Trumpington Street, Cambridge CB2 1RP
32 East 57th Street, New York, NY 10022, USA
296 Beaconsfield Parade, Middle Park, Melbourne 3206, Australia

© Cambridge University Press 1983

First published 1983

Printed in the United States of America

Library of Congress Cataloging in Publication Data
Rivers, Wilga M.
Communicating naturally in a second language.
Bibliography: p.
Includes index.
1. Language and languages – Study and teaching.
I. Title.
P51.R5   1983   418'.007   82–23620
ISBN 0 521 25401 9 hard covers
ISBN 0 521 27417 6 paperback

Contents

P
51
. R5
1983

WILLIAM F. MAAG LIBRARY
YOUNGSTOWN STATE UNIVERSITY

Preface

How varied is the language teaching enterprise! The readers of this book have, or will have, students of all ages, of all kinds of cultural and educational backgrounds, with varied reasons for wanting to acquire a second language (some frankly pragmatic and utilitarian, others cultural or personal). Their students learn the language in short courses, intensive courses, or in long sequences. In their native languages, some are literate, some illiterate. Some are migrants, some refugees, some small children, some retired persons, some college students. Some love languages and all kinds of verbal activities; for others the learning of a language is a chore from which they have found no way of escaping. The teachers are an equally diverse group: Some have been trained as language teachers; others have drifted into it because they know the language well; still others have moved over from the teaching of social studies, elementary school reading, or some career outside of education. Some are well informed on research in language learning and related areas; some are neophytes. How can one book address all of these needs?

First of all, second-language teachers should be thoughtful professionals, not mere day laborers. Knowledge that can help them understand their students better, and the way they learn various aspects of language use, is proliferating in a number of tangential disciplines. Teachers absorbed in their daily, demanding tasks have neither the time nor the energy to seek this information in research reports and books that are not readily accessible to them. This book endeavors to make their task easier. From conclusions of experts in linguistics; psycholinguistics; sociolinguistics; cognitive psychology; studies of personality, motivation, and child development; educational theory; and curriculum experimentation I have drawn together the most pertinent findings. I have tried to explain these clearly, while demonstrating in practical recommendations how this information can be of use to second-language teachers — stimulating them, I hope, to imaginative efforts to incorporate this new knowledge into their own teaching. I have tried to give them both a historical perspective and a panorama of the present scene. For those facing unexpected difficulties in a new situation, I hope the theoretical notions brought forward will help them to see how some of their most baffling problems can be approached. In second-language teaching, we cannot expect to find ready-made solutions that we can apply without reflection. Each situation must be approached according to its own logic, and we are frequently on our own as we decide what to do next.

The theme of this book is centered in Chapter 8: "The Natural and the Normal in Language Learning." Student learning is central; teaching is facilitative of learning. To be able to communicate naturally, students must know the forms of the language native speakers normally use in all kinds of circumstances. In other words, they must possess linguistic skills they can use to express their own intentions and feelings and understand those of others, whose cultural background and ways of conveying meanings may be very different.

This book will be useful in methods courses, for in-service training, in refresher courses and summer institutes for practicing teachers, in training courses for teaching assistants in colleges, in the departmental library, or for an individual teacher's private reading. It can provide the applicational element in a theoretical course in linguistics or psycholinguistics directed toward teachers. It will bring the untrained teacher (and one long in the profession) up to date with the field, providing a wealth of ideas for self-training and improvement.

Many extra readings are indicated in the notes for those who wish to continue with a specialized study of any particular topic or issue. Like the rest of the book, these provide an overview of earlier work as well as explication and evaluation of current trends with which the teacher should be conversant. (There is much to be learned from our predecessors as well as our contemporaries.) The notes are placed at the end of the book for easy consultation. In this way these constitute a more useful reference tool. The reader should note that the Bibliography comprises only books; references to articles can be found by looking for the author's name in the Index.

For further study, cross-references are given to the parallel volume, *Speaking in Many Tongues: Essays in Foreign-Language Teaching*, 3d ed. (Cambridge: Cambridge University Press, 1983), in which I have dealt in greater depth with many subjects alluded to briefly in this book; and to my methods books: *Teaching Foreign-Language Skills*, 2d ed. (Chicago: University of Chicago Press, 1981), and the *Practical Guides to the Teaching of French, German, Spanish, English as a Second or Foreign Language, and Hebrew* (Rivers, 1975; and Rivers et al., 1975, 1976, 1978, in preparation). The latter are referred to as the *Practical Guides*.

The questions at the end of each chapter should provoke reflection and stimulate discussion within a class group or among colleagues. Many will be useful for term papers or short investigative projects;

others will encourage readers to design their own activities in order to direct their language teaching toward more natural communication.

I have had the good fortune during my career to have met some inspirers of teachers and lovers of students, whose influence on me has been incalculable. Here I am thinking particularly of Professor Wilfred H. Frederick and Miss Dorothy J. Ross, who shaped so much of my approach. Much of what I have written has been inspired by the many teachers and students with whom I have interacted over the years – as colleagues, in seminars and at meetings in many places, or through correspondence. Each of these in one way or another has led me to reflect more deeply on our collective task. To all of you, wherever you may now be, I owe grateful thanks. Since "I am a part of all that I have met,"[1] I am I because you are you. This, then, is your book as well as mine.

My especial thanks must go to Ann Julie Boruvka and Reed Wood-house for their devotion, friendship, and untiring assistance in the many tasks book production involves. They, with me, would wish this book to go far and be a help to many.

Wilga M. Rivers

Harvard University
Cambridge, Massachusetts
November, 1982

1 Linguistics, psychology, and language teaching: an overview

The "miracle" of language acquisition

Parents and teachers alike are struck by the ease with which small children acquire language – the language or languages of their parents, their grandparents, or their playmates. They compare this with the often painfully slow and discouraging acquisition of second or third languages by teenagers or adults and wonder how one can replicate natural language learning in school situations. They want to see school learners using the language with some spontaneity and confidence, and this also is seen as a desirable goal by the learners themselves. But how to achieve this goal in a reasonable amount of time, before discouragement sets in, has been, and continues to be, a major preoccupation of language teachers who care about motivation and the students' satisfaction in learning.

Linguistics or psychology?

The obvious disciplines to which to turn for help in achieving this goal are linguistics and psychology: the sciences that investigate respectively the content and the process of language learning. In other words, we ask "*What is language?*" so that we may see how best to present language material to facilitate student learning; or we ask "*How do individuals acquire a language* so that they can use it effectively in life situations?" and then try to apply answers developed by behavioral research in psychology to language learning in and out of the classroom. The importance of both of these questions, and the many unresolved issues that linguists and psycholinguists face, have, rightly or wrongly, kept language pedagogy, as an applied field, in a ferment for nearly half a century, to go back no further. Linguistics is an ancient preoccupation of scholars and a relatively

Revised version of an article that appeared as "Psychology and Linguistics as Bases of Language Pedagogy," in F. M. Grittner, ed., *Learning a Second Language*, 79th Yearbook of the National Society for the Study of Education, Part 2 (Chicago: University of Chicago Press, 1981), pp. 44–66.

young science, as is psychology. Modern psychology and modern linguistics have both burst into full vigor since the latter part of the nineteenth century. They have thus shared in the evolving spirit of the times that can be seen through history to influence scientists in various disciplines at approximately the same period, as new findings radically modify previously unquestioned theoretical models. We will now trace the influence of the switches and changes in theoretical orientations in linguistics and psychology on the teaching of second languages.

Language use as patterned oral behavior

In the 1920s and 1930s, most behavioral psychologists were committed to a *nonintrospective study of human behavior*, which concentrated on what could be objectively observed, described, and measured, without resort to the presumption of inner motives or innate mechanisms as determinants. Since much of overt human behavior takes the form of actions repeated in similar circumstances (that is, in response to similar stimuli), learning theorists of this period *focused on habits* and tried to determine how they are acquired. They observed and measured events that co-occur when habits are formed (*stimuli* and *responses*) and manipulated the consequences of responses to study the effect these had on repeated occurrence. They tried to find out why habits sometimes disappeared. Extending Thorndike's work on reward and punishment (his law of effect, elaborated at the turn of the century), *reinforcement theorists* maintained that an action was most likely to recur when pleasurable consequences followed immediately upon its appearance, and that the continuation of this sequence of stimulus-response-reward increased the probability of specific actions recurring in response to particular stimuli, thus establishing a habit pattern.

Language behavior was regarded by reinforcement theorists as being the same in kind as other forms of behavior and therefore subject to the same laws of learning. In this paradigm, language acquisition would be described as follows. As an infant is babbling, it utters a sound that resembles the appropriate word for some person or object nearby. This utterance is rewarded or reinforced with approving noises and smiles from the person attending to the child, and as a consequence the probability of the emission of the same groups of sounds in a similar situation is increased. With repeated reinforcement a habit is established, and the child continues to name the person or object in the same way. Inappropriate responses disappear through lack of reinforcement. As more combinations of sounds are reinforced and as the use of these is generalized to similar stimuli, the child learns to combine verbal responses in more and more complex ways. Oral responses are gradually refined through differential reinforcement in actual communication situations.

During the years when the reinforcement theorists were elaborating this model of learning, *structural linguists* were taking specimens of language as emitted (often for little-known languages, such as the American Indian languages) and endeavoring to describe the regularities of their phonological and grammatical patterning, without having to resort to the nuances of meaning particular speakers intended to convey. They were thus able to bypass in their descriptions of linguistic behavior the murky quagmire of semantics, which, as Bloomfield expressed it, "is equivalent to the sum total of human knowledge."[1] Following the lead of the cultural anthropologists of the period, the structuralists viewed language use as *a set of habits acquired within the social group* in which the child was growing up. The set of arbitrary vocal symbols that constituted the language of the group was clearly encountered in *spoken* form first, and this was the form acquired by the child. Because through the ages written language in many cultures has been (or is) nonexistent, the spoken language was regarded by the structuralists as of primary importance, writing being considered "merely a way of recording language by means of visible marks."[2]

A number of structural linguists were language teachers in universities. During World War II, others became interested in language teaching when the American defense authorities called on the linguists to help develop as rapidly as possible a large pool of interpreters for different languages, many of which were not generally taught in academic institutions.

Not surprisingly, linguists trained to describe and analyze recurring surface forms of language, without necessarily having recourse to meaning as the key to use, found compatible a psychological approach to habit formation that similarly did not require presumptions of unobservable mental processes at work in determining behavior. The methods the structural linguists as language teachers developed for language learning similarly emphasized overt patterned behavior of responses to stimuli. This combination of habit-formation techniques became known as the audiolingual approach.[3] Because of its success in the army training programs, the techniques of the audiolingual approach gradually became the predominant methodology in teaching English to foreign students, who were flocking into the universities. In the late fifties it began to spread to foreign-language classrooms in colleges and high schools. It retained the emphasis on spoken language of the structuralists and on teaching the language as it is spoken in everyday circumstances by native speakers.

The audiolingual approach

The hallmark of audiolingual teaching is emphasis on presentation of the language in its spoken form first. Only after practice in the aural-oral mode (first listening, then producing utterances) are students presented with a graphic representation of what they have been learning. They then read before they write.

Initial language study usually takes the form of *memorization of dialogues*, which are composed of useful situational utterances that can be varied to meet a number of conversational needs within the foreign culture. Students learn to give responses to the stimuli of the dialogue sentences, at first in the exact form memorized, then with variations. Grammar is learned through *drilling in substitution, expansion, or conversion* of elements in the language patterns.[4] These drills often concentrate on points of contrast between the structure of the native language and that of the foreign language, as being areas of probable interference from well-established first-language habits. Explanation, which usually comes after the initial practice, is kept to the minimum required for comprehension of the working of particular structures. In this pattern or structure drilling, quick-fire response with *immediate confirmation of the correct form* is the focus.

Reading is introduced systematically, beginning with the reading of what has been learned orally, with careful attention to sound-symbol correspondences. Texts move through various levels of reading difficulty until the student can read all kinds of materials. *Writing* acts as a supportive exercise to oral learning in the early stages. Translation does not figure prominently in learning activities, except that native-language stimuli are used occasionally to elicit responses in the foreign language during structure drill. A few written exercises may involve translation when this is the most direct way to elicit complex responses, such as idiomatic expressions, which it is preferable not to analyze.

The objective of the audiolingual approach is to provide students, as soon as possible, with *useful building blocks* of language material (usually in the dialogues), which they can use in communication and from which they can generalize by analogy to parallel forms and functions. These useful expressions and structures are to be learned to a level of automatic production through saturation practice. *Choral response* is frequently elicited in class to provide every student with many opportunities to produce acceptable responses in a situation where confirmation of the right response is immediately available. *Practice in the language laboratory*, or with recorded cassettes, also gives students ample opportunity to practice structures in a stimulus-response format, with immediate confirmation by the recorded model of the correct response. Both the learning materials and the classroom situation are structured in such a way that the student rarely makes mistakes, and in this way correct habits are presumed to be formed. To ensure transfer to real-life conversational situations, all language material is presented with *authentic native accents and intonation* at a speed of utterance that is normal for speakers of that language. The ultimate aim is for students to achieve near-native mastery of the language, and this presumes a long sequence of study, even though quite spectacular results in language use within structured bounds can be observed very early in the learning process.[5]

Modifying the audiolingual approach

In the early 1960s, criticisms were leveled against the audiolingual approach.[6] These focused on the overemphasis on tedious, mechanistic processes to which the student was not expected to make any spontaneous, personal contribution. Critics questioned whether real learning could take place when students were giving automatic responses in drills, *without understanding the crucial element* they were practicing or its relationship to other features of the language system. It was found that students who could use with facility language material in the exact form in which it had been practiced, in dialogues or drills, were at a loss to adapt this material for the expression of a multitude of personal meanings in communication with others. The value of learning by *trial and error* began to be reemphasized. Structured situations in which students would rarely make errors were found to provide insufficient preparation for spontaneous expression, which requires flexibility, alertness, and audacity in extending what one has learned to new contexts. Teachers began to realize that if students were to communicate, they needed practice in communicating *personal messages*, not just formulas presented by the teacher or the textbook writer. Finally, *individual differences* in students received fresh consideration. It began to be recognized, once again, that some students learn efficiently through oral materials, whereas others need the support of a visual representation; some students feel traumatized when they are expected to produce rapid foreign-language responses, while others feel stimulated.

As a result of these criticisms, modifications were made to prevailing audiolingual practices. More explanation was provided before or during practice. More attention was paid to the creation in the classroom of situations as close to real-life language interaction as possible, and new materials attempted to present the culture in which the language is embedded in a more authentic way. Above all, teachers felt the need to relax the tension of early language learning. They sought to introduce more variety of activity, more friendliness and humor, within an atmosphere in which the students felt at ease with the teacher and with each other, in what could otherwise be an ego-threatening situation.

The mentalistic trend

The tide in linguistics and psychology soon turned definitively. Linguistic theorists declared themselves to be frankly "mentalistic," and cognitive psychology became active in studying processes of the mind. Perception, memory, thinking, how meaning is encoded and expressed, and how information is processed became areas of major concern. Languages were no longer regarded by the linguists as distinct sets of arbitrary vocal symbols, nor as systems of habits acquired through conditioning by the psychologists. Transformational-generative linguistic theory pointed out that apparent similarity of surface forms of a language in different utterances may camouflage important differences in meaning. Hence, indiscriminate selection of surface features for drill exercises can result in students' making serious errors when they begin to extend by analogy the use of structures that have been practiced in a mechanical, unthinking fashion.

Chomsky, the protagonist of the revolution in linguistic theory, categorically rejected the notion that language was acquired by children through a form of conditioning dependent on reinforcement or reward. He asserted that children come into the world with innate language-learning abilities, a *faculté de langage* that takes the form of a language acquisition device (LAD) that proceeds by hypothesis-testing. Consequently, children acquire a language by making hypotheses about the form of the grammar of the language with which they are surrounded. They then compare this with their innate knowledge of possible grammars based on the principles of universal grammar. In this way, the child internalizes a knowledge of the grammar of the native language (this Chomsky calls "competence"), and this competence makes language use (or "performance") possible. Language use is thus rule-governed behavior that enables speakers to create new utterances that conform to the rules they have internalized.[7]

The terms "rule-governed behavior," "creative language use," and "hypothesis-testing" soon replaced "building in habits" and "saturation practice" as the catchwords of language teaching.

Rule-governed behavior

The term "rule-governed behavior" as a description of language use aroused the interest of those teachers who had criticized the inductive procedures of the audiolingual approach, which they felt neglected the teaching of grammar. They proposed a return to systematic presentation and explanation of grammar rules first. This, they contended, would involve the reasoning processes of the students in their learning of a language, in contrast to what they considered to be the "mindless" drilling of audiolingual classes. Emphasis on explanations of grammatical functioning was a major feature of what came to be known as *cognitive code-learning*.

Chastain claimed as the "one basic tenet of the cognitive approach" that "students never be expected to meet new structures prior to the explanation of those forms." "The term 'cognition,'" he continued, "implies proceeding from mental understanding and awareness to practice; from studying a structure to seeing it used in context."[8] Chastain's deductive order of learning was the following: step 1, comprehension of new grammatical concepts, which are presented deductively; step 2, practice in selection of linguistic forms to fit the context in exercises; step 3, the study of reading and listening materials, with some opportunity provided for students to produce messages intended to communicate their thoughts to others.[9] This approach put language analysis before language use and instruction by the teacher ahead of student practice of forms, presumably providing a more "cognitive" approach to language learning. That a deductive instructional approach is more "cognitive" than the inductive, discovery approach to grammar of audiolingual methodology (and the direct method) is difficult to sustain on the basis of psychological evidence, since *inductive thinking requires just as much cognitive processing as deduction*. Moreover, Chomsky's concept of "rules" in rule-governed behavior in no way resembles the explanations of language functioning in traditional foreign-language textbooks. Chomsky's rules, "of great abstractness and intricacy," are inherent in the structure of the language and operate below the level of conscious awareness.[10] However, the spirit of the times was such that these facts were usually ignored in the rush to be in the vanguard.

Carroll, who had first advanced the term "cognitive code-learning" in an article in 1965,[11] came forward again in 1971 to express his alarm at the growing tendency to oppose "rule-governed behavior" and "habits" as incompatible concepts in language learning. He de-

7

WILLIAM F. MAAG LIBRARY
YOUNGSTOWN STATE UNIVERSITY

fined a "habit" as "any learned disposition to perceive, behave, or perform in a certain manner under specified circumstances." He further maintained that "to the extent that an individual's language behavior conforms to the habits of the speech community of which he is a member, we can say that his behavior is 'rule-governed.' " To Carroll, *a rule is an abstraction, but a habit is what has actually been learned;* in other words, "the notion of 'habit' is much more fundamental, psychologically, than the notion of 'rule.' "[12] Carroll's 1971 article was heeded by those who had ears to hear, but overlooked or not discovered by others.

Creative language use

Chomsky drew attention to the fact that most sentences one utters have never been heard before in that particular form. They have been created by the speakers in conformity with the grammar they have internalized (the individual's "competence," in Chomsky's terms). Miller supported this viewpoint graphically, with the following explanation:

> If you interrupt a speaker at some randomly chosen instant, there will be, on the average, about ten words that form grammatical and meaningful continuations. . . . A simple English sentence can easily run to a length of twenty words, so elementary arithmetic tells us that there must be at least 10^{20} such sentences that a person who knows English must know how to deal with. Compare this productive potential with the 10^4 or 10^5 individual words we know – the reproductive component of our theory – and the discrepancy is dramatically illustrated. Putting it differently, it would take 100,000,000,000 centuries (one thousand times the estimated age of the earth) to utter all the admissible twenty-word sentences of English. Thus, the probability that you might have heard any particular twenty-word sentence before is negligible. Unless it is a cliché, every sentence must come to you as a novel combination of morphemes. Yet you can interpret it at once if you know the English language.[13]

Statements like these caused teachers to reevaluate the audiolingual technique of requiring students to memorize long dialogue sentences that they would then practice using in the precise form they had memorized. Where dialogues were used, greater emphasis was laid on using dialogue sentences as a springboard for creating new utterances – the students would use the phrases they had learned, and variations of these phrases, to express new meanings. Teachers realized that students needed to understand the operations of the grammatical system if they were to use it effectively to generate new utterances. It began to be realized that, if students were to develop flexibility in creating new combinations to fit different circumstances, they needed encouragement in using, from the beginning stages, the small amount of language they had acquired to express personal meanings. More opportunities were provided in class for student-sustained discussion and for extempore dialogue in situations that simulated those in which students might find themselves in the second culture.[14] Materials writers changed their approach to dialogues and presented much shorter exchanges of six or eight lines, from which students could memorize useful building blocks of language that they could adapt and vary to express meanings of their own devising.

Hypothesis-testing

Chomsky's theory of an innate language acquisition device that proceeds by hypothesis-testing had considerable influence for a while on studies of the acquisition of a first language by children. Researchers interested in the acquisition of second and third languages followed suit. If there was an innate LAD, was it also operative, they wondered, when a second language was acquired, and, if so, until what age? If the LAD were still operative, should the teaching of second languages seek to recreate the kind of situation in which first languages were learned and expect students to pass through similar stages of development?

Brown discovered that children learning English as a first language acquired the first fourteen morphemes in a certain order. For instance, the child subjects, Adam, Eve, and Sarah, were observed to acquire the *-ing* morpheme (as in "eating," "walking") very early, and then the functors "in" and "on." Next came the indicator of the plural of nouns, the irregular past of common verbs (e.g., "went"), the possessive "s," the uncontractible copula ("Where is it?"), the definite and indefinite articles, the regular past tense form, the third person regular form, and the third personal irregular; the auxiliary "be" form came lower down the list and, once again, the uncontractible form was acquired before the contractible form, which was acquired a little later than the contractible copula. This order correlated very highly with that obtained by the de Villiers.[15] Both Brown and the de Villiers considered the morpheme order obtained to reflect the degree of grammatical and semantic complexity the child had to master.

Some early researchers in second-language acquisition looked for a similar order of acquisition of grammatical morphemes of English by second-language (L_2) learners. They felt that this would show that first- and second-language acquisition were similar processes, follow-

9

ing the same developmental path and using comparable strategies. This would, they considered, demonstrate that the LAD was still operative for L_2 acquisition. Results showed that the same morphemes as those for L_1 were among the first acquired by L_2 learners, but in a somewhat different order. (The order of acquisition reported for L_2 was considered by some to be an artifact of the measuring instrument.[16])

Of interest in this discussion is the fact that the order of acquisition reported for L_1 was found to correlate highly with some features of the language L_1 learners were hearing from their mothers and other caregivers.[17] Furthermore, a study of the morphemes listed reveals that they are essential for the functions language performs for the young child, being related to the "here and now," to the position, quantity, and possession of objects, and their relevance at the moment ("the dog"). It is not surprising that perceptually salient features of English, like "ing," are acquired before nonsalient features, like the contractible copula and contractible auxiliary ("It's a dog"; "Mummy's here"), especially since "-ing" is one of the earliest features relevant to the child's activities. That the innate structure of the LAD is as concrete and nonuniversal as the particular surface structure morphemes of individual languages seems highly improbable. (Chomsky spoke of abstract features of universal grammar as being innate.) To base any language-learning theory on a presumed natural order of acquisition of morphemes by L_2 learners seems to ignore the fact that morphemes of specific languages will be acquired as uses of language dictate, and it is these functions that are being acquired. When using language for different functions is emphasized, as in communicative teaching, the necessary morphemes will follow. The acquisition of language essential for the performance of these functions should be the central concern of L_2 teaching.

L_1 acquisition researchers also observed that children seemed to pass through a series of interim grammars, from simple to more complex, as they tested hypotheses about the form of the language they were learning. This phenomenon interested L_2 acquisition researchers, who began to use the term "interlanguage" to describe the systematic language an L_2 learner was using at a particular stage of learning, that is, the learner's version of L_2, which deviated in certain ways from the target forms.[18] This interlanguage was regarded as an indication that L_2 learners too were testing hypotheses about the form of the grammar of the new language. Presumably, when interlanguage speakers produced utterances that were not comprehended by speakers of the language, they would reject their former hypotheses and develop others, gradually bringing their interlanguage into closer conformity to the accepted forms of the L_2.

Controversy raged as to whether deviant forms in the interlanguage were the result of interference, or negative transfer, from the L_1 of the L_2 learner or were developmental errors of the same type as those to be observed in the interim grammars of young children learning this language as a first language. Some researchers, opposed to a habit-formation view of language acquisition, refused, on theoretical grounds, to accept interference or negative transfer explanations for L_2 errors that showed similar patterning to L_1 surface forms. (Positive transfer is more difficult to distinguish from new learning and so is less frequently discussed.) Later, longitudinal L_2 acquisition studies[19] did bring forward examples of what certainly looked like negative transfer by learners of L_1 features in L_2 use (or at least of L_1 grammatical and semantic concepts), and this phenomenon, so frequently observed by classroom teachers, again became a research issue. (Some of these errors become ingrained or "fossilized.") Corder has suggested that what appears to be interference from L_1 language knowledge may be the result of testing the hypothesis that L_2 structure and semantic distinctions are similar to those of L_1.[20] It may, on the other hand, be an example of the common learning strategy of drawing on what one knows (in this case, L_1 syntax and semantics) and adapting it, when one is unsure of the L_2 system.

A continual thorn in the side of the hypothesis-testing theorists has been the persistence in L_2 speech of "fossilized errors," that is, incorrect forms that remain in the speech and writing of L_2 learners for years, despite the fact that they have been taught the rules and appear to understand them. (Sometimes they have even taught these rules to others.) In hypothesis-testing theory, a serious or continued disconfirmation of the hypothesis leads one to seek a different hypothesis that fits the facts and to adjust one's testing accordingly. The fact that L_2 learners are unable to do this, often despite awareness of the nature of the discrepancy and a strong desire to produce the correct form, throws doubt on hypothesis-testing as a sufficient explanation of the phenomena of L_2 learning.

Corder and others consider that pronunciation, as distinct from grammatical structure and semantic distinctions, may be acquired by a process of habit-formation and that pronunciation errors may be considered examples of interference from well-established L_1 articulatory processes. It is evident that native-like pronunciation is very difficult for older L_2 learners to acquire, even after much effort and study of articulatory differences.[21]

The hypothesis-testing and interlanguage (interim grammars) approach had considerable influence on classroom practice. Teachers trained in audiolingual techniques had learned to structure classroom situations so that the students would make the fewest possible errors. They did this by using drills where the logic of the exercise led the students to produce correct responses along the lines of the patterns presented, by immediately correcting any errors that were produced, and by prompting in a low voice when the student hesitated. With more emphasis on creative language use in the classroom, they were encountering more student errors. Now hypothesis-testing and interlanguage theorists were telling them that these errors were a natural part of the language-learning process, helpful to students in providing opportunities to test their hypotheses about the functioning of the L_2 system, and helpful to teachers in revealing to them the interim grammars on which students were basing their utterances and the strategies they were employing to express meaning with the meager means at their disposal. As a result, teachers became more tolerant of errors in L_2 production and began to experiment with unobtrusive means of helping students to improve without overt correction, by the use, for instance, of expansions and restatement of students' deviant utterances.

Natural language learning

The convergence of these three insights from Chomskyan theory has led to the revival of an older approach to the learning of another language. Called "natural language learning," it recalls efforts in the middle of the nineteenth century to simulate in the classroom an environment that will approximate the context in which children acquire their first language, as they create utterances to express their own thoughts.[22]

In its latest form, natural language learning does not overlook the need that many adolescent or adult learners feel for the security of structured learning. *Students are encouraged to study the grammar of the language out of class* as they feel the need for it (with programmed or individualized materials from the textbook or through language laboratory practice), so that class time can be devoted to *communicative interaction*, which is considered the more important activity. This means skill-getting out of class and skill-using in group activities in class.

The basic principle of natural language learning is the distinction Krashen has drawn between *acquisition* of a language ("through the pores" learning) and *learning* (in the formal cognitive sense, with teacher or structured materials). Acquisition, it is claimed, takes place during episodes of authentic communication in the language and is considered to be the source of the student's ability to use the language in unstructured interaction. Formal learning of the language, in this hypothesis, may contribute to the self-monitoring, or self-editing, of output that sometimes occurs when speakers have time to reflect and focus on the form of their utterances. Krashen considers that formal learning of features of the language or practice in the use of these features is of very little importance in the development of communicative ability for most language learners, whereas active interaction in the language is, and should be, the major activity in the classroom.[23]

In this approach, much listening to the language is advocated before production is expected or encouraged (since first-language learners typically develop comprehension long before they speak). Early listening is usually accompanied by some form of activity. Recommended techniques are physical responses to instructions given in the new language, as in Asher's Total Physical Response (TPR),[24] and simple verbal or nonverbal responses to pictures or to comments by the teacher on what other students are wearing or doing (as in the direct method). The visible and tangible makes the linguistic input comprehensible to the students, who are not expected to respond verbally, in other than one-word responses, until they comprehend and feel ready to contribute of their own accord. (Terrell suggests that the prespeaking period for elementary school children may be as long as several months, for high school students at least a month, and for college students a week or so.[25])

The proponents of natural language learning maintain that, through these techniques, the innate capacities to acquire a language that all individuals possess will be tapped; students will have ample opportunities to test their hypotheses about the nature of the new language; their interim grammars will be accepted and tolerated while they are refining their hypotheses through experience in communication; and they will get much practice in creating new utterances in meaningful contexts (a process also called "creative construction"). In order to succeed, this approach requires a low-anxiety situation where students feel at home with each other and the instructor and are willing to express themselves freely. To maintain this atmosphere, Terrell advocates that students not be corrected during acquisition activities,[26] although reconstruction and expansion of students' deviant utterances by the instructor in a conversational, unpressured mode are used. When students begin to speak, much use is made of enjoyable and natural activities, like games, problem-solving tasks, sharing experiences, and discussing slides or artifacts – all of which are activities that concentrate the students' attention on meaning, not form of utterance.

Meaning in sociocultural contexts

Sociolinguistics developed rapidly during the 1960s and 1970s. Concentrating on language as it is used for *communication within the*

13

social group, it employs the concepts and research techniques of sociology and social psychology, as well as those of linguistics. Research in this field has brought to the attention of linguists and language teachers important information about language in organized communicative interaction within a community, domains of language use, speech varieties within a community, language behavior of different ethnic groups, bilingualism and multilingualism, and language planning.

Communicative competence

Sociolinguists and psycholinguists soon found Chomsky's competence–performance distinction to be too restricted to account for language in use. To Chomsky, competence was the internalized knowledge of the system of syntactic and phonological rules of the language that the ideal speaker-hearer possesses in the native language; and performance was language in use by the individual (full of hesitations, false starts, and convoluted syntax), which was not a faithful reflection of the individual's competence. Consequently, to Chomsky performance was of little theoretical interest. His critics, however, felt that there were aspects of what he labeled "performance" that were obviously rule-governed, although the rules to which the speaker was conforming were not syntactic, in Chomsky's sense of the term. They felt that these aspects of language behavior, which were related to the sociocultural context in which the speaker-hearer was operating, should be considered part of the language user's competence.

Soon the term "communicative competence" was coined to cover this extended notion of competence. Hymes described communicative competence as "what a speaker needs to know to communicate effectively in culturally significant settings."[27] According to Hymes, a child learning a language acquires, along with a system of grammar, "a system of its use, regarding persons, places, purposes, other modes of communication,...patterns of the sequential use of language in conversation, address, standard routines."[28] Hence, the most important task for sociolinguistic research was the identification of the "rules, patterns, purposes and consequences of language use" and an account of their interrelations.[29] A theoretical formulation of communicative competence, Hymes believed, should take account of whether something was formally possible (i.e., could be expressed with the linguistic means available); whether it was feasible in virtue of the means of implementation available (the psycholinguistic aspect); whether it was appropriate in relation to a context (the sociolinguistic aspect); and whether it was in fact done, actually performed, and what its doing entailed (the reality aspect).[30]

14

Hymes's emphasis on the importance of context in determining appropriate patterns of behavior, both linguistic and extralinguistic, appealed to teachers who found an overemphasis on accurate use of language structures to be confining and unrealistic. Although the term "communicative competence" was at first batted around as though it meant "creative language use," an understanding of Hymes's concepts soon began to permeate second-language teaching circles. Teachers and writers of materials began to recognize the fact that students needed to be able to do more than express imposed ideas in correct grammatical form, or their own ideas in incorrect forms, as they struggled to express meanings for which they did not yet possess the linguistic means. If they were really to communicate with speakers of the language, they needed also to know the *culturally acceptable ways of interacting orally with others* – appropriate levels of language for different situations and different relationships; conversational openers and gambits and when it was appropriate to use these;[31] how to negotiate meaning in various circumstances, and when and how to use appropriate gestures and body language; the message content of pitch, loudness, and intonation patterns; the questions and comments that were acceptable and unacceptable in the culture; and the importance of distance in communicative encounters.[32]

Soon the study of the culture in which the second language is embedded became a preoccupation of second-language teachers. Teachers and students alike realized that, if this type of culturally based competence was to be acquired, lectures and readings were not enough. Students must also have opportunities to interact with native speakers in natural settings. Foreign-language teachers began to organize exchange and study-abroad programs (particularly in home-stay situations),[33] ethnic festivals, and language camps with native speakers, where communicative interaction might take place in authentic social contexts. Teaching aides were also recruited from nearby communities where the language was spoken to add authenticity to the classroom experience. Second-language students were encouraged to mingle with the local community, often through one-to-one contacts organized by the second-language department, group outings with speakers of the language, or phone friendships to encourage regular communicative practice. It was realized that liking people of other cultures and their ways could not be mandated, but tolerance and understanding of cultural differences could increase the individual's ability to cope with new circumstances.

Semantics and pragmatics

Meanwhile, some theoretical linguists had become conscious of the neglect in linguistic research of meaning and context, which were given summary treatment in Chomskyan theory. The case grammar of Fillmore,[34] the generative semantics of J. R. Ross, G. Lakoff, and J. D. McCawley,[35] and the meaning-structure grammar of Chafe[36] all considered semantics to be basic to any theoretical model of language. There being a thin line between semantics and pragmatics, the latter also rose in importance. Meaning was seen to depend to a large degree on the sociocultural contexts in which speech acts occurred.[37] Sociocultural aspects of language in use had been particularly stressed by the functionalists, who considered the *purposes language serves in normal interaction* to be basic to the determination of syntactic functions.[38]

These approaches soon influenced research in first-language acquisition. R. Brown[39] and I. M. Schlesinger,[40] for instance, found that children's early utterances could be more readily explained in semantic terms, such as agent, action, instrument, patient, or experiencer. Bruner and Halliday preferred to emphasize functions. "Use," said Bruner, "is a powerful determinant of rule structure,"[41] and Halliday analyzed his son Nigel's initial utterances in terms of distinct functions (instrumental, regulatory, interactional, personal, heuristic, imaginative, representational, and ritual).[42] Tough proposed as functions important to children 3 to 7 years old the following: self-maintaining, directing, reporting on present and past experiences, logical reasoning, predicting, projecting, and imagining.[43]

To language teachers, the functional approach seemed more promising for application in the classroom than the more abstract linguistic models we have discussed.[44] Classroom activities centered more and more on simulating interactional contexts, in which language might be used in a normal everyday way. Teachers began to recognize how artificial and stilted many language exercises were and set about adapting them so that they would reflect more authentic uses of language.[45] In this they were supported by materials writers. Textbooks soon began to provide more realistic activities, in which language could be used in a likely context.[46]

There were proposals to reconstruct the language syllabus so that learning communicative conventions would become as important as learning grammatical conventions. Wilkins proposed a notional syllabus, that is, a syllabus "organized in terms of the purposes for which people are learning language and the kinds of language performance that are necessary to meet those purposes."[47] A *notional syllabus*, as Wilkins conceived it, implies a careful analysis of particular communicative situations in order to identify what students should most usefully be able to communicate in those situations. Only then, Wilkins believes, can one decide the most appropriate linguistic forms to be learned by the students. "In short," he says, "the linguistic content is planned according to the semantic demands of the learner."[48] A notional syllabus, then, places "emphasis on the meanings expressed or the functions performed through language – in broad terms on the speaker's or writer's intentions."[49]

To meet the demands of a notional syllabus, Wilkins identifies three categories of meaning that must be taught: *semantico-grammatical or conceptual* (the formal features of the grammar and lexicon), *modal* (expressing attitude and degree of certainty), and *communicative function* (speech acts).[50] Each of these is important, and Wilkins insists that the structural component (implicit in the semantico-grammatical and modal categories) cannot be ignored. "The notion that an individual can develop other than a rudimentary communicative ability without an extensive mastery of the grammatical system," he says, "is absurd."[51] However, the orientation of the teaching is essentially toward the purposes and social uses of communication, rather than the understanding and acquisition of linguistic features.

A notional syllabus deals with such categories as time, quantity, space, relational meaning, judgment and evaluation, suasion, argument, rational enquiry and exposition, personal emotions, and emotional relations, rather than such traditional grammatical areas as definite and indefinite articles, moods, tenses, and relative and interrogative pronouns. For the learning sequence, Wilkins proposed *a cyclical, rather than linear, presentation* of concepts and functions, so that as students advance they will be learning to express the same semantic notions with greater finesse and nuance. *Role playing* becomes an important activity in this type of learning, and students are brought into immediate contact with authentic language in teaching materials.

Elaboration of a notional syllabus was undertaken by the language specialists of the Council of Europe, particularly to meet the needs of adults within the European Economic Community. A threshold level, or basic course, was developed that sets out in specific detail exactly what students with minimum requirements should know in order to communicate in particular situations.[52] Later, the threshold level materials were adapted to the needs of secondary schools and incorporated in television programs for a wider public.

In 1978, New York State issued a curriculum guide, *Modern Languages for Everyone*, which aimed at meeting the needs of foreign-language students who wished to learn a language with particular purposes in mind. This curriculum proposed a basic course that would be followed by a series of options: a four-skill sequence, a listening-speaking sequence, a reading-writing sequence, and special-interest courses (such as "French for Travelers," "German for Auto Mechanics," "Music and Dance in Hebrew," "Spanish for Community Service"). This curriculum culminated nearly a decade of experimentation in the schools with diversified options, minicourses, and the like.[53]

Language and cognition

In the early 1970s, some of the cognitive psychologists who had been working in areas of acquisition, production, and comprehension of language began to have doubts about the *psychological reality of the transformational-generative linguistic model*. A number of psychological experiments had been conducted to see whether such aspects of the model as transformations represented cognitive operations that language users actually performed and whether constituents of phrase structure were perceived as units when one listened to speech. Results indicated that listeners did assign to the language they were hearing a systematic structure that conformed with the rule system of the language. It also appeared that sentences that were more complex, involving more transformations, required more time for cognitive processing, which lent some credence to the existence of more complex operations. It was also demonstrated that listeners extract and retain in memory the gist of what is said in simple, active, affirmative, declarative sentences, which are the closest surface forms to the base component of deep structure. However, as Chomsky had long warned his readers, his transformational-generative model was an attempt to describe and account for "the ability of a speaker to understand an arbitrary sentence of his language and to produce an appropriate sentence on a given occasion."[54] He was not attempting to explain how hearers and speakers do in fact perceive, comprehend, retain, and produce meaningful messages – the very areas that most interest psychologists and language teachers.[55]

Meanwhile, linguists went on refining their theoretical models, arriving at their conclusions as a result of introspective judgment. Consequently, psychologists, whose conclusions could be reached only after lengthy experimentation, sometimes found that their findings, when ready to be announced, were already somewhat irrelevant, since the premises on which their experiments had been based were no longer accepted in current linguistic theory. Refusing to act any longer as toolmakers for the linguists[56] (devising tests to prove the reality of processes that the linguists had predicated to their own satisfaction, following their own methodology), some well-known *psycholinguists declared their independence from schools of linguistics*. They began to draw their own conclusions, based on their discipline's experimental methods and standards of evidence, and develop their own models of perception, processing, retention, and production of language by living, breathing human beings. Concluding a

18

study of the strategies children employ in learning to extract meaning from a stream of sound, Bever stated, "I do not know anything about how language (or anything else) is learned, while I do have some initial understanding of the mechanics of perception....The most obvious behavior constraint on language acquisition is the development of memory in the young child."[57] Bever developed a model of a psychogrammar in which perception and production use different processes, independently represented in behavior.[58] Schlesinger developed separate models for comprehension and production of utterances, both of which were basically semantic in operation, with syntax playing a minor role.[59] Perception and memory processes became major areas of concern in cognitive psychology.[60]

With the flurry of psychological attention to perception, it is not surprising that the language teaching profession began to give serious attention to listening and reading, which have much in common since they involve similar processes. Postovsky, who was teaching Russian at the Defense Language Institute at Monterey, began experimenting with *an initial listening period of some length* before students would be expected to produce any material orally. Students listened, without repeating or creating oral utterances, for about a month (in a six-hours-a-day intensive course), during which time writing was the supporting activity. Students wrote out structure drills, took dictation, and wrote dialogues from memory. Thus, reading (of what they had written) was developed as a corollary activity. Postovsky found that students began to speak when they felt like doing so, and, when they did speak, they had a better accent and more control of structure than those who had spent the same amount of time practicing oral production, accompanied by written exercises.[61]

Other experimenters became active in this area. Winitz and Reeds developed a series of pictures of actions that students identified as they were listening,[62] and Olmsted Gary's students matched pictures with sound, physical actions with sound, and reading with sound (through identification of written multiple-choice items).[63]

The comprehension approach to initial language learning gained a number of adherents. Whether teachers adopted this approach or not, listening was in the air, and teachers realized that if students were to understand native speakers they would need much practice in *listening to authentic materials* recorded in natural situations, rather than to the stilted, artificially concocted laboratory materials that accompanied many textbooks. As reasonably priced videocassettes and videodiscs became generally available, teachers were able to bring the student into contact not only with the natural spoken language but also with the situational context, the appearance of the speakers, and their nonverbal forms of communication.

19

Since, at this time, much research was being conducted into *the nature of the reading process*, and since extraction of meaning from oral output has many features in common with the extraction of meaning from graphic symbols, teachers became aware of the neglect into which the teaching of second-language reading had fallen. They began to recognize that falling back on the assumption that many L_2 students "already knew how to read," and leaving them to their own devices with texts, was merely sweeping a real problem under the mat, especially as many students were poor readers in their native language to begin with. Goodman's research into reading as "a psycholinguistic guessing game" made teachers aware of the *roles of expectations and inference* in drawing meaning from texts,[64] and books for teaching reading began to appear that encouraged students to draw on their natural cognitive abilities and prior knowledge, as they selected the graphic cues that would enable them to recreate the author's meaning.[65]

With so much emphasis on cognitive processes, it was not surprising that, in the area of L_1 acquisition, psychologists were now more willing to accept as innate not just a specific language-learning capacity, but certain *cognitive and perceptual processes* that were basic to all forms of human learning. This approach made it possible to align studies of L_1 acquisition and use with the findings of Piaget and his colleagues in Geneva. Although Piaget's work was already well-known in Europe in the 1950s, it was only in the 1960s and 1970s that it received the serious attention it deserved from American developmental psychologists. Piaget had identified a series of natural, maturational stages in cognitive or intellectual development from infancy to adolescence: the sensory-motor stage of practical intelligence and two stages of operational intelligence, concrete thinking operations and formal thinking operations, the latter being characterized by the ability to cope with abstract logical thought (processes like hypothesis and deduction).[66]

As Piaget's work became better understood, developmental psychologists began to relate their studies of L_1 acquisition to this growing body of experimental research findings, and some L_2 researchers followed suit.[67] Teachers began to realize that L_2 *learning by young children and adults must necessarily differ*, children learning more easily through action and manipulation of materials, whereas adults would feel the need for more formal explanations of what they were learning and doing. It became increasingly clear that the many studies of L_2 acquisition by young children in informal situations did not necessarily throw much light on L_2 learning by adolescents and adults in formal instructional settings. Studies began to appear that were directed toward the learning problems of these older groups.[68]

As teachers realized the importance of involving the adult learner's reasoning processes more directly in language learning, some adopted Gattegno's *Silent Way*, which forces students to listen attentively to material that will not be repeated and to produce utterances based on inductive discovery of syntactic structures. Students then explore by trial and error the possibilities for generalization of these structures to new situations. In this approach, the teacher acts as a support and yardstick for the student's own learning.[69]

As researchers delved more deeply into *the workings of the mind*, second-language teachers gained much insight into the way new information is transformed by receivers as they relate it to information already stored; how what is perceived is recoded and organized for storage, not as atomic items but in conceptual networks; how recoded information moves from short-term to long-term storage; and how the processes of retrieval operate. Much interest developed in what neuropsychology was revealing about the roles of the *left and right hemispheres of the brain* in language use – a complicated issue by no means resolved.[70] Since people not only acquire languages but also forget them rapidly, research began into the problems of *language loss*.[71] Much work remains to be done in these areas, but at least a start has been made.

As computers became more and more powerful, much energy went into computer simulation of human language use, in what came to be known as *artificial intelligence* (AI) research. Since computers begin with a tabula rasa, it was necessary to develop a model of the knowledge human beings possess that enables them to comprehend and produce speech. This resulted in much research into semantics, which structures meaning and our experience of the world, just at the time when some theoretical linguists were developing a system of generative semantics, which analyzed lexical units in terms of their underlying semantic structure. To provide computers with a store of semantic notions on which to draw, artificial intelligence researchers had to establish relations among concepts such that some representation of the real world could be activated as the computer processed the data. This detailed knowledge of the world was called the "script," and this the computer had to have in its memory store in order to draw inferences from the elliptic and often informationally reduced statements characteristic of normal human interaction. This research threw much light on the complicated nature of the lexical component in language and revealed the active role that memory plays in interpretation and production of utterances.[72] As a result, teachers became even more conscious of the immensity of the task confronting the second-language learner.

21

The affective element

Sensitive teachers have always recognized the very important role tension, anxiety, and emotion play in communicating in a second language. Unless students feel at ease with their teacher and their fellow students, and relaxed within themselves, they withdraw from expressing what they really think in another language, as they would in their own. Speaking in another language involves not only stripping oneself of the protective devices a well-known language makes available to us but also reverting to a much less mature level of expression that can make adolescent and adult learners feel foolish and vulnerable. (Of course, anger can also reduce inhibitions, but L_2 students at an early stage do not know the words and phrases to express this emotion, so they tend to relapse into an uncooperative silence instead.) Once, as language teachers, we move beyond the study of rules and paradigms, or the drilling of structural patterns and the reciting of dialogues, and encourage a genuine communication of ideas, emotions, and interests, we have much to learn from dynamic and personality psychology and theories of motivation. With changes in approach to the second-language teaching task in the 1970s, affect-based approaches to learning began to have an impact, in particular humanistic psychology (as elaborated by Maslow, Rogers, and Brown) and Curran's Counseling-Learning approach.[73]

Maslow maintained that the individual has a hierarchy of needs to be satisfied. In ascending order, he listed physiological needs, needs for security, belongingness, esteem for self and for others, and self-realization, the latter being attainable only after the lower-level needs have been satisfied.[74] These needs of our students lead to complex interrelationships within the class group, which consists at any one time of individuals who are in need of support and fulfillment at different levels of the hierarchy. As we have observed, for genuine communication to occur, students must feel at ease in the situation; consequently, the interrelationships among students and between teacher and student affect the success of every attempt at communicative interaction, even apart from the differing levels of language control within the group. Affective factors also determine what is meaningful and absorbing for students at any particular moment, and motivational factors are not the least among these.[75]

In practice, the humanistic approach has brought to the teacher's attention the need to include in language-learning materials vocabulary and activities for expressing one's feelings, sharing one's values and viewpoints with others, and developing a better understanding of their feelings and needs as well as one's own.[76] Where students of a number of different cultural backgrounds find themselves in the same class, this also provides an opportunity to learn about the enthusiasms and reticences of other cultures. It also requires of the teacher even greater sensitivity to the variety of responses the students are willing and able to offer.

A second-language class is a particularly suitable environment for meeting affective needs, since content to flesh out the language structures is unlimited. Much of the activity can take the form of role playing, simulation games, and small-group discussions. Masks and puppets help the more inhibited to express themselves with less risk. The expressive arts (drama, music, and song) allow for free flow of imagination and self-expression. Yet, in all these activities, without concentrating on "grammar," students must seek from among the L_2 expressions they know the appropriate forms to express the nuances of meaning they have in mind.

With this reemphasis on individual worth and difference, language teachers began to accept the fact that their students have preferred modalities of learning: Some learn best through the ear, some through the eye. They also learn at different rates and employ quite different strategies for understanding and retaining the material to be learned. With this new understanding, teachers were no longer satisfied with a monolithic "what is good for one is good for all" approach. They wanted to do more to meet the needs of their students. The 1970s saw a flowering of experimentation with individualized learning programs,[77] diversified content, and courses of differing lengths and intensity. There was also much research into students' individual learning strategies.

Confluent learning

Brown's confluent learning emphasized the importance of working with both feelings and intellect at the same time, in both group and individual learning. As described by Galyean, confluent learning comprises four components: "(1) Learning in the '*here and now*' ongoing interests and energies of the class. (2) *Student offered material* as the basis for learning and practicing language structures. (3) *Interpersonal sharing* and student-to-student communication. (4) *Self awareness and self realization.*"[78] Although the emphasis is on personal material that reflects the attitudes, likes, dislikes, hopes, fears, and imaginings of individual students, correct production of language structures is emphasized. The types of exercises used are introduced by the teacher and designed for the practice of certain structures, but they are open-ended, so that they may be developed and sustained by the students. "The key," says Galyean, "is a personal awareness of what is interesting and energizing to oneself and to others, and the ability to encourage reflection upon and discussion of these momentary interests in the course of language practice."[79] Lively exchanges on topics that enable students to express their own ideas and feelings are encouraged between student and teacher, student and student, and in small groups. Thus, provision is made for the cognitive, affective, and interactive aspects of language learning. In keeping with the close attention to affective needs that this approach advocates, teachers are cautioned to wait until individual students are ready to reveal themselves in this intimate way and never to push individuals to share more than they wish to share. The approach realizes its full potential only with a nonauthoritarian teacher who is willing to share and to grow in self-awareness along with the students.

Counseling-Learning/Community Language Learning

The affect-based approach to second-language learning was most fully realized in Curran's Counseling-Learning/Community Language Learning (C-L/CLL) model.[80] Curran's approach also requires on the part of the teacher a yielding up of the desire to direct and decide, and a willingness to experience emotionally along with the students.

Curran, a psychiatrist, began with a consideration of "the relation of conflict, hostility, anger, and anxiety, to learning."[81] Conscious of the risks being taken by second-language learners, and the strong emotions involved, he advocated a group-learning situation where students, in an investment phase, created and recorded their own utterances in the second language, with the teacher as a supportive, nonjudgmental Knower, remaining on the periphery. Later, in a reflective phase, the students considered and commented in their native language on what they had produced, learning from the Knower as they felt able. Curran found that, as the learning proceeded, "an atmosphere of enthusiasm and shared achievements" developed, "similar to that of amputees beginning to walk on artificial limbs."[82] There was also a significant change in the students' "positive self-regard."[83]

Lozanov, a Bulgarian psychiatrist, also recognized the need to involve the whole person in the learning process: both the conscious and the unconscious self. He found that by breaking down the students' sense of the limitations on what they could learn, real learning could be greatly enhanced. For this to take place, a relaxed, cooperative atmosphere was necessary. He applied these principles in a method of language teaching called Suggestopaedia. To ensure that students were experiencing positive and pleasant feelings at an unconscious level, he advocated that they take on new identities in the language classroom, with names, addresses, and occupations that they could bring into play in classroom activities. The occupations selected were interesting, even prestigious, to give the students a deep-seated sense of worth.[84]

Drama in language teaching

With the emphasis on letting people be themselves and helping people to know and express themselves, the idea of using drama techniques came to the fore. As early as 1966, Via, an actor and stage manager from Broadway who was visiting Japan, began experimenting with the production of plays as a way of teaching English, and this met with great success. Via was not advocating a return to the literary approach of staging one great masterpiece, with much expenditure of time and effort on the part of the few, in order to boost the prestige of the language department. His approach involved the whole class in learning what actors learn about expressing themselves in the roles of the characters they represent. By immersing themselves in their roles, students focused on what they were doing, not the fact that they were doing it in a second language. (Via's seminars took place during six-week periods, when students met for four hours a day. His approach has been tried with success in other areas of Asia, and it is particularly suitable for summer or between-semester sessions.)

According to Via, "*A play is all communication....* We don't talk in pattern practices and drills. We talk in ideas. We talk with emotion. We talk with feeling – and we must learn to add this to the words if we are going to have true communication."[85] In performing a play, students are working cooperatively with a purpose. They are using English for every aspect of the production: staging, lighting, makeup, costuming, acting, operating curtains, or advertising. All students can be actively involved.

In Via's system, all learn to act as well. The success of the projects depends on a relaxed atmosphere, where students and teachers all know each other as persons and explore their feelings together, thus forming a confident working group. Students learn to speak up. They do not memorize parts, but through a "talk and listen" method, with access to the script, they acquire their parts through speaking them and listening to others. Thus, all concerned have much practice in listening carefully, as well as in expressing themselves in the language, with attention to the motivation behind the words.

Even in *classroom role playing*, Via maintains that students should always be themselves, thinking how they would act and relate in these circumstances in a different culture. He calls this "the magic *if* of theater: *If* I were in this situation, what would *I* do?"[86] As students involve themselves in their roles, gestures and intonation follow. Via does not correct, but allows students to grow through what they are doing.

If plays are too ambitious for some (and such projects are usually undertaken after a basic course), there is plenty of room for *improvisations* in class. Via suggests that one plan a situation with a conflict, which different students act out extempore, trying to solve the problem on their feet with other students coming forward with suggestions. There is again much listening and speaking by the students themselves.[87]

A similar approach was advocated by Di Pietro, in what he termed the *open scenario*. Di Pietro's interest was in the real-life roles we play, both on a long-term basis and in episodes of interaction. He believes that culturally acceptable behavior in these roles can be learned through interactional games and classroom scenarios.[88] In the open-ended scenario, new information is introduced into a fully described situation, so as to force decisions and alter the direction of the action. Students prepare in groups for one role in the scenario; then one member of each group acts out the situation, adapting extemporaneously to the unpredicted course the other players are taking. Di Pietro's open scenario approach is much more structured than Via's improvisations, in that students prepare their versions carefully in groups.[89]

Scarcella's concept of the *socio-drama* also calls for student discussion of a story with a clearly definable problem and a dilemma point, from which the students are to continue the story with improvisational acting. "Socio-drama," Scarcella states, "is a problem-solving activity which simulates real life situations and requires active student involvement."[90] As some students extemporize the solution, the others decide on the effectiveness of the solution. New solutions are proposed and acted out, until some consensus is reached. The socio-drama is usually followed by written work, a reading assignment, or an aural comprehension exercise.

Still others have advocated the techniques of *creative drama* to relax students and overcome their resistance to being other than their cultural selves. In this approach movement and sound, in imaginative situations and implausible roles, precede actual use of the second language, which then becomes less intimidating.[91] In these activities, all participate, the individuals lose themselves in the group, and all become less inhibited, thus preparing them for the experience of sounding and acting differently, while cooperatively developing new communication skills.

Rassias, at Dartmouth College, introduces a dramatic element that depends much more on the histrionic abilities of the teacher, and this sets the atmosphere for "bringing out the uninhibited child" in the student, once again to facilitate self-expression in the new language.[92] "First you have to secure an emotional reaction," Rassias says. "To do that I will go to any extreme,"[93] and this includes breaking eggs on students' heads, pretending to mow them down with a machinegun if they make errors, kneeling beseechingly before them to bring out a correct response, and kissing effusively those who give correct answers. The major part of the course in the Dartmouth Method is very structured, with audiolingual-type drilling in small groups directed by undergraduate apprentice teachers (ATs). (The course is intensive, with five hours in class, five hours in drill sessions, and five hours of language laboratory exercises.) Some time in class is used for acting out dialogues and micrologues (one-minute culturally based scenarios), with costumes and props. Dramatic activity may also take place during the drill sessions with the ATs.

Maley and Duff provide many activities of a dramatic nature that can be woven into any class structure. As they point out, a statement takes its meaning from the intentions of the speakers and their relations to each other, so that even a simple statement like "It's eight o'clock" can have a number of meanings and varying forms of emotional content.[94] The drama approach enables students to use what they are learning with pragmatic intent, something that is most difficult to learn through explanation. Forcing the teacher from center stage, it gives students space to work with language in ways that are enjoyable, memorable, and continually varying.

In all of these approaches we can see the levels of Maslow's hierarchy of needs being satisfied: Physiological needs for movement and expression, security in feeling part of a caring, sharing group, esteem for oneself and for others as the contribution of each is seen to be essential to the activity of all, and finally self-realization (discovering not only who one is but also who one can be and what one can achieve in cooperation with others). We see the breaking up of traditional authority structures and postures in the classroom, as well as the disappearance of the traditional classroom setting of thirty or forty desks lined up facing the teacher, who is at an (often elevated) desk or table that is considerably larger than those of the students.

HOW DOES THE INEXPERIENCED TEACHER BEGIN?

Not all teachers can produce plays, even short ones within the classroom, but all can introduce the dramatic element, allowing imagination and creative energy to flow in the use of the language, at the level of knowledge the students possess, and this can be done with very few words in the early weeks. The imagination of the students is often more vivid and creative than that of the instructor.

For a start, teachers experiment with student role playing, with small groups acting out situations from the material they have studied. Next, they extend these situations (for which students know the vocabulary and expressions) to include problems that are not solved in the textbook material – Via's "magical *if.*" Then new situations are presented, with an element of potential conflict, and different groups work on possible solutions, as members from one group act out the situation with members of other groups. At this point, the unpredictable takes over, and students must extemporize to resolve the issue. Sometimes these improvisations lead students to prepare skits for presentation to the class or other classes.

Students are now ready for *simulation games.* In this type of activity, a particular situation is outlined with distinctively defined participants who have conflicting interests in the project under discussion (a new road to be built through a country club estate or through a well-established housing project, for instance), and the parties involved work out a solution acceptable to all. (With larger classes, different groups have different simulation situations to work with. This makes for more interesting final presentations.) Paralleling this stage, the class may embark on improvising characters and situations of their own devising. Finally, the class may feel ready to produce a short one-act play to be presented to other classes, parents, or the community. At every stage of dramatic activity *videotaping* is a valuable accompaniment, allowing students to see themselves and each other and cooperatively work toward more genuine, uninhibited expression in the language they are learning.

What of the future?

During the period discussed in this chapter there has been much change and flux in the second-language teaching and learning enterprise. The flow of ideas, complementary and contradictory, may seem overwhelming; on the other hand, it opens up a future of choice. Teachers now feel free to select and choose, to invent and innovate, developing a personal style of teaching and techniques that meet the needs of the particular students with whom they are working. As informed professionals, they have to be adaptable as new pressures bring new demands. Yet, they press forward toward their primary goal of providing for their students the mind-expanding and personality-liberating experience that learning a second language can be, with the contact it provides with new modes of thought, new behaviors, new forms of expression, and, best of all, new friends with whom to communicate.

Let's discuss

1 Which psychological problems of classroom language learning do you consider to be most urgently in need of research?
2 Have you found a knowledge of linguistic theory to be of value to you as a language teacher? If so, in what ways? For which problem points in the language do you feel most need for linguistic guidance?
3 Of the various approaches to language teaching described in this chapter, which one would you consider most appropriate for:
   a) young immigrant children who do not speak English and whose parents do not speak English?
   b) 12-year-olds of a low level of academic achievement?
   c) adult migrant workers who are illiterate in their native language?
   d) senior citizens about to embark on a trip abroad?
   Discuss your reasons.
4 From your own experience of language learning and teaching, how do you feel about the habit-versus-rule controversy? How do you think the grammar of the language can best be "internalized"?
5 Is "communicative competence" as Hymes has defined it attainable in a formal language-learning situation? If so, which seems to be the most fruitful approach?
6 Design a listening and reading course that takes account of what you have learned about these two processes in this chapter.
7 How would you design a course to involve the whole person of the student in the learning process?

2 Rules, patterns, and creativity

In 1966, Chomsky shocked many participants at the Northeast Conference by casting doubt on the validity of the direct and uncritical application of linguistic theory to teaching practice. "I am, frankly," he said, "rather skeptical about the significance, for the teaching of languages, of such insights and understanding as have been attained in linguistics and psychology."[1] "It is possible," he continued, " – even likely – that principles of psychology and linguistics, and research in these disciplines, may supply insights useful to the language teacher. But this must be demonstrated and cannot be presumed. It is the language teacher himself who must validate or refute any specific proposal."[2]

With an obvious, though unstated, reference to methods of language teaching then in vogue, which it had been believed were consistent with what was known of the nature of language and of the learning process,[3] Chomsky declared: "Linguists have had their share in perpetuating the myth that linguistic behavior is 'habitual' and that a fixed stock of 'patterns' is acquired through practice and used as the basis for 'analogy.'"[4] To Chomsky, "language is not a 'habit-structure.' Ordinary linguistic behavior characteristically involves innovation, formation of new sentences and new patterns in accordance with rules of great abstractness and intricacy."[5] For this reason, he speaks continually of the "'creative' aspect of language use."[6]

Linguistic science has made teachers very conscious of the fact that *grammar is the core of language*. Without an internalized set of rules, or syntax, they are told, no one can understand or use a language: Language is "rule-governed behavior."[7] In the past, many teachers have uncritically adopted habit-formation techniques because language, it appeared, was "a set of habits."[8] Following Chomsky's declaration, many were ready to seize upon a new slogan and began to inculcate rules in the hope of establishing rule-governed behavior, even though

Revised version of an article, "Grammar in Foreign Language Teaching," *Modern Language Journal* 52 (1968), 206–11 (Madison, Wis.: University of Wisconsin Press); reprinted as "Rules, Patterns and Creativity" in *English Teaching Forum* 8, 6 (1970).

they had only a vague concept of what this phrase meant as used by linguists and psychologists.[9] In this way they hoped *to take their students beyond the arid fields of mechanical repetition*, where pure habit-formation techniques seemed so often to have left them, *into the greener pastures of creative production* of their own utterances.

Before deciding on any particular approach, we need to clarify our ideas about the essence of language use (which in Chomsky's terms is a question of performance based on competence). We then select methods appropriate to the type of learning involved in its effective acquisition. This seems to be a straightforward progression, but it is at this point that there is the most confusion.

Linguistic and pedagogic grammar

First, it is important to distinguish, as Chomsky has done, between a linguistic and a pedagogic grammar. A linguistic grammar, as Chomsky sees it, aims to discover and exhibit the mechanisms that make it possible for a "speaker to understand an arbitrary sentence on a given occasion," whereas a pedagogic grammar attempts to provide the student with the ability to understand and produce such sentences.[10]

This leaves the question wide open for the second-language teacher. *A linguistic grammar* is an account of competence (the knowledge of the language system that a native speaker has acquired) expressed in terms of an abstract model that does not necessarily represent, and may not even attempt to parallel, the psychological processes of language use. It can give the informed teacher insights into language structure and clarify various aspects of the subject matter, but methods of linguistic description do not per se provide any guidance as to how a student can learn to communicate in a second language. This is the preoccupation of the writer of *a pedagogic grammar* who, in the light of what the linguistic grammar has established about the subject matter, decides what are psychologically (and, in this context, pedagogically) the most appropriate ways of arranging and presenting the material to the students. The form a particular pedagogic grammar will assume will depend on such factors as the objectives of the language course (which devolve from the felt needs of the students); the age and intellectual maturity of the students; the length and intensity of the study; the major differences between the second and native languages, which may affect how the teaching of the language is to be approached; and how communicative needs are to be provided for early in the course.

31

Internalizing the rules of the language

How, then, can the language teacher establish rule-governed behavior that will enable students to produce novel utterances at will? In conformity with Chomsky's position, we need to make it possible for the language learner to internalize a system of rules capable of generating an infinite number of grammatical sentences that will be comprehensible and acceptable, when uttered with the semantic and phonological components appropriate to specific communication situations.[11] With the word "internalize" we are at the heart of the problem: *Rule-governed behavior, in the sense in which it is used by linguists or psychologists, does not mean behavior that results from the conscious application of rules.*

According to Chomsky, "a person is not generally aware of the rules that govern sentence-interpretation in the language that he knows; nor, in fact, is there any reason to suppose that the rules can be brought to consciousness." Neither can we "expect him to be fully aware even of the empirical consequences of these internalized rules,"[12] that is, of the way in which abstract rules acquire semantic interpretations. *The behavior is rule-governed in the sense that it conforms to the internalized system of rules.* These rules are not the pedagogic "grammar rules" (often of doubtful linguistic validity) of the traditional deductive, expository type of language teaching, according to which students docilely construct language sequences. They are rules, as Chomsky puts it, of "great abstractness and intricacy" inherent in the structure of a language, which, through the operation of various processes, find expression in the overt forms that people produce.

Generate, in the mathematical sense in which Chomsky uses the term, does not refer to some unexpected production of language sequences that reflects originality of thought on the part of the speaker, but to a mechanical process: The outworking of the internalized rules will automatically result in what are recognizably grammatical utterances. When Chomsky talks, therefore, about the "'creative' aspect of language use," he is not referring to the type of free play with language elements where students, with glib abandon, "create language," grammatical or ungrammatical, to suit their immediate purposes. He is referring to the fact that, once the system of rules of the language has become an integral part of the students' store of knowledge, *they will be able to produce, in order to express their meaning, an infinite variety of language sequences, whether they have previously heard such sequences or not* – sequences that are grammatically acceptable, and therefore comprehensible, to the persons to whom they are speaking. The mere supplying of pedagogic grammar rules, and subsequent training of students in their use for the construction of language sequences, is not in itself sufficient to ensure the "internalizing" of the linguistic system so that it will operate in the production of sentences, without the students' being conscious of its role. Unless language teachers are aware of the technical meaning of the terms Chomsky was using in his lecture on language teaching, they may be left with erroneous impressions of his viewpoint.

Creative use of language

Exercising the language teacher's prerogative that Chomsky has so clearly assigned us, we may well question his statement that it is a myth that linguistic behavior is "habitual" and that a fixed stock of patterns is acquired through practice and used as the basis for "analogy."[13] "Repetition of fixed phrases," he says, "is a rarity," and "it is only under exceptional and quite uninteresting circumstances that one can seriously consider how 'situational context' determines what is said."[14] Here Chomsky is overstating his case. *He is ignoring the role of "building blocks" of language* that help the speaker create utterances with new meanings (such frames as "in the X"; "I'll X tomorrow"; "Is that X?"; "Do you have any X?" and very frequent expressions like "Wait a minute"; "Don't do that"; "He's wrong, you know"; "I'll be ready soon"). Despite his assertions, Chomsky would be the first to admit that a theory of language performance has yet to be developed, and it is here, surely, that *situational context quite obviously plays a role* in what is said, as witness the way speakers change their sentences in mid-utterance in response to their interlocutor's reaction or other situational clues.[15]

Chomsky's emphasis on creative and innovative use of language is salutary.[16] It fixes our attention on the true goal of all second-language teaching: to produce students who can communicate about anything and everything in the second language, comprehending and creating at will novel utterances that conform to the grammatical system of the language (whether in speech or writing). He does not, however, indicate how this may be done. He expects teachers themselves to reflect on this. It is we who must map out the progression that will facilitate such free and unfettered language use, by providing our students with the linguistic means to create novel utterances through a carefully designed and presented program they can digest (internalize?) and enjoy.[17] Our error in the past has been to concentrate on the program, while ignoring the goal (perhaps considering it unattainable for many). Now we realize that, while providing the means, we must encourage students to use these means immediately, frequently, and pleasurably to express meanings they themselves wish to communicate, at the level of expression of which they are capable.

Creative and innovative use of language still takes place within a restricted framework, a finite set of formal arrangements to which the utterances of speakers must conform if they are to be comprehended and effective communication established. *Speakers cannot "create" the grammar of the language as they innovate*: They are making "infinite use of finite means."[18] Innovative ability will exist only to the degree that underlying competence exists – that the set of rules has been internalized. Second-language students must acquire the grammar of the new language so that it functions for them as does the grammar of their native language: as a vehicle for meaning that they do not even realize they are using.

Basically, the question of how to inculcate the grammar of a language will depend on the type of activity we believe communication in a second language to be: *Is it a skill or an intellectual process, or is it a blend of the two?* If learning to use another language implies the acquisition of a skill, or a group of interrelated skills, then our students need intensive practice until they are able to associate, without hesitation or reflection, the many linguistic elements that are interrelated in a linear sequence. If, on the other hand, second-language use is an intellectual process, then a different type of practice is necessary to ensure that students can make correct choices of rules, and modifications of rules, in order to construct utterances that express their intentions.

Two levels of language behavior

If we can identify two levels of second-language behavior for which our students must be prepared, then it is clear that one type of teaching will not be sufficient for the task. These two levels may be designated: (1) the *level of manipulation* of language elements that occur in fixed relationships in clearly defined closed systems (that is, relationships that will vary within very narrow limits), and (2) the *level of expression of personal meaning* at which possible variations are infinite, depending on such factors as the type of message to be communicated, the situation in which the utterance takes place, the relationship between speaker and hearer or hearers, and the degree of intensity with which the message is conveyed. If we recognize two such levels, a place must be found for the establishment of certain basic linguistic habits as well as the understanding of a complex system with its infinite possibilities of expression.[19] The problem is to define the role of each of these types of learning and their interrelationships in the acquiring of a usable knowledge of a second language.[20]

It is essential to recognize first that *certain elements of language remain in fixed relationships in small, closed systems*, so that once the system is invoked in a particular way a succession of interrelated formal features appears. Fluent speakers are able to make these interrelated adjustments irrespective of the particular message they wish to produce. The elements that interact in restricted systems may be practiced intensively in order to forge strong habitual associations from which the speaker never deviates (this applies to such elements as inflection of person and number, agreements of gender, fixed forms for interrogation or negation, and formal features of tenses). These elements do not require intellectual analysis: They exist, and they must be used in a certain way in specific environments and in no other way.[21] For *these features, intensive practice exercises of various kinds can be effective learning procedures*, with the teacher supplying a brief word of explanation where necessary to forestall hesitation or bewilderment. Lengthy explanations can be a hindrance rather than a help for this type of activity, because it is *how* these systems operate that matters, not *why*.

Practice of this type should not be given in solid, tedious blocks in a determined attempt to stamp in these formal features once and for all. *Shorter exercises, reintroduced at intervals over a period of time, with interspersed opportunities to use these features in association with other language elements in a communicative interchange*, no matter how simple, will be more effective in establishing the necessary control. After such attempts at use to express personal meaning, the attention of the students will be more directly focused in subsequent practice on areas they have found to be of persistent difficulty. Structural practice of this type may be considered effective only if these formal features are observed to be readily available to the students when their attention is concentrated on constructing a message – an act that involves the second level of language behavior. They will not become readily available, however, unless students have early and constant practice in expressing personal meanings.

At the second level, decisions more intimately connected with contextual meaning may bring into play any of a variety of syntactic structures, so that students will be continually reusing what they have learned. A decision at this higher level has structural implications beyond the word or the phrase, often beyond the sentence. A slight variation in the decision will often mean the construction of a quite different form of utterance. Naturally, then, decisions at the second level involve a more complicated initial choice, which entails further choices of a more limited character. In order to express exactly what one wishes to say, one must view it in relation to the potential of the structural system of the language as a whole and select accordingly. This is the higher-level decision that sets in motion operations at lower levels that are interdependent. The decision to make a particular type of statement about something that has taken place recently involves a choice of register, a choice of degree of intensity, the use of lexical items in certain syntactic relationships that will involve the production of certain morphological elements, certain phonemic distinctions, and certain stress and intonation patterns. The interrelationships within the language system that are involved in these higher-level decisions often need to be clarified in deductive fashion by the teacher or textbook. For effective practice at this level, *students must understand the implications and ramifications of changes they are making*. This understanding will be achieved only if they are involved in making decisions in real communication situations devised in the classroom, rather than in artificial drills and exercises. In such interchanges, the feedback from other participants in the communication brings a realization of the effect of the decisions the speaker has made.

There must be in the classroom, then, *a constant interplay of learning by analogy and by analysis, of inductive and deductive processes* – according to the nature of the operation the student is learning.[22] It is evident that higher-level choices cannot be put into operation with ease if facility has not been developed in the production of the interdependent lower-level elements. Thus, both learning by intensive practice and analogy have their place. Genuine freedom in language use, however, will develop only as the student gains control of the system as a whole, beyond the mastery of patterns in isolation. This control will become established only through much experience in attempting to counterbalance and interrelate various syntactic possibilities, in order to convey a comprehensible meaning in a situation where its expression has some real significance.

It becomes clear that the second level of language use, which we have just considered, is more sophisticated than the first level. It demands of the student *understanding of the interrelationships and options the language system allows*. This understanding guides the higher-level choices, yet full comprehensibility depends on skill in manipulation of the numerous lower-level elements that are set in operation by the higher-level decisions. Too often in the past, language teaching concentrated on an understanding of the language system as a whole, without providing sufficient practice in rapid production of the lower-level elements. This led to hesitancy in language use. On the other hand, more recent methods have worked out techniques for developing the lower-level manipulative skill while leaving the student unpracticed in making decisions at the higher level. The language course must provide for experience at both levels.

It would be a mistake, however, to believe that practice at the second level should be delayed until the student has learned all the common features of the manipulative type (that is, until the student has first learned to manipulate elements in fixed relationships), leaving aside for a year or two practice in the selection process of the higher level. If students are eventually to understand a complex system with its infinite possibilities of expression, they must develop this understanding little by little. Students will learn to make higher-level selective decisions by being made aware at every step of the potential for meaningful use in communication of the operations they are learning at the manipulative level. No matter how simple the structural pattern they are practicing, they will become *aware of its possibilities for communication*[23] *when they attempt to use it for their own purposes*, and not just to complete an exercise or to perform well in a drill.

As each structure becomes a medium of communication, it takes its place in the evolving system of meaningful expression that the students are internalizing; by using it in relationship with what they have already learned, they see this isolated operation as part of a whole, with a definite function within the language. As they acquire more knowledge of the language, they will need further explanation of how the various elements they have become accustomed to using interact within sentences and sections of discourse. Such explanations will be brief and to the point. Since their sole purpose is to prevent mislearning through mistaken assumptions about relationships, they will be fruitful only if followed immediately by meaningful practice in the expression of these relationships. Such practice is essential, until it is evident that the student has internalized the underlying rules so effectively that they govern the production of utterances without conscious and deliberate application on the part of the speaker.

Whether at the first or second level, practice does not have to be boring and meaningless. It can take the form of games, competitions, and spontaneous role playing that call for the production of the types of structures being learned, or conversational interchanges within a directional framework.[24] With a little thought, the classroom teacher can find interesting, even exciting ways to practice all kinds of structural combinations and interrelationships, until the student has acquired confidence and assurance in their potentialities of expression.

Understanding the language system

As a further step, and this will be sooner or later according to the age and maturity of the class, the students will *need to see the parts and the interacting sections they have learned in relation to the whole functioning system* of the language. (Having learned, for instance, different ways of expressing past action, they will need to see how these forms fit into the general expression of temporal relationships in this particular language.) Since they are already accustomed to the system of their native language, they will often be tempted to identify specific similarities and differences between the two languages at this higher level of conceptualization (that is, of overriding systems that reflect the semantic organization of the language: ways of looking at time, of expressing the general and the particular, of classing and categorizing aspects of experience).[25] When in doubt, or unaware of important distinctions, they will tend to fall back on native-language ways of looking at things, and this will be reflected in their selection of linguistic means. It is essential, therefore, for them to see how these apparent similarities and differences interact within the complete system of the language they are learning, without reference to an external, and therefore irrelevant, criterion such as their native language.[26]

This advanced stage of comprehension of the complexities of the second-language system is frequently neglected, and students have to piece it together inductively, without confirmation or guidance, from their personal observations of the language in use. *A careful balance has to be maintained at this point.* The student cannot realize the understanding of the whole before experiencing, through practice and active use, the functioning of the parts. Students who attempt to possess the whole too soon will achieve only rote learning of grammar rules and the ability to describe, rather than use, the grammatical system. On the other hand, when teachers can present the system as a whole to students who already have some practical knowledge of the functioning of the parts, they can draw maximum benefit from the use of authentic language materials, aural and graphic, in which is demonstrated what they wish to convey. *By showing how the grammatical system works for real purposes*, teachers can convey far more to their students than by giving numerous abstract explanations, supported by isolated, out-of-context examples.

Textbooks and courses of study – and teachers – must make ample provision at appropriate stages for both types of learning discussed here. Neglect of the practice needed to acquire such things as interrelated inflectional systems will force students to make decisions for each element as they proceed, and their use of the language will remain hesitant. On the other hand, it is only by going beyond the practice stage, and trying out what they know in communication, that students can learn to make the higher-level choices that will bring the lower-level adjustments they have learned into operation at the appropriate moment.

There has been much experimentation with techniques for the lower-level manipulative operations. We need to give more thought to effective ways of inducing language behavior at the second level, the expression of personal meaning. Learners will understandably take their cue from their teachers. They will see that the use of what they are learning in spontaneous production is their most important task only when their teacher is convinced, and convinces them, that this is so, and when every exercise and classroom activity leads frankly and naturally to a further opportunity for personal expression in the language. It is often easier for teacher and students to keep on working at the manipulative level, finding immediate satisfaction in the mastery of small elements. The necessary and eagerly anticipated liberation in second-language use, however, will not occur unless concentrated effort is directed at all stages toward this end.

Let's discuss

1 Make a list of features of the second language that "remain in fixed relationships in small, closed systems," that is, first-level features. How would you propose teaching these features (a) so that students may use them effortlessly, and (b) so that students may realize the role they play in a more comprehensive overriding system?
2 What are the implications for the language classroom of Carroll's reconciliation of the terms "habit" and "rule" in note 19 to this chapter?
3 List a number of activities that are proposed in a commonly used textbook for the language you teach. Which of these provide for the first level and which for the second level of language behavior? Is there a reasonable balance between activities for the two levels? What proposals would you make for improving this balance?
4 Which systems of the second language seem most difficult for your students? For all or some? Can you identify any influence of the native language in the students' confusion about these systems?

How could you improve the teaching of these aspects of the language?

5 Discuss possibilities for directional frameworks that would give students practice with problem features of the second language in conversational interchanges. (See note 24 to this chapter.)

3 Talking off the tops of their heads

In a description of the Defense Language Institute program (1971) I read: "After basic patterns and structures are mastered, the student can proceed to more and more controlled substitution and eventually to free conversation." How delightfully simple it sounds! We breathe the fresh air of the uncomplicated. Our students master the basic patterns and structures; we provide them with carefully controlled practice; and hey presto! – they speak freely in unstructured situations.

There were times, in days that seem now to belong to another age, when faith in the efficacy of structured courses and controlled drills to produce fluent speakers of another language went unchallenged. We knew where we wanted to go; we knew how to get there; we were happy with our products – or were we? And were they? Are such cries of frustration as "I can't say anything off the top of my head, it all comes out as phrases from the book" new to our ears?[1] This student complaint of the seventies sounds almost like a paraphrase of the more academic remark of 1948 that, "while many students could participate in memorized conversations speedily and effortlessly, hardly any could produce at length fluent variations from the basic material, and none could talk on unrehearsed topics without constant and painful hesitation."[2]

Autonomy in language use

In almost a quarter of a century we have still not come to grips with our basic problem: How do we develop communicative ability in a second language? We may intensify practice in the classroom (practice of patterns, practice of variations of patterns, practice in selection of patterns), but how do we engineer the great leap? Children learn all kinds of swimming movements while loving parents hold them, let them go a little, but are there to support them if they lose

Revised version of a paper delivered at the Defense Language Institute English Language Branch, Lackland Air Force Base, Texas, on June 30, 1971 (TESOL Project). Originally published in *TESOL Quarterly* 6 (1972): 71–81. © 1969 by Teachers of English to Speakers of Other Languages. Reprinted with permission of the publisher.

confidence; then at some moment they swim. One moment they are nonswimmers, then they are swimmers, if only for a very short distance. The movements are the same, the activity is of a new kind – the difference is psychological. How do nonswimmers become swimmers? They draw on their own resources; they cease to rely on somebody else's support; they become autonomous in their control of their movements; they take off and they are swimming. *How do we get our students to this autonomous stage in language use?* This is the crucial point of our teaching. Until we have solved this problem we will continue to mark time, developing more and more efficient techniques for producing second-language cripples, with all the necessary muscles and sinews but unable to operate on their own. "Spontaneous expression," "liberated expression," "creative language use," "authentic communication" – the terms may vary with changing emphases in our profession: The goal seems still to elude us.

We must examine the problem at the point at which we are stalled. How can we help the student pass from the storing of linguistic knowledge and information about how this knowledge operates in communication to actual use of this knowledge for the multitudinous, unpredictable purposes of an individual in contact with other individuals? We do not need new ways to help the student acquire linguistic knowledge – we know of many from our "twenty-five centuries of language teaching"[3] and each in its heyday has seemed to be effective for this purpose. Here we can pick and choose according to our theoretical persuasion, our temperamental preferences, and our assessment of the learning styles of the particular groups of students with whom we are dealing. In any case, these students will learn according to their personal strategies in the ultimate secret of their individual personalities, even when they appear to be doing as we direct.

Essential processes in learning to communicate

We need a model of language teaching activity that allocates a full role to the student's individual learning in communication. I propose the following division of essential processes (see schema).

Ability to communicate, to interact verbally, presumes some knowledge (*cognition*) both in the perception of units, categories, and functions, and in the internalizing of the rules relating these categories and functions (which is a process of abstraction). I am not concerned here with how this knowledge is acquired, and I am willing to concede the validity (and probably the necessity) of a variety of ap-

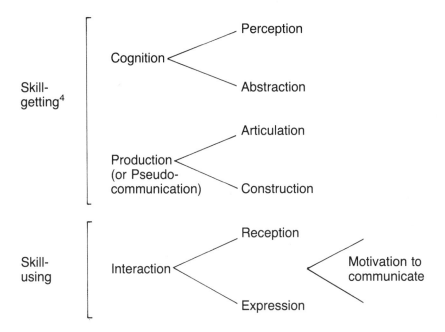

proaches to this acquisition. Linguistic knowledge must, however, be acquired. In the process of acquisition students learn the *production* of language sequences: They learn through doing. Whether we use the terms "exercises," "drills," "intensive practice," or "activities" is immaterial; some kind of practice in putting together smoothly and confidently what they are learning is also essential. Each student must learn to articulate the sounds of the language acceptably and construct comprehensible second-language sequences by rapid association of learned elements. No matter how much we relate these skill-getting activities to real-life situations this practice rarely passes beyond *pseudo-communication*. It is externally directed, not self-originating; it is a dependent, not an independent, activity. The utterances may even be original in their combinations of segments, but the students are not communicating anything that is of real import to them nor are they receiving any genuine messages from others. This is practice in formulating messages, and as such it is valuable practice. *It is near-communication with all the outward appearances of communication*, but in these activities the student does not have to demonstrate that great leap into autonomy – the leap that is crucial. Our failure in the past has been in our satisfaction with students who performed well in pseudo-communication. We have tended to assume that there would then be automatic transfer to performance in *interaction* (both in the reception and expression of messages). We may have encouraged some sketchy attempts at autonomous interaction, but always with the supporting hand: the instructor or the native speaker leading the group, drawing the student out, directing the interchange.

Problems with drills

Wolfe suggests that progress toward autonomy is hindered by the artificiality of language learning through drills and exercises that force the student to lie. "From the point of view of true linguistic communication," he says, such "seemingly harmless sentences" as *Yesterday I went to the movies, Last night I went to the game,* or *Last week I went to the game* "border on the nonsensical."[5] I do not think this is the problem. We may even maintain that lying is a common form of real communication, but, this aspect aside, sentences in drills of this type are merely pseudo-communication, and it may be clearer to students that this is the case if they are sometimes also incredible or absurd. In a foreign-language text coauthored by the playwright Ionesco, the nonsensical, shall we say whimsical, approach to adult learning is purposefully exploited with students playing manipulatively with such sentences as "The teacher is in the pocket of the vest of the watch"; "The crocodile is more beautiful than Mary-Jane"; and "He says his parents are as big as the Eiffel Tower."[6] Such manipulations are intended to force students to *think of the meaning of what they are saying*, which is one step toward autonomy, and pure nonsense may on occasion be more effective in this regard than the colorless, socially correct actions of Dick and Jane, or Maria and Pedro.

Communication drills

In recent writings on second-language teaching there has been increasing emphasis on communication and on what have been called *communication drills*. I myself have spoken elsewhere of the necessity for relating the content of drills to the student's own interests: "Participation in the drill can be innovative: providing for practice in the repetition and variation of language segments, but with simultaneous practice in selection, as students express their own meanings and not those of a textbook writer.... Practice in selection should not be considered a separate activity for advanced classes: it can and should be included in class work from the very first lessons."[7] Moreover, "many drills may be given the appearance of a game, or of elementary communication, by provoking the students into asking the teacher a series of questions in response to cues; or the items of a drill may develop a series of comments about the activities and interests of teacher and students.... *The more students are interested in an activity in the target language, the more they feel the desire to communicate in the language,* and this is the first and most vital step in learning to use language forms spontaneously."[8]

Paulston has developed the communication drill concept in more detail.[9] She groups drills into mechanical drills, meaningful drills, and communicative drills.

In *mechanical drills*, there is complete control of the response so that the student does not even need to understand the drill to produce the correct response (as in simple substitution drills). Paulston suggests that if a nonsense word can be inserted as effectively by the student as a meaningful word, then the drill is of the mechanical type (for example: "This is a box"; "Wug"; "This is a wug"). Drilling of this type is pure production: sometimes merely practice in articulation, at others in constructing an orderly sequence. As such it has its place in the initial phase of introducing a new structure or for practicing some problem of pronunciation or intonation. An example of a mechanical drill would be:

> Pattern: I'm holding a book.
> Cue: Magazine.
> Response: I'm holding a magazine.
> Cue: Banana.
> Response: I'm holding a banana.
> Cue: Wug.
> Response: I'm holding a wug.

In *meaningful drills*, "there is still control of the response (although it may be correctly expressed in more than one way...) but the student cannot complete the drill without fully understanding structurally and semantically what he is saying." The following is an example of a meaningful drill:

> Question: When did you arrive this morning?
> Answer: I arrived at nine o'clock.
> Question: When will you leave this evening?
> Answer: I'll leave at six o'clock.

In a *communicative drill*, however, "there is no control of the response. The student has free choice of answer, and the criterion of selection here is his own opinion of the real world – whatever he wants to say." This sounds like autonomous interaction, but Paulston continues: "Whatever control there is lies in the stimulus.... It still remains a drill rather than free communication because we are still within the realm of the cue-response pattern." She gives the example: "What did you have for breakfast?" with its possibility of an orthodox response such as "I had toast and coffee for breakfast," or the unorthodox "I overslept and skipped breakfast so I wouldn't miss the bus." It is clear that the unconventional student may well turn this into real interaction, but my guess is that the majority of students, feeling insecure in their knowledge of the language and fairly certain of what the teacher expects, would remain in the area of pseudo-communication.

Palmer suggests what he calls *communication practice drills*. "In communication practice (CP) drills, the student finds pleasure in a response that is not only linguistically acceptable, but also conveys information personally relevant to himself and other people." As outlined, this is an interesting technique. Palmer maintains that "the most powerful technique at the teacher's disposal is his ability to verbally create situations which could be relevant to the student's own life and then to force the student to think about the meaning and consequences of what he would say in such situations."[10] Palmer's CP drills are drills in that they center on practice of particular structures such as:

> I would tell him to shut the door.
> her   turn on the light.
> them   bring some food.

He develops these, however, by a somewhat Socratic method:

> Teacher: Karen, if you and Susan came to class at 8 a.m. and it was winter and the room was dark at 8 a.m., what would you tell Susan?
>
> Karen: (with any luck at all) I would tell her to turn on the light.
>
> Teacher: And how about you, Paul, if you were with Mary and you wanted to read, what would you do?
>
> Paul: I would tell her to turn on the light.
>
> Teacher: (in student's native language) You as a boy would tell a girl to do that for you?
>
> Teacher: (continuing in the target language) Paul, if you came alone, and if I was in the room, what would you do?
>
> Paul: I would tell you to turn on the light.
>
> Teacher: Then I would throw you out of class.

In this type of drill Palmer is moving toward interaction in that students who give mechanically what appear to be correct responses may well be pulled up short because they have not thought about the implications of their responses in the imposed setting. With training in such drills, average students would possibly produce more original responses than in Paulston's communicative drills, because of the goad of the teacher's teasing and their natural desire to show that they had recognized the pedagogical stratagem. This type of drill teeters on the brink of interaction, but it is still in the area of pseudo-communication and production practice because the whole interchange is teacher-directed, with the specific intention of eliciting certain structures.

Using language freely for normal purposes

Where do we go from here? We must work out situations, from an early stage, where our students are on their own, trying to use the language for *the normal purposes of language*: establishing social relations; seeking and giving information; expressing reactions; learning or teaching others to do something; hiding intentions; talking their way out of trouble; persuading, discouraging, and entertaining others; sharing leisure activities; displaying their achievements; acting out social roles; discussing ideas; and playing with language for the fun of it.

When I say students are "on their own," I mean they are not supported or directed by the teacher: They may well be working with other students. In this type of practice students should be allowed to use anything they know of the language and any aids (gestures, drawings, pantomime) to fill out their meaning, when they are "at a loss for words."[11] *In this way they will learn to draw on everything they know at a particular moment* in their acquisition of the language, and fight to put their meaning over, as they would if they suddenly found themselves surrounded by monolingual speakers of the language. This experience is not intended to replace the careful teaching of the language we already supply (the skill-getting activities we organize) but to expand it with regular and frequent opportunities for autonomous interaction (skill-using), thus making full provision for a dimension of language learning, which at present is, if not completely neglected, at least given insufficient place in our programs. As I have said elsewhere: "Perfection at the pattern-drill level, no matter how impressive to the observer, cannot be an end in itself. It is a fruitless activity unless care is taken to see that the result of all this effort is the ability to use the language to express some message of one's own."[12] In 1964, I spoke of the need for developing "*that adventurous spirit* which will enable the student to try to meet any situation by putting what he knows to maximum use."[13] In 1968, I wrote

47

"students should be encouraged, at the advanced level, to try out new combinations of elements to create novel utterances. This is what the advanced student would do were he to find himself in a foreign country. He would make every effort to express his meaning by all kinds of recombinations of the language elements at his disposal. *The more daring he is in such linguistic innovation, the more rapidly he progresses.*"[14] On looking back I feel it was a mistake to tag this recommendation specifically to "the advanced student" (a vague entity at best). Where we have been failing may well be in not encouraging this adventurous spirit from an early stage, with the result that our students find it difficult to move from structured security to the insecurity of reliance on their own resources, just as young would-be swimmers cling to their mother's hand or insist on having one foot on the bottom of the pool.

In Savignon's interesting study, students in the experimental communicative skills program (which consisted of one hour per week supplementing the regular audiolingual type of course) "were given the opportunity to speak French in a variety of communicative settings. These ranged from short (1–2 minute) exchanges between a student and a fluent speaker of French in a simulated situation to whole group discussions on topics of current interest. Emphasis was put on getting meaning across; students were urged to use every means at their disposal to understand and in turn to make themselves understood. Grammar and pronunciation errors were expected and were always ignored when they did not interfere with meaning. In other words, the experimenter and the other fluent speakers who participated in these sessions reacted to what was said, not to how it was said."[15] One student commented: "These sessions taught me to say what I wanted to say instead of book conversations."[16] If we compare this comment with the student's remark quoted at the beginning of this chapter it seems that these students did begin to "talk off the tops of their heads."

Autonomous interaction in the language program

Just how practice in autonomous interaction can be incorporated into the program will depend on the type of program, but incorporate it we must, giving it a substantial role in the students' learning. We must not feel that interaction is somehow "wasting time" when there is "so much to learn." Unless this adventurous spirit is given time to establish itself as a constant attitude, most of what is learned will be stored unused, and we will produce learned individuals who are inhibited and fearful in situations requiring language use. As Carroll has said, "When utterances are not generated to attain communicative goals, they can hardly be rewarded by the attainment of such goals, and language learning is deprived of its true meaning."[17] With careful selection of the activity, *some genuine interaction can be a part of every lesson*, even early in the learning process, with expansion of the complexity of the demands as the student advances.

Practice in autonomous interaction should be individualized in the sense that it should allow for the different ways students learn, the different paces at which they learn, the different things that interest them, and the different situations in which they prefer to learn. *Students should be offered a choice of tasks* (things to do, things to find out, problems to solve, situations to which to react) and then be allowed to choose their own way, their own place, time, and company for handling them. Some may prefer to work regularly with one other person; some will prefer to work consistently with a small group; some will choose to work with the teacher. Some who are loners will prefer to work through certain situations by themselves, demonstrating their capacity as individuals (and many of these in a quiet way may outpace their fellows through sheer single-mindedness of purpose).

Students cannot be set down in groups, or sent off in pairs, and told to interact in the foreign language. *Motivation to communicate must be aroused.* Occasionally some fortuitous incident or combination of personalities will cause a desire to communicate something in the second language to emerge spontaneously, but in most instructional situations it will need to be fostered by the intrinsic attraction of the task proposed and the students' interest in developing it. Such interest will make the interaction that follows autonomous: a genuine communication from one person to another, not just another imposed act of pseudo-communication. Because of the personal nature of the activity we are promoting, *the type of reaction to be displayed will always remain consistent with the personality of the particular student.* Some people are temperamentally incapable of interacting with a babble of words; to force them to do so is to force them back into pseudo-communication and into mouthing learned phrases. The quality of the interaction will be judged by other criteria: ability to receive and express meaning, to understand and convey intentions, to perform acceptably in situations and in relations with others.

Earlier I suggested various normal uses of language in interaction that can be incorporated in this type of activity. Here I will expand on these and set down a few elaborations of each.[18] Any imaginative teacher will think of others.

Communicating naturally

(1) *Establishing and maintaining social relations:* greetings between persons of the same and different age and status; introductions; wishes for special occasions; polite enquiries (with attention to the permissible and the expected questions in the culture); making arrangements; giving directions to strangers; apologies, excuses, refusals, mild rebukes, hedging (the gentle art of noncommunication); encouraging, discouraging, and persuading others. Students may be sent to find out from a monolingual native speaker (or one who pretends to be monolingual) how these are enacted in the cultural context of the language being learned.

(2) *Seeking information* on subjects for which students have some basic vocabulary. (At some point finding out specific technical vocabulary can be part of this type of interaction.) Once again the native speakers or informants involved act as though they were monolingual. The information may be useful for (1), for (3), for (4), for (8), or even for (11).

(3) *Giving information* about oneself, one's background, one's country, or about some subject in which one is proficient. The student may be giving information to other students learning to do or make something (4), or passing on information gained in (2). Simulated settings like bank or airline counters, customs desks, workshops, or restaurants may be used where the students are confined to a school setting.

(4) *Learning or teaching how to do or make something.* The possibilities here are limitless. The pressure of intensive courses can be relieved by organizing actual sessions in the second language where students work with real-life materials and activities (sports, physical exercise, hobbies, crafts, music, dance, cooking, making clothes).

(5) *Expressing one's reactions.* Students can be put in real situations or simulated situations where they have to react verbally throughout a television show, at an exhibition of pictures or photographs, or during a friendly sharing of slides.

(6) *Hiding one's intentions.* Each student may be given a mission that must not be revealed under any provocation but must be carried out within a given period of time. This type of activity carries purposeful use of the language beyond course hours as students try to discover each other's missions.

(7) *Talking one's way out of trouble.* Simulated or real situations of increasing verbal difficulty should be set up where students must use their wits to extract themselves from some dilemma.

(8) *Problem solving.* A problem may involve (2) or (4), or even (6) and (7). The problem represented should be an active one whose solution requires verbal activity or enquiry. As early as 1953, Carroll posed the question whether aural-oral methods might not be more

successful "if, instead of presenting the student with a fixed, predetermined lesson to be learned, the teacher created a 'problem-solving' situation in which the student must find...appropriate verbal responses for solving the problem," thus being early forced "to learn, by a kind of trial-and-error process, to *communicate* rather than merely to utter the speech patterns in the lesson plans."[19]

(9) *Sharing leisure activities.* Students should have the opportunity to learn and become proficient in the games and diversions of the target culture. They should be able to participate in verbal competitions. Where there are special activities associated with festivals or national holidays these should be engaged in.

(10) *Conversing over the telephone.* This is always difficult in a second language and should be practiced early. The student should use a phone book in the second language and, where possible, make actual calls enquiring about goods, services, or timetables for transport. The help of monolingual contacts outside the course should be enlisted. (Some incapacitated persons and older people living alone would enjoy participating in this type of communication.) This activity can be linked with (2) or (8) and will often involve (3).

(11) *Entertaining others.* Students should be given opportunities to use their natural talents or encouraged through role-playing sessions and skits to act out in front of a group. They may conduct radio call-in programs or a TV talk or game show. Groups of students may prepare and present radio or TV commercials (these may involve more or less talking interspersed with mime and are therefore very suitable for the early stages of a course). A continuing serial story, with episodes developed successively by different groups, keeps interest alive.

(12) *Displaying one's achievements.* Students may tell the group about what they did in (4), (5), (6), (7), or (8), or they may present and explain special projects. This can be a regular culminating activity to draw together more individualized efforts at interaction.

(13) *Acting out social roles.* In our social life, we are continually acting out roles: the hostess, the guest, the employee, the leader, the impressive achiever, the long-suffering noncomplainer. Improvisations, where students act out various roles in relation to each other, are not only useful and interesting but also provide a cover for those more inhibited students who do not mind expressing feelings and viewpoints when they are presumed to be those of others. These activities also bring in aspects of (1), (3), (5), (7), and (11).

(14) *Discussing ideas and opinions.* This is one of the most frequent verbal activities in any language. It can be linked with understanding the target culture and similarities and differences in ways of acting and reacting between speakers of the first and second lan-

guages. Discussion groups, debates, panel discussions, lecturettes or oral reports with questions and comments from the listeners, and frequent classroom discussion of second-language material read or seen are obvious ways to develop this ability, which also involves (2), (3), (5), and (8).

(15) *Playing with language.* This is another frequent activity of all language users. We love jokes, puns, word games, crossword puzzles, and so on. Students can make up poems and learn nonsense and counting rhymes. Charades, in which students act out the various syllables of a word and then the complete word, are useful. As students go further, they become interested in word histories and word formation and learn to create their own words in acceptable ways. They also learn to distinguish levels of language (formal from familiar, standard usage from slang and jargon) and become familiar with regional and subgroup variants.

All of these activities will obviously not be possible for all students from the earliest stage of learning. The teacher will *select and graduate activities from these categories* so that the attitude of seeking to communicate is developed early in an activity that is within the student's growing capacity. An impossible task that bewilders and discourages students too early in their language learning is just as inhibiting of ultimate fluency as lack of opportunity to try what they can do with what they know.

Noncorrective approach to interaction

Some people will have deep-seated doubts about accepting such an approach, because they foresee that the student will make many errors that may become ingrained and ineradicable. It was because of such problems that many turned away from the direct method, seeking something more systematic that would seem to ensure more accurate production. Unfortunately, the emphasis on correct production at all times and the firm determination to create a learning situation where students would not make mistakes seem to have led to an impasse for many students. If we wish to facilitate the "great leap" into autonomous communication that I have described, then *a change of attitude toward mistakes during interaction practice is imperative.* It is during production (or pseudo-communication) practice that immediate corrections should be made. It is then that we should make the students conscious of possible errors and so familiarize them with acceptable sequences that they are able to monitor their own production and work toward its improvement in spontaneous interaction. In interaction practice *we are trying to develop an attitude of innovation and experimentation* with the new language. Nothing is more dampening of enthusiasm and effort than constant correction when students are trying to express their own ideas within the limitations of their newly acquired knowledge of the language. What is required is that the instructor note silently the consistent and systematic errors made by each student (not slips of the tongue and occasional lapses). These errors will then be discussed with students individually at a time when the instructor is helping them evaluate their success in interaction, with particular attention being paid to those types of errors that hinder communication. Such an analytic session may be conducted from time to time with a tape of an actual communication sequence, the student or group of students being asked to detect errors in their own spontaneous production and suggest corrections and improvements.[20] This technique makes the students more alert to their own mistakes and to other possibilities for expressing their meaning that they have not been exploiting.

Many of the types of activities listed have already found their place in our courses. The originality of the approach lies not so much in the novelty of the activities as in the way in which they are approached. *To develop autonomous control of language for communication we must at some time allow the student autonomy* and, conversely, we must discourage dependence. We must give students practice in relying on their own resources and using their ingenuity, so that very early in their language learning they realize that only by interacting freely and independently with others can they learn the control and ready retrieval essential for fluent language use. As Jespersen once said, "The first condition for good instruction in...languages would seem to be to give the pupil as much as possible to do with and in the...language; he must be steeped in it, not only get a sprinkling of it now and then; he must be ducked down in it and get to feel as if he were in his own element, so that he may at last disport himself in it as an able swimmer."[21]

Let's work it out

1 Take some structural pattern drills from the textbook you have been using and try to turn them into meaningful drills. Now try to rewrite them as communicative drills. Try these out on others in your group. What did you learn from this exercise?

2 Design some classroom conversational practice as pseudo-communication (that is, "near communication with all the outward appearances of communication"). What would you have to do to convert these activities into genuine communicative interaction?

3 Design some role-playing activities for practice in establishing and maintaining social relations, talking one's way out of trouble, and acting out social roles.

4 Draw up some lists of words and expressions in the second language that students would need to know to express various kinds of reactions (appreciation, frustration, hesitancy, suspicion, enthusiasm, etc.). Begin to use these with the class you are teaching.

5 Plan in detail some leisure activities in which students can use the language with each other in a purposeful way. (These may be for a club, festivity, national celebration, dinner, or international day, among others.)

4 Bridging the gap to autonomous interaction

In Chapter 3, I emphasized the need for providing students from the earliest stages with a great deal of practice in using language for its normal purposes, that is, practice in interaction (skill-using), and I proposed a number of activities that involved spontaneous use of language. I wish now to consider the gap in the model between skill-getting and skill-using, and will make proposals for *a smooth and natural transition from production practice to interaction*.

If free, spontaneous interaction is an attractive extra in a program that is rigid and mechanical, we should not be surprised to see our students develop a kind of schizophrenia: *Personality A, which is submissive and malleable*, produces correctly constructed sequences as directed by the teacher in intensive practice, whereas *Personality B asserts its own individuality*, completely ignoring, when engaging in autonomous interaction, what Personality A has been so laboriously practicing. How can we develop our program so that such a schizophrenic situation will not develop?

The route is not the goal

The important questions to be considered in movement toward spontaneous expression or autonomous interaction are: *Where are we going?* and *By what route?* Some instructors unfortunately are not quite sure where the goal is or which is the best route. They take their students by routes that are circuitous, lead to deadends, backtrack, and make the going rough and difficult, so that attention is on the going instead of the destination, and students begin to feel that the journey itself is the most important thing, completely losing sight of the goal.

We see examples of the route-as-goal when instructors are chiefly interested in eliciting near-native pronunciation in imitation and choirlike perfection in construction exercises. We see instructor and students

Revised version of an article originally published in *TESOL Quarterly* 7 (1973): 25–34, as "From Linguistic Competence to Communicative Competence." © 1969 by Teachers of English to Speakers of Other Languages. Reprinted with permission of the publisher.

settling down in cozy comfort on the way when smooth and effort-less production of correctly constructed sentences, even complicated and intricate ones, satisfies. These students become completely pre-occupied with good performance in pseudo-communication and rarely engage in authentic interaction. Production practice is necessary for developing linguistic control, without which there can be no solidly based fluency in interaction, but it is less demanding for instructor and students than trying to develop communicative ability itself. Consequently, many find it an unexciting but comfortable haven and never reach the goal at all. At least, they feel, here is something tangible for their efforts.

Other routes, through similar country, lead to the destination di-rectly but they demand effort and persistence. The students to whom these routes are indicated know where they are going and what they will be able to do when they get there. They are prepared psychologi-cally and practically for the goal of autonomous interaction and all their activities are directed toward it and toward it alone. These students never allow themselves to become absorbed in any activity on the way as an end in itself, but always as a means to the clearly recognized goal of spontaneous communication and as an activity of the same generic nature.

A program directed toward skill-using

Merely adding interaction activities of the kind elaborated in Chap-ter 3 to a conventional course will not provide the answer. *Skill-using activities should not be supplemental, but should spring naturally and inevitably from the types of activities engaged in for skill-getting.* The only way to avoid the schizophrenia of Personality A and Per-sonality B is to develop the whole program with Personality B in mind, so that Personality B is free to operate imaginatively at all times. This will not be possible with a patched-up program – some-thing added here and something added there while the bulk of the program is based on wrong assumptions. We must rethink the pro-gram so that all efforts are directed toward the perceived goal.[1]

In many programs much effort is put into the production of what are sometimes called "controlled drills," and reliance is placed on a carefully organized step-by-step progression toward the goal. Yet, despite careful planning and fastidious practice, students still stumble and falter when trying to express their own ideas in the second language.

I would like to suggest that we look here for the source of our schizophrenia. *Our conventional controlled drills are based on as-sumptions that make them incompatible with our ultimate goal of autonomous interaction.* They are usually based entirely on manipu-lation of language elements as though that is all language learning consists of. Nor is the answer, as some would suggest, merely a matter of switching over to the learning of explicit grammar rules that we then attempt to put into operation in language material, important as the comprehension of the syntactic rules of a language may be. We must recognize that "knowing" involves not one but several types of cognitive processes.

Three systems for processing information

Bruner posits three parallel systems in human cognition for process-ing information and storing it for use, all capable of partial transfor-mation one into the other.[2] They reflect the three ways people can "know" something.[3] If we understand these three ways (enactive, iconic or perceptual, and symbolic) we can analyze in practical fash-ion what the student has to learn in learning a second language.[4] We can then categorize the various aspects of linguistic knowledge as belonging largely to one or another of these systems and devise the types of practice most appropriate for the kind of learning involved in each case. Here we must not be discouraged by people who tell us that nobody knows just what "knowing" a language involves. If we had to wait until complete and irrefutable theoretical knowledge were attained in such a complex area as language acquisition, we would be forced to give up all activity in language teaching. Theoret-ical advances are sparked and verified through practical observations. We must act on what is known at a particular stage and continually adapt and readapt our procedures as new knowledge becomes available.

The first representational system in human cognition, according to Bruner, is the *enactive. This system is acquired through manipulation and action by a process of stimulus-response conditioning.* In this case we "know" by a habitual pattern of responsive action. Mediat-ing responses transform the stimulus prior to the response, and these are processes of understanding that make the response a personal one. Because of this internal transformation of the stimulus, different people require different time intervals for making the response. In a second language what we can "know" through active response are such things as the arbitrary structural associations that can be set out in paradigms. In actual meaningful language use, however, the other two cognitive systems are immediately involved: Knowing the form of a verb ending after a particular pronoun subject may be a habitual reaction, but knowing when to use that particular ending in the expression of a message is much more complex. There is, therefore, a role, but a limited one, for stimulus-response conditioning in making automatic the production of certain arbitrary elements of surface structure. (Bruner suggests it is also appropriate for learning the production of strange sounds, although, once again, learning when to use the sound as it has been learned and when to adapt and modify it in context involves other types of representation.)

Bruner's second system of representation is the *iconic*,[5] *acquired through perceptual organization and imagery*, that is, auditory and visual pattern recognition. Here we build on the inductive recognition of the gestalt: the whole consisting of systematically distributed, interrelated parts. The identification of patterns in what we hear and see aids memory. We must devise methods for recognition and assimilation of recurring systematic arrangements of formal features and their acceptable rearrangements. Such features as fixed word order in sentence types or in syntactic relationships and structural patterns that continually recur in association with each other are appropriately listed here. Bruner warns us that "affective and motivational factors affect imagery and perceptual organization strikingly." For this reason we must look for individual differences in perception of auditory (and visual) patterning and realize that the disconcerted or embarrassed student will often fail to recognize auditory patterns and may develop, as a result, an emotional block against all auditory activity. The bored student will simply not retain them.

Third, we have the *symbolic representational system, which operates through internalized language and logical processes in the formation of concepts*. This symbolic system enables us to categorize and to establish hierarchies of categories, principles, and rules, to bring order into the complexity of what is being learned, permitting "a transition from merely orderly behavior to logical behavior."[6] This systematization of the language may be established inductively by the student, but in many cases it can be acquired more rapidly through the deductive medium of the explanations of the teacher or the textbook (using language, "the second signal system," as Pavlov called it). Nevertheless the student, whether guided or not, must abstract features and synthesize them into rules of operation that will create new meanings. It is the symbolic representational system that processes the many complexities of syntax through which formal features and arrangements of features attain vigorous life in the expression of infinite nuances of meaning.[7] Students go beyond the specific instances in which they have seen the forms of language in operation into the creative use of language in novel situations.

These three types of representation coexist in an adult student's cognitive system – they are not stages of learning. Any or all may be appropriately activated at any point in a learning process: It is for us to analyze the aspects of language learning for which they are appropriate and continually interweave them in learning activities as they are interwoven in actual language use, if we wish our students to do more than perform well in exercises of a specific kind.

Types of intensive practice exercises must then be varied. Mere repetition and manipulation will help with only a minor portion of what must be known. The associations in a paradigm are arbitrary (*I get, he gets*), but the notion of paradigmatic variations (the fact that the new language has more or fewer paradigmatic associations than the student's native language) is conceptual and must be understood before knowledge of the details of the paradigm can be effective in use. Similarly, formal features of tenses are paradigmatic and may be learned by rote, but of themselves they are so much useless baggage. Using them appropriately involves conceptual understanding of the way in which the new language expresses time relationships.

We must develop more and better ways of dealing with the conceptual aspects of language: the patterns of arrangements and the intricate complexities of interacting systems and subsystems of rules.[8] These cannot be assimilated absentmindedly. In each of these cases, "knowing" depends on awareness of abstractions such as similarities, differences, functions, and interactive relationships. Without such awareness the student cannot operate confidently within the new system. This awareness can only develop when the student focuses on abstract operations. Such focus depends on the degree of personal involvement in correct selection from among the possible variations of the system. We must concentrate on the types of activities that elicit this personal involvement.

Implications for classroom practice

In the model presented in Chapter 3, I referred to production exercises as pseudo-communication, and I emphasized the first segment of this term, *pseudo*-communication, in order to contrast it with real interaction activities. Here I wish to emphasize the second segment, pseudo-*communication*, because this, I believe, is the way we can bridge the gap between skill-getting and skill-using. Unless production practice is always regarded as pseudo-*communication*, our schizophrenic situation will continue, and our students will not apply what they have practiced in articulation and construction when involved in interaction. Let us elucidate, then, the ways in which production exercises can take the form of pseudo-*communication*.

Passive exercises do not prepare students for active use of language; completely controlled and directed activity does not prepare students for autonomous expression.

Each exercise must demand of the student close *attention, abstraction* (recognition of the requirements of the particular situation), and *active construction* (requiring recall of stored cognitive information and judicious selection). Exercises that can be performed mechanically are useful only for demonstration of associations of forms, of systematic patterning, or of relationships. They allow the student time to see the picture – to observe the interplay of surface elements or grasp the principle. They serve an introductory function, after which they are no longer of use unless it appears later that the student is confused, at which time they may be reintroduced for clarification or confirmation. They must lead directly to intensive practice in the types of constructions that require students to produce utterances they themselves have selected – practice that will continue until they demonstrate control of these constructions. Opportunity must then be given without delay for students to use what they have been learning within the wider syntactic system they have been building up. Thus, *every extension of linguistic knowledge is tested out immediately in natural communicative use.* Luria has pointed out that grammatical speech will not arise if there is no objective necessity for speech communication.[9] We must create that necessity by the design of our activities.

How then can intensive practice exercises become pseudo-*communication* and gradually lead to real communication? Here I shall set out some guidelines.

1. As each exercise is designed, it should be given a *situational context and a lexical content that are readily transferable to interchanges* between instructor and student, or student and student.

Are we practicing question forms? Then what is the transferability of items that produce questions with zero probability of occurrence?

> We are sitting in the hall.
> Are we sitting in the hall?
> Janet and I are at the movies.
> Are Janet and I at the movies?

How often in conversation do we move from statement to question anyway, unless there is a change of reference as in:

> "I've been waiting a quarter of an hour. Have you been waiting too?"

2. After a brief presentation of forms (that is, *teacher-directed practice*) to develop familiarity with a particular aspect of the language, the activity should move to interchange between student and student. *Student-directed practice* may take the form of a chaining activity in a large group (for example, question-answer, question-answer from student to student), or of a small-group activity with a student leader. In a small-group activity students teach and learn from each other while the instructor listens to see what further directed practice may be required. Self-selected small groups also provide for those variations in ability and pace that are so necessary for individual learning.

Student-directed activity moves smoothly into some interteam competition or game that enables groups to test each other's knowledge. For any aspect of language structure a game or simulated activity can be invented that forces the students into *autonomous activity* in which they produce responses similar to those in an artificial teacher-directed exercise, but this time of their own volition for their own purposes. This conscious and intentional progress at all times from teacher-directed demonstration to student-directed application to autonomous student production makes the further step to *communicative interaction* natural and attainable. In this way Personality B is involved early in the practice sequence and is not suddenly called into play in an artificial "extra" activity.

3. With a little imagination even the simplest of structures can be practiced in autonomous production.

Are we practicing affirmative and negative statements? Students can compete in producing the most improbable statements or set themselves up as a Liars' Club:

"I borrowed a thousand dollars but I didn't pay it back."

"Last night I flew to the moon and I didn't come back."

Are we practicing question forms? A simulated telephone link may be set up. Students are required to ask questions until they have been able to identify the person calling, until they have found out what a presumably diffident caller wanted to ask them, or until they have extracted from the caller what he or she wanted them to do. Although this is a simulated situation, it parallels a possible communication situation.

Another realistic way of eliciting question forms is for the teacher to give Student A vague instructions to transmit to Student B. Student B must continue to ask questions of Student A, and Student A of the teacher, until Student B is quite clear about what to do. Upon completion of the required task, Student B reports back to the teacher on what has been done, so that the teacher can verify that the original message was accurately transmitted.

Are we practicing indirect speech? The teacher transmits information very softly to one student, who is expected to pass on to the class what the teacher has said:

> "She said she saw an accident on the way to class."
> "She said one person was injured."

This can be a three-way transmission:

> Instructor says to Student A: I don't like rock music.
> Student A says quietly to Student B: He says he doesn't like rock music.
> Student B says to the class: He said he didn't like rock music.

Although this is a structured exercise, it simulates a possible situation where, for instance, people at one end of a table cannot hear what their fellow guests are saying.

Another variation of the same activity is the familiar parlor game of "Confidences" where one student whispers to the next along the line what the preceding person thought was said by the originator of the message. The last person in the line repeats aloud the message as it has finally been received, and this is compared with the original message. This can be a very amusing activity because of the distortions that creep in as the message is inaccurately perceived and reconstructed by different persons in the group.

4. Whether we are using expansion, completion, or translation exercises we have the possibility of two types: Type A, which provides only for Personality A, and Type B, which encourages the emergence of the innovative Personality B.[10]

A Type A expansion exercise is purely manipulative. Students are supplied with elements they must insert at the correct places in a basic sentence frame. *A Type B expansion exercise provides students with the opportunity to create new sentences* from the basic frame by expanding it as they wish as often as they wish. (This activity can become a competition to see which students can expand the meaning of the utterance still further through the addition of another word or phrase.)

TYPE A EXPANSION EXERCISE
> Basic frame: He goes to town.
> Instructor: Often.
> Student(s):   He often goes to town.
> Instructor: On Saturdays.
> Student(s):   He often goes to town on Saturdays.

TYPE B EXPANSION EXERCISE
This may be a competition or a chaining activity.
> Student A: He goes to town.
> Student B: He often goes to town.

Student C: He often goes to town on Wednesdays.
Student D: He often goes to town by train on Wednesdays.
Student E: In summer he often goes to town by train on Wednesdays.

The competition continues until students run out of inspiration or possibilities of insertion. Note that students not only have the opportunity to develop the meaning as they wish, but in so doing they also reproduce the whole expanded sentence each time as part of their own production.

A similar division can be made in types of *completion exercises.* In a Type A completion exercise a fixed segment is retained, varying perhaps in tense or person in concert with the element the instructor supplies. In a Type B completion exercise, students can make their own semantic contributions within the syntactic framework they are acquiring.

TYPE A COMPLETION EXERCISE
Students are presented with a model sentence; for example, "I took her pencil because she took mine." They are told that, throughout the exercise, they must retain a concluding segment of similar meaning to "because she took mine," but as the introductory segment varies they must vary the person referred to in the concluding segment.

Model: I took her pencil because she took mine.
Instructor: She took my book.
Student(s): She took my book because I took hers.
Instructor: We took their seats.
Student(s): We took their seats because they took ours.

TYPE B COMPLETION EXERCISE
Students are asked to invent excuses for aberrant behavior on their own part or on the part of other students in the group.

Student A: I sat in his place because he sat in mine.
Student B: I ate her lunch because she ate mine.
Student C: Mary broke John's pencil because he broke hers.
Student D: My father used my mother's car because she used his.

The Type A activity may be useful to allow the student time to assimilate the operations of the basic structure, but the Type B activity is essential if students are to develop the command and confidence they need for interaction activities.

Sometimes *oral translation exercises* are used, when the class has a homogeneous language background and the instructor is familiar with their language. In this case, we again have the possibility of Type A and Type B exercises.

In a *Type A oral translation exercise* students translate rapidly a series of unconnected sentences linked only by their central attention to a difficult point of grammar or an idiomatic turn of phrase. In a *Type B oral translation exercise* the same attention can be paid to a specific problem of grammar (for example, use of past tenses), but the sentences in the sequence have a semantic relatedness or a situational development such that the students can simulate a simultaneous interpretation situation or pretend to relay the information sentence by sentence to a presumably monolingual visitor in their midst. Once again the activity is the same, but the situation has an authenticity that prepares students to use the language in real situations when the opportunity arises.

So we could continue. To avoid schizophrenia let us keep most of our production practice time for Type B activities, which develop quickly and easily into interaction, that is, use of language for the normal purposes of language.[11] In this way, we will wean our students early from dependence on direction from without, thus preparing them psychologically for the uninhibited autonomy of the confident language user.

Let's discuss

1 Work out a Type A and a Type B substitution drill. What problems did you have? What does this indicate about substitution drills?
2 How can you ensure that skill-using activities "spring naturally and inevitably from the types of activities engaged in for skill-getting"? Give precise examples.
3 What types of exercises would you propose for acquiring language by way of each of Bruner's three systems of "knowing" (enactive, perceptual, symbolic)?
4 Discuss the difference between *pseudo*-communication and pseudo-*communication*. Give examples of types of exercises and activities that fall under each of these headings.
5 Discuss in detail activities for teaching the use of the possessive forms that move from teacher-directed practice to student-directed practice, then to autonomous activity and communicative interaction.

5 Individualized instruction and cooperative learning: some theoretical considerations

Individualization of instruction, or of the learning environment, is not a new concept, nor an American one. It seems to have skipped across the Atlantic at various periods. Rousseau and Pestalozzi in Europe influenced Horace Mann and John Dewey in the United States.[1] The same beliefs that Dewey held were reflected in the British informal elementary school of the 1960s,[2] which applied ideas drawn from the research of Piaget in Geneva.[3] This British movement in turn inspired Weber's Open Corridor in a school in Harlem.[4] Nor should we forget the enduring and pervasive influence on early childhood education everywhere of Froebel, Montessori, and Susan Isaacs.[5]

These influences cannot be clearly delimited within precise episodes in educational experience, although the names of certain schools and school systems do spring to mind. The beliefs they embody have persisted, as a constantly surfacing underground, wherever teachers have cared more deeply about their students than about their subject matter. Lest anyone think individualized instruction emerged full-grown on the educational scene in the seventies,[6] allow me to quote from a history of American education published in the early fifties:

> In city school systems around the country it was found in 1948 that 40 percent of the cities had adopted some form of individualized instruction. More than half of the cities over 30,000 population had adopted such programs, and the trend toward still more individualized instruction for those cities that used it was strong.[7]

Individualized approaches such as the Dalton or Contract Plan, the Winnetka Plan, and the "unit method," which achieved worldwide recognition, were on their way in the twenties.[8] Technical implementation has evolved and concepts have been enriched, with an *emphasis on individual development* rather than the earlier emphasis on individual differences, but the "unipacs" and LAPs (learning activity packets) of today and the "assignments" of yesterday are in the same

Revised version of an article originally published in Gerhard Nickel, ed., *Proceedings of the Fourth International Congress of Applied Linguistics.* Vol. 3 (Stuttgart: HochschulVerlag, 1976), pp. 437–54.

family line.[9] Why then, we may ask, is there such a resurgence of interest and energy in this area in this late twentieth-century period?

The philosophy of individualized instruction

We will gain some insight into this question if we first identify the essential philosophy that is basic to what we may regard as intermittent waves of an ebbing and flowing tide. This essence is captured in the following quotation. Each person

> is born a unique individual, and development is *in* this individual. His world of inner needs and meanings is personal, lived out in the human relationships into which he is born and with people whose world has been equally individually determined. He has particular, specific bits of experience and particular, specific expectations, and it is these that he brings to his relationships – meeting people with differing experiences and expectations. His development is individual and uneven in pattern and pace and made even more individual by the personal route of his interests.[10]

In this quotation, we have all the emphases of the contemporary individualization movement, and from it we can also see what individualization is not. Our students have their own inner needs. They come with *an individual perception of what is meaningful and valuable*, which they have acquired within a cultural milieu (in which ethnic, socioeconomic, and subcultural influences have played a role). *They are maturing (developing) at an individual rate*, so that they have their own preferred pace, mode, and style of learning, which may vary at any particular stage. They have individual goals and expectations, and therefore *their motivation is intensely personal but purposeful.* The "personal route" of their interests dictates the content that will absorb them. They learn through active experience, particularly as they interact with others. This experience is genuinely shared, because each individual in the group contributes his or her personal experiences to the communal enterprise; *the individual's inner world is thus "lived out" in human relationships.* Consequently, individualization cannot be equated with "isolated learning,"[11] as in independent study, although some individuals may prefer to work on their own on certain occasions (or even a great deal, depending on their preferred style of learning). We may note that no mention is made in this quotation of "abilities" or "aptitude," which are comparative expressions. The proponent of individualization does not compare students, but allows each to learn as his or her individual nature permits. *There are no nonlearners in the human family.*

A fine philosophy and one with a distinguished and respectable ancestry, you may say, but is it relevant to our day and age? In order to determine relevance, we need to study carefully what distinguishes the world in which our young people are growing up. The trends I seek to identify are worldwide, even if they may appear more slowly in some cultures.

The world in which our students learn

Ours is an era of mechanization, standardization, and homogenization. It is the throwaway age. It is *an age of anonymity and depersonalization.* In the United States, we are our Social Security numbers, which computers devour or reject. It is interesting that the U.S. Internal Revenue Service and the Blue Cross/Blue Shield Health Plans, among others, depend on the computer to spit out those returns and claims that do not conform to certain patterns. You give too much to charitable causes for a person of your income bracket: This is suspect. You have had too many illnesses this year for a person of your age, occupation, or social milieu: This must be investigated. You must not stand out from the crowd. Of course, investigation may show that you are just a harmless oddity, in which case you can be reinserted in the computer and ignored. The skills of many of our generation have become rapidly dispensable, since automation and robotized production demand only a few who can be trained rapidly for specific tasks, and replaced as rapidly if they fall out. No wonder it is an age of the alienation of the young, who have never experienced a period when they really counted, when their contribution to society was considered essential. The brief euphoria of 1968 when young people were heeded because they were a substantial statistic has faded, and society has again turned its attention away from those for whom there is as yet no place, and perhaps never will be. This is the kind of world we have created or allowed to creep up on us.

It is not, however, a world with which many of our young people feel satisfied. They see it as a world careering ahead without direction – careening perhaps toward disaster. Our young people know more about what is going on in the world – what is being done with their world – than any previous generation and they don't like it. Many do not perceive a role in society with which they care to identify. The more vocal among them demand a voice in their future. They see the need for responsible individuals independent of the system, willing to stand out and live by other values than those of the corporate yes-man on the make – *self-directed individuals who can work and think*

67

with others. They see the need to reassert the values of cooperation over those of individualism in the service of one's own interests. They wish to be able to choose. They need an education that will help them to develop their ability to think, to weigh alternatives, to work without compulsion, and to accept responsibility for their choices.

This is a world that has dedicated its efforts to universal education, frequently referred to as "mass education" – a formula clearly indicating that we are talking here of instruction, not education. There cannot be education of a mass. There can be manipulation of a mass or exploitation of a mass. *There can be education only of persons, of individuals.* Even the concept of universal instruction can be a cruel delusion and a frustrating deception when it means trying to pour new wine into old bottles. Instruction for failure in the system of another age is not good enough. Even where the school system is willing to face reforms, so that the uneducated become educated and the "disadvantaged" become advantaged, this will not suffice unless society can provide opportunities for all to play a self-fulfilling and satisfying role, even in modest circumstances. Education must provide individuals with the kinds of opportunities for development that will enable them to create worthwhile lives for themselves, not merely prepare them to fit into a pattern or temporary slot.

Knowledge, or at least factual knowledge, is accumulating at an exponential rate and becoming obsolete almost as fast as it is accumulating. This is not the time for merely acquiring a body of knowledge. It has become imperative for our young people *to learn how to learn, how to assess facts, how to evaluate new knowledge, and how to put knowledge to use.* Education, then, must encourage creative, heuristic thinking, boldness in application, and ability to function autonomously.

So now more than ever we need to educate, rather than instruct. Much of what we taught in an earlier period our students already know from informal sources: television, magazines, personal experience through travel, and extended contacts.

What can education do?

These, then, are forceful reasons for a reconsideration of our educational approach. Where education and societal needs do not keep pace something must crack, and the breakdown in many educational systems throughout the world is clearly observable. Our education must, in some way, face up to the world as it is today and prepare our young people to do something in it and about it. From these preoccupations springs the present resurgence of emphasis on the individual, on the person, and on developing educational procedures that maximize opportunities for participation by students with teachers in cooperatively planning and implementing purposeful activity. Procedures must be developed for *involving students in responsible decision making and self-direction:* for building a strong foundation of self-confidence and appreciation of one's uniqueness, and for raising levels of aspiration. Originality and creative endeavor must be encouraged, as well as the flexibility of mind that enables each person to adapt to new circumstances and recognize new opportunities. This is not an easy task, but it is most certainly an urgent one.

We may wonder what this can possibly have to do with second-language teachers who surely know that their task is implanting another language. No new knowledge there. For too long, language teachers have claimed a place apart, rarely recognizing that theirs is an educational task like that of any other teacher. It is not for second-language teachers to train for rigid performance and unthinking reproduction, while their fellow educators are seeking to develop flexibility and willingness to experiment. Here a word from the generative semanticist Green seems appropriate.

Two meanings of "teach"

In an interesting linguistic analysis of the verb *teach*, Green shows that in English we are really dealing with two homophonous verbs, as indicated by their semantic and syntactic properties.[12] In other words, the verb *teach* does not behave in all respects like the verb *give*. The two sentences

1a Mary gave John an apple
1b Mary gave an apple to John

are synonymous, whereas the two sentences

2a Mary taught John linguistics
2b Mary taught linguistics to John

are not.

3a The teacher taught Jane the meaning of responsibility

implies that Jane learned it, whether the teaching was explicit and voluntary or implicit and involuntary, whereas

3b The teacher taught the meaning of responsibility to Jane

implies an explicit act on the teacher's part, but does not presume learning by Jane. This distinction is particularly appropriate in the present discussion. *What we think we teach is not necessarily what our students learn.* Much of what they learn comes from their associations with other significant contacts in and out of school (parents, peers, other teachers) and from all kinds of activities. What is learned in the long run is determined by the personal perception of the situation by each student – what is important to them individually and how the situation affects their sense of well-being (of security, belonging, and self-esteem, to use Maslow's terminology).[13] We should, therefore, be much more sensitive to the learning environment we create and the qualities of the relationships within it, rather than attribute to our organization of explicit teaching the major role in student learning.

Let us look now at second-language teaching and see what kinds of demands this change of attitude lays on our profession by requiring a change of attitude on our part. How, then, can second-language teaching fit into the picture I have just drawn and still be true to its own nature as a discipline?

Second-language acquisition research

Research in second-language acquisition in natural environments makes it abundantly clear that different people at different ages acquire a second language in different ways and at different rates. Hatch, after an in-depth analysis of fifteen observational studies of forty children learning a second language without formal teaching, concludes that "the differences seem very great indeed."[14] One child with two-and-a-half hours' exposure to English a day was able to speak the language like a native after five months, another with greater exposure to English each day had said only a few words of English in two years.

Hatch distinguishes in these studies[15] "*rule-formers,*" who sorted and organized the input from the beginning, from "*data-gatherers,*" who seemed merely to accumulate segments of language without any identifiable systematizing, yet the members of each of these groups seemed to acquire the language in their own good time and in their own way. Some learners experienced interference from their first language in expressing themselves; others did not, but explained items to themselves in their first language. Some switched and mixed languages; others did not. Some merely inserted second-language vocabulary items, as they acquired them, into a first-language matrix; others occasionally used direct translations from the first to the second language, and so on. In a study of an adolescent Spanish speaker learning English, again without formal training, we find the subject trying to express adult ideas on a wide variety of topics, employing strategies of simplification and reduction, circumlocution for words he could not remember, gestures and repetition of words for increased intensity, and borrowing features of his native-language structure when he thought it could help him.[16]

The individual second-language learner

Such is the diversity of natural language learning. Hatch concludes that, in natural environments, *learners will do whatever is within their power to communicate*, making the most of what they have in the second language and supplementing this, where necessary, with what they can transpose from their other means of communication: their first language. How familiar such a variety of communication strategies sounds to the language teacher who has tried to encourage students, at whatever stage, to express themselves freely with what they have learned![17] Yet many teachers still try to push students through the same series of hoops, expecting the "right" answer as output. Where ability to communicate is our aim, as in so many programs, we must relax and allow a place for the varied developmental and idiosyncratic processes of the individual to operate, while ensuring that the student has frequent contact with a wide variety of language structures and expressive vocabulary. *We must encourage our students to struggle to express what is within them*, to fight their way out of the straitjacket of their minimal knowledge. This is by no means easy for them to do. With our help, however, they can develop confidence in themselves and learn that what one wants to do one can do with perseverance and imagination. While increasing their satisfaction in personal achievement, we will be contributing something beyond mere language knowledge to their development as individuals.

The little research we have from natural second-language learning thus supports the observations of every experienced teacher of languages in a formal setting: There is in any class, no matter how large or small, a wide range of *individual differences in styles, strategies, and pace of learning*. We must do something about this. Students who cannot learn a language at the pace we set and in the way we present it must no longer be sloughed off like so much dead tissue.[18] By not allowing them to learn at their own pace and in their own way, we attack them at the level of security, a very basic level in Maslow's hierarchy of needs. The rickety foundation to which the student is

71

required to add level after level of unconsolidated information cannot but give way, and the student, it seems, is a "failure." We find it so easy to blame the student, rather than ourselves or the system. If we, as second-language teachers, are to have a role in the "education of the masses," which is the education of a mass of individuals, then something must be done to face up to this "problem." Let us say rather "situation" and acknowledge openly that "problem" is another word by which we shift the responsibility from ourselves to others. The mechanics of providing for different paces and styles will have to be worked out in relation to any particular situation.[19] This is not my province in this chapter. The Gerry Logans, Steve Levys, and Fred LaLeikes[20] have made it work in areas as widely separated physically and situationally as California, New York City, and Wisconsin. We can learn from their experience.

Is this a return to programming?

Ah! programming! the initiated murmur, as soon as the question of individual pace of learning is raised. It always seems so much easier to find an answer for this aspect of personal style than for the others. We just lift time restrictions and let our students learn as quickly or as slowly as they comfortably can, allowing for learning and relearning, testing and retesting, until they have mastered the material. The answer seems purely organizational – complicated perhaps, but feasible.

There are several other questions to be considered, however, at this point: What kind of programming are we talking about? Do we mean one program for all students? Can programming, as we know it, really teach language use as we now understand it?

For kind of programming, except for very sophisticated computer programs not yet readily available to most second-language teachers,[21] we are, for the most part, talking about refinements of the two classical types of programming: linear programming with minimal-step progression, originally developed by Skinner, and Crowder's intrinsic programming with built-in trial-and-error factor and opportunities for branching to accommodate faster and slower learners.[22] In both cases the program is basically the same for all students, although intrinsic programming allows for more variation in assimilation of the material, because it provides extra practice for the student who does not select the right answer according to the program. This summary statement is not intended to ignore the diligent work of second-language programming researchers who have tried to develop more sophisticated versions of these basic types, by taking into consideration, for instance, Carroll's proposals for "designed learning"[23] and by incorporating the auditory and oral aspects of spoken language and the inferencing that is essential for fluent reading. Nevertheless, step-increment and feedback (reinforcement through immediate knowledge of success or failure) remain the basic principles of most programs.[24]

The programming system shows a clear relationship with some types of individualized instruction. *Programming requires precise specification of the terminal behaviors the student should be able to demonstrate* after completion of the program, just as some forms of individualized instruction require the writing of performance or behavioral objectives. The latter do not seem to differ in any significant way from the specifications of terminal behavior of the programmers.

A *performance objective* explains the purpose for requiring a particular form of behavior, the conditions under which this behavior will occur, and how it will be evaluated (the criterion by which students will demonstrate that they have achieved the required behavior). Valette and Disick[25] give the following example of a performance objective:

1 *Purpose:* To demonstrate knowledge of twenty vocabulary words.
2 *Student Behavior:* Write out and spell correctly the word that corresponds to each of the twenty definitions given.
3 *Conditions:* On a twenty-minute classroom test.
4 *Criterion:* At least thirteen of the twenty items must be entirely correct in order to pass.

The constant use of the word "behavior" and the precision of the specifications in statements of objectives show clearly the line of descent from behavioristic programming. It seems clear also that *only the most trivial or mechanical aspects of language use can be so specified for all students.* It is disheartening to see a fine ideal like individualized instruction being equated with such precise dissection of living wholes of language and language use into atomistic morsels. These segments have an undeniable place, since there is much detail to be mastered in any language (what I have called the micro-language learning, which is important for skill-getting).[26] When, however, attempts are made to deal in the same way with macroaspects of language use, or skill-using, we realize the simplistic view of language learning on which the approach is based, despite the elaborate paraphernalia involved in carrying it through to its logical conclusion.[27]

The following examples will demonstrate what I mean.

73

(I) OBJECTIVE FOR ORAL PRODUCTION
After completing all the written assignments and the laboratory practice drill accompanying Unit 8, the student will go to the laboratory and record his oral responses to eight aural stimuli of the following form:
    Stimulus: I like ice-cream. Does Martha?
    Student: Yes, Martha likes ice-cream too.
A response is acceptable if, and only if,
1) the appropriate subject is used.
2) the correct verb is used.
3) the response is complete.
4) the pronunciation is good enough to be easily understood by the teacher.
At least five of the eight responses will be correct.[28]

(II) OBJECTIVE FOR LEVEL I INTERACTION
The student will make a comment about the weather and will follow the comment with a question which he will ask a classmate. When the class-mate answers his question the first student will follow the answer with another question. The classmate will answer this question; then the first student may pose a second question to his classmate.[29]

(III) OBJECTIVE FOR A LITERATURE ASSIGNMENT
Each student will write a description of the protagonist describing at least four physical characteristics and three personality traits.[30]

(IV) OBJECTIVE FOR CLASS DISCUSSION
The student *will volitionally participate* in each class discussion by con-tributing a total of *at least three* questions and/or complete-sentence comments per discussion.[31]

Naturally one would expect teachers to have clear ideas on the direction in which they wish the class to progress, and students will need precise instructions on what is expected of them in an assign-ment or task. In Carroll's model of school learning,[32] one important element determining the amount of time a student *needs* to spend in learning is the quality of instruction, defined by Jakobovits in his application of Carroll's model as "the extent to which it is made clear to the learner what it is that he is supposed to be learning."[33] Whether what is to be done is clear to the student is dependent to some degree on ability to understand instructions. That these instructions should, however, take the form of elaborate "behavioral objectives" has yet to be demonstrated to the satisfaction of this author, who continues to feel that *behavioral objectives and individualized instruction are incompatible terms*. Behavioral objectives imply that someone, the teacher or the materials writer, will decide precisely what someone else will do and how.

The fact that the writer of Objective (iv) could use the expression *volitionally participate* in an objective that stated the exact number of interventions required of each student in a class discussion illustrates a certain blindness to the authoritarian nature of behavioral objectives. Even when students are working with individual packets, their learning may be even more teacher-directed than in many classrooms. (No one has yet suggested that all behavioral objectives should be tailored to the needs of each individual student, thus making the task of writing them infinite.) As usually presented, they leave very little room for flexibility or for adaptation by students who may not feel inclined to do just what has been stated, but who may very well be learning a great deal in their own way.

Individualization must imply choice and some latitude in modality and style of learning; otherwise, the only individual thing about it is the pacing: Students are allowed to complete the predetermined, detailed assignments with which the teacher confronts them at their own speed of learning. This is precisely what programming was supposed to do, and for this we do not need another name. Let us use programming where it is appropriate (for learning basic features of phonology and language structure, for instance), and let us keep the name "individualized instruction" for the richer, more humanistic approach outlined in the earlier part of this chapter.

Since teachers are individuals too, let us say that performance objectives are an integral part of some programs that are individualized, but that they are neither a sufficient nor a necessary feature of individualization. For those teachers or students who feel comfortable with them they may be a helpful prop, but those who enjoy the challenge of adapting to an evolving situation may ignore them.[34] Either way, let us raise our sights and those of our students to a fuller and more normal use of language than can ever be confined within the limits of a circumscribed "objective."

The "personal route" of our students' interests

In a preoccupation with pace of learning, we may well change the outward form of the learning situation in highly visible ways while retaining the same old content. To do this, after all, may require only technical manipulation: adapting the textbook, writing assignments, and putting our usual handouts, exercises, and tests into folders with answer keys. Attention to the students' interests requires much more of us: It requires a fundamental rethinking of what we are about.

In recent years, as a profession, we have felt the pressures of a narrowing world. When one group changes its major objectives, we all seem to change. So we have moved to a worldwide emphasis on oral communication skills, often to the almost total exclusion of reading and writing; from an overemphasis on literature and literary style, we have moved to a wide-scale rejection of anything that might be branded "literature"; from a translation-burdened course we have moved to the vilification of translation. Now we seem to be drifting imperceptibly back to a reemphasis on reading, and discussion of Language for Specific Purposes seems to turn inevitably into an analysis of reading materials for science and technology. In many cases, the swing has occurred without personal conviction on our part that the change had anything to do with our own students in their unique situation. Now is the time for assertion of individual priorities, thoughtfully established in consultation with our students and their community.

As teachers of languages we have great freedom. A language may be learned for a number of different purposes, each with a variety of possible contents. Anything in the language, anything that can be expressed in the language, facts about the language itself, facts about language – all or any of these are our province. It is we, and we alone, who have restricted ourselves to a certain approach, to certain procedures, to a certain type of content. Our students avoid language study because they do not know the choices available to them, or because we do not allow them to choose. If we are convinced of the need to tailor opportunities for learning to the individual, *we must take seriously the individual's personal interests in learning a language.*[35] Individualized instruction implies diversification of objectives and content. Some students may want only to read and to read in a narrowly defined area; this is their prerogative. Some may want to communicate spontaneously; some may want merely to be able to pronounce the language acceptably (as for opera and newscasting). Others may wish to be able to communicate freely in the aural-oral mode, but not to write; still others may want to read poetry, or to find out about the customs and daily lives of the speakers of the language, or to translate instructions for making prestressed concrete. Individualization, sympathetically conceived, makes such diversity possible, as no previous system has done. Again, *it is a matter of attitude on our part:* We must work with our students in establishing what they are really seeking in learning the language, rather than imposing on them our view of their needs. This may add further organizational complications, but we cannot speak sincerely of "individualization" without it.

Cooperative learning

In our enthusiasm for techniques adopted by colleagues in mathematics or science, we may forget that we are seeking an approach that is true to the nature of our discipline. Unless we are careful, packets, carrels, and individual tests may conspire to isolate students from their fellows. The term "individualized instruction" itself may be leading us astray with its connotations of separateness and segmentation and its seeming focus on receptive learning. For both language-related and educational reasons I propose we use the term "cooperative learning."

Language is essentially a vehicle for the communicating of ideas, emotions, and experiences, whether in the oral or graphic medium. We call languages "dead" when they no longer function in this way, and we rediscover them in tombs and caves or in the sepulchral depths of silent libraries. If our students' new language is not to be stillborn, it needs at all stages to be used for some form of real communication.

The essence of language is macro-language use: listening to something someone wants to share (ideas, songs, plays, news, plans, and projects); telling something we want others to hear; writing something we intend to be read (by ourselves at a later date or, more frequently, by others); reading what others want to communicate (to inform ourselves or enjoy), and then sharing what we have read with others through action or discourse. Students do not move easily from isolated micro-language learning (learning about facts of language and how smaller elements combine into larger segments) to normal uses of language. Whitehead has said that in training a student "to activity of thought, above all things, we must beware of...'inert ideas' – that is to say, ideas that are merely received into the mind without being utilised, or tested, or thrown into fresh combinations."[36] How peculiarly appropriate this is to language learning! Facts we learn about language are "inert ideas" until they are tossed about, recombined in original ways, and tested for their communicative potential in the natural give-and-take of interaction between individuals or in the dynamic interchange within groups. "The acquisition of skills," said Dewey, "is not an end in itself. *They are things to be put to use*, and that use is their contribution to a common and shared life."[37]

One of the demands on modern education, as outlined earlier in this chapter, is to reestablish the values of cooperation in an increasingly depersonalized world. It has been suggested that we need an interdependent learning model "in which cooperation is structured to be as productive of results as competition."[38] Since language use, if it is to be developed with confidence, needs just such an accepting, cooperative atmosphere, free of cross-comparisons, here is an area in which we can take the lead. *In cooperative learning, all can succeed because each has something unique to contribute to the enterprise* and because success is not an external standard contrived to exclude, but the individual perception of the attainment of a self-selected goal. With acceptance of diverse goals, and individual emphasis on how the language will be used, this is not a vain dream. Ongoing individualized programs have shown us how it may be implemented.

Cooperative learning implies full participation of both teacher and student and the interaction of student with student. It implies participation in planning and the opportunity to make effective choices. It implies student helping student, student helping teacher; it implies small-group activity, large-group instruction, interacting in pairs, or leaving another individual alone if that is what he or she prefers. It implies sharing what one has discovered with others. This is surely what education, as opposed to instruction, is about: "a deliberate and conscious sharing of responsibility for learning."[39] *As students are given responsibility, they develop responsible attitudes,* even if for a while there are "shavings on the floor."

Cooperative learning means a new role for the teacher, as well as for the student. Instead of dispenser of knowledge from a podium to which all eyes are raised in expectant vacuity, *the teacher becomes an adviser, guide, helper, supporter, and partner* in a cooperative venture. Since so many of the problems the student has in developing confident language use are emotional ones, this new relationship cannot but promote better language learning through the reduction of tensions. In education, "it is the *process* and not merely the result that is important."[40] Through cooperative learning, sound language learning becomes sound education as well.

Let's discuss

1 What applications to second-language teaching can you see in the findings of second-language acquisition research on pp. 70–71?
2 Discuss what is implied by considering the language-learning/ language-teaching enterprise as education, not instruction. How does this affect what we do in the classroom? Be specific.
3 Have you observed natural "rule-formers" and "data-gatherers" in your classes? What kinds of materials are most appropriate for each of these types?

4 What have you observed in the way of individual learning strategies among your students? Which activities irk some of them and
 which are most compatible? How can you accommodate different learning styles in the one class?
5 Gather some information on the personal interests in learning a
 language of students in a class with which you are presently associated. Share these with others in your group.
6 Discuss how learning to communicate can be developed in the cooperative mode. Cite specific activities that demonstrate this
 potential.

6 Student-centered trends: a rationale

In 1968, in *Teaching Foreign-Language Skills* I took my readers on a tour of four classrooms, all engaged in different activities, but all devoted to the *teaching* of a language.[1] Now I think it's time for us to take a tour of our Language Institute again and visit three classrooms, all devoted to the *learning* of a language.

Three classroom visits

In Classroom X, there is a long silence; the teacher looks encouraging; a student constructs a sentence; the teacher nods, changes the positions of some rods,[2] and gestures to another student who, after a moment of contemplation, puts together an utterance and is encouraged by the teacher's reassuring smile. If the student's response is incorrect, the teacher nods to another student, who supplies the expected response.

In Classroom Y, a small group is seated in a circle with a tape recorder in the center; the recorder is there not to give but to receive language material. The teacher is not the focus of this scene but, with some aides, is outside the circle, waiting for students to take the initiative. One student is speaking, occasionally seeking a word from an aide. Another student cuts in, rather aggressively, refusing to accept what the first student has just said. The other students murmur further objections, seeking help for stronger expressions of their displeasure from the teacher or from the aides. The latter supply exactly what is requested in a low tone without intervening in the exchange. All the utterances are being recorded for later analysis by the group in discussion with the teacher.

In Classroom Z, baroque music is playing. Soft light falls on the pastel walls and the students look pleasantly relaxed as they recline, breathing rhythmically, and listen to a dialogue being recited, alter-

Revised version of an article that appeared in C. A. Yorio, K. Perkins, and J. Schachter, eds., *On TESOL '79: The Learner in Focus* (Washington, D.C.: TESOL, 1979), pp. 67–70.

nately in a normal tone of voice, then in a persuasive whisper, and then triumphantly. The dialogue is quite long, so we leave before the end of the rendition.

Why now?

What can these three ways of approaching the language-learning task have in common, and how is it that they have all come to the fore at this particular time? We may note that they are not newly forged. Gattegno clearly described the Silent Way, in Classroom X, in his 1963 book. At that time, he stated that it was based on thirty-five years of language-teaching experimentation in fourteen countries on five continents. Curran's Community Language Learning, in Classroom Y, was first described in the *Bulletin* of the Menninger Clinic in 1961.[3] Lozanov's Suggestopaedia, in Classroom Z, was the subject of experimentation in Bulgaria in the 1960s, although detailed accounts of it did not appear in the United States until 1970.[4] The reasons for the sudden prominence of these approaches in language-teaching circles can be found in particular emphases that evolved in second-language teaching in more recent years.

In the grammar-translation period (before World War II in most languages and continuing in English teaching in many parts of the world today) the emphasis was on "*Why* teach a modern language?" The justification, for reasons of respectability, was based on intellectual rigor and cultural enrichment, with the result that the teaching of modern languages became as much like the teaching of the highly regarded classical languages as possible – with great emphasis on the understanding of a formal grammatical system and the ability to read literature and philosophy.

Modern language teachers then passed through the *What* and *How* of the audiolingual era, asking such questions as "What is language?" and "How do people learn languages?" The structuralists believed they knew what language was. It was "a system of arbitrary vocal symbols by means of which the members of a society interact in terms of their total culture," as Trager expressed it;[5] and the behaviorists knew how it was learned: by acquiring language habits through reinforcement (or confirmation of their efficacy).

The emphasis on *what* and *how* continued during the transformational-generative period, when the so-called cognitive code-learning approach was much discussed (though rarely described). *Language, we now knew, was an innate structure,* and our language learners, through their innate language-acquisition device, were hypothesizing about the form of the grammar to which they were attending and matching it against their innate knowledge of potential grammars of a human language. In the cognitive code-learning approach, as proposed in the literature, students had little opportunity, despite the theory, to hypothesize about the form of the grammar. Because language use was considered to be "rule-governed behavior" (a term largely misunderstood[6]), it behooved students to understand and apply the rules. We were back to a deductive presentation of grammar, with conscious practice in the application of rules before authentic passages of discourse were to be encountered.[7]

Individual learning and learning styles

More recently has come emphasis on the individual as learner. *Who are our language learners? How do individuals learn? What are their personal learning strategies?* Second-language teachers became wary of presuming they could *teach* a language and began to seek ways in which students could be given opportunities, situations, and time to *learn* as their individual proclivities permitted.

The three approaches we are discussing all fit into this new mood of emphasis on the individual and on personal learning strategies. Each one tries to *give the student room and time to learn with as little intrusion of the teacher into the learning process as possible.* Gattegno, for instance, speaks of "techniques which made it possible for the teacher to say less and less as the lessons advanced, while the pupils were saying more and more and using their own inner criteria."[8] He speaks of throwing the learning upon the students themselves.[9] Although all three approaches structure the learning situation, and structure it in very specific ways based on theoretical convictions, they each envision the teacher's role as indirect. This applies even to Suggestopaedia where the teacher's role is highly structured, but the emphasis is still on allowing time and space for the students to use their language-learning capacities to absorb and assimilate the material. In the Silent Way, the teacher leads from behind, in the sense that the progression and the appropriate materials are carefully planned, but in ways that are not obvious to the students, who are encouraged to think for themselves and discover the way the language works through using it. Community Language Learning is deliberately nondirective and not prestructured.

What else do these three very different approaches share?

These approaches also have in common the following characteristics:

1. They all endeavor to involve the *whole person* of the student. Curran calls one of his books *Counseling-Learning: A Whole-Person Model for Education.*[10] Gattegno considers breathing and kinesics of tremendous importance in speaking a new language, as well as the conscious application of the intellect. Lozanov tries to draw on the powers of the unconscious mind to assimilate positive suggestive factors in an act of communication or a pedagogical process. "The purpose of suggestopaedia," we are told, "is to put those 'mental reserves' to work by organizing a coherent system whereby the suggestive, emotional, more or less unconscious signals we receive, are coordinated."[11] He recognizes the impact of the aesthetic, using fine arts and music. Curran draws these notions together when he speaks of learning as a "unified personality encounter."[12] Curran is particularly concerned with the emotional and interactional facets of communicating in a second language.

2. All view *the learning of a second language as quite different from the learning of the first.* Gattegno calls it "radically different."[13] In the first-language learning situation, parents and caregivers frequently repeat what they have said for young children, often with expansions and restatements, a technique that is not encouraged in the Silent Way. The Lozanov procedures also make no attempt to reproduce child native-language learning situations, and Curran encourages students to draw freely on the native language in early attempts to communicate.

3. All three are *inductive in the initial encounter of the student with the language.* Curran's students learn through use, Gattegno's through inductive analysis of the teacher's (limited) output, and Lozanov's students assimilate structure in the dialogue, which they memorize but without conscious effort. All three provide explanation at a later point in the learning as students require it. Initially, however, all three present material and let the students do what they can with it. To quote Gattegno, "the synthetic, the intuitive, precedes the analytic."[14]

4. All three approaches are *noncorrective and give the students time.* They aim to reduce the anxiety and tension of language learning (although the rigorous inductive demands of the Silent Way do raise tension and create frustrations for some). Corrections when supplied are done so in a supportive way, as information rather than

reproof, and as the students show a need or desire for them. Gattegno makes a strong statement in this regard: "I do not correct learners," he says, "I only throw them back onto themselves to elaborate further their criteria and to use them more strongly."[15] Curran found that students wanted time. "The counselor had to be very sensitive...," he noted, "to discern when he was really needed or when, on the contrary, persons wanted time to find, on their own, the required word or phrase."[16] Lozanov's "concert" allows the students this time, as they relax and listen to the dialogue.[17]

5. Each of these approaches encourages *active use of the language in communicative situations from the beginning.* Curran's clients try to express their feelings and opinions from the first moment with the help of the counselor or an aide. Gattegno's communication situations are structured by the teacher with rods, but the students are expected to express in the new language information about these situations that they themselves have put together. Lozanov's students act out the material of the dialogue as soon as it has been assimilated and, by the structuring of the dialogue material, are "thrust directly into a communication situation."[18]

6. Finally, we may note that each of these approaches tries to *create a community feeling* of "all pulling together,"[19] which decreases inhibitions against expressing oneself in front of others in a language of which one still knows very little.[20]

Each of these six factors can be reproduced in other approaches in the usual classroom situation: involving the whole person of the student (affective, cognitive, and physical); an inductive approach to language material; a noncorrective, encouraging attitude on the part of the teacher; active use of the language in communication as soon as possible; and the building of an esprit de corps so that students begin to care for each other's progress and form a language-learning community. These are aspects of the language learning and teaching enterprise that have been urged on teachers for some years. Surely it is now time to take action.

Let's discuss

1 Can all structures be learned inductively? Make a list for the language you teach of structures you think would have to be learned deductively (that is, by explanation of the rule before practice). Discuss ways in which these structures could be approached inductively.

2 Do you think these three methodologies successfully respond to the need to provide for individual learning styles?
3 How do you feel about correction of students' errors? What is your own approach? What approach was most helpful to you as a language learner?
4 Is it possible to "involve the whole person of the student" in a structured learning situation? To what degree do you consider these three methodologies succeed in doing this? How could you apply this principle more fully in your own teaching?
5 Read some of the references in the notes about these three methods and find out for each:
  a) how vocabulary is treated;
  b) how communicative situations are developed;
  c) how reading is incorporated;
  d) how pronunciation is dealt with.

7 The second-language teacher and cognitive psychology

The psycholinguist Martin Braine tells a story about his 2½-year-old daughter who had the habit of using "other one" as a noun modifier, as in "other one spoon." On a number of occasions he tried to induce her to utter the correct form "the other spoon." A typical interchange went as follows:

        – Want other one spoon, Daddy.
        – You mean, you want THE OTHER SPOON.
        – Yes, I want other one spoon, please, Daddy.
        – Can you say "the other spoon"?
        – Other...one...spoon.
        – Say..."other."
        – Other.
        – Spoon.
        – Spoon.
        – Other...spoon.
        – Other...spoon. Now give me other one spoon?[1]

Braine uses this as an example of *the difficulty children have in using negative information (that is, correction)* for the development of their syntax, a feature of child learning that has been observed by many researchers.

Most second-language teachers will nod appreciatively on hearing a story like this and think of similar experiences they have had: when, for instance, after careful and apparently successful practice of the form of an information question, a student will blithely ask, "What means this word, Miss X?"[2] And so our problems continue perennially. External arrangements may change; our attitude to our students' learning may evolve, so that the pace of activities, even the type of activity, is adjusted to individual styles, but the problems of language learning remain – those peculiar problems that make the learning of a second language a different proposition from the learning of history or science or calculus.

Revised version of an article that appeared in Wilga M. Rivers, *Speaking in Many Tongues*, 1st and 2d eds. (Rowley, Mass.: Newbury House, 1972 and 1976).

First- and second-language learning: same or different?

We certainly do not lack statements on how to go about the task of helping students acquire a second language (L$_2$). In fact, we seem at times to be almost deafened by a babble of voices. One rather prevalent (and to my mind oversimplified) view is described by Cooper in the following terms: "There seems to be little evidence that the actual language-learning *processes* differ for the child and the adult. Somehow, both have to abstract the linguistic rules underlying the language as well as the sociolinguistic rules underlying its use. Some second-language learners may do this more quickly than others. . .but they must do it nonetheless if they are to learn the language. The question which confronts us as language teachers is how we can best structure the language-learning situation so as to exploit the language-learning abilities of the student."[3] The type of restatement in the last sentence, if taken at its face value, obviously does not throw a great deal of light on the problem. It does, however, highlight the need for us as teachers to *know as much as we possibly can about the way our students learn and learn language.*

When we discuss language-learning processes at the level of generality of Cooper's statement, we must not be surprised to read that these "processes" do not differ for the child and the adult. It is almost self-evident that second-language learners must "abstract" and internalize, as a part of their own cognitive structure, the system of linguistic and sociolinguistic rules, if they are to function autonomously in the language independently of their teacher. We are not surprised, at this undifferentiated level, when the writer tells us that the learner must do this "somehow."

Chomsky's language acquisition device

Basic to Cooper's statement is a theory, expounded in several places by Chomsky,[4] that the child has *innate language-learning abilities* in the form of "a linguistic theory that specifies the form of the grammar of a possible human language"[5] and a "strategy for selecting a grammar of the appropriate form that is compatible with the primary linguistic data."[6] This innate strategy enables child learners to match with the language they hear around them the form of a particular grammar from a "fairly restricted set of potential languages."[7] The "strategy" of which Chomsky is speaking is a language acquisition

87

device (LAD)[8] that proceeds by hypothesis testing. Child learners make hypotheses about the form of the grammar of the language to which they are attending from what Chomsky calls "the meager and degenerate data actually available" to them.[9] They compare this with their innate knowledge of the grammar of a possible language[10] that is congruent with the abstract principles of universal grammar and that is capable of generating the many surface variations of this specific language. (Note that *the hypotheses the child is presumed to be making are about deep structure relationships, not the peculiarities of surface structure.*) Work in first-language (L$_1$) acquisition based on this theory has tried to describe linguistically the series of interim grammars that result from the learner's hypotheses and reflect the child's competence at a particular stage of learning.

Proposals for classroom teaching: a critique

It is against this theoretical background that we can now consider Cooper's proposals for an actual language-teaching situation. Quoting from Cook (1969),[11] Cooper suggests that the teacher should "permit, and indeed encourage the learner to produce sentences that are ungrammatical from the point of view of the target language. This would be done on the assumption that... the second-language learner's deviations are not random but systematic and reflect implicit hypotheses as to the nature of the language being learned.... When he produces sentences which deviate from those of the target language, the teacher's reactions can help him change the hypotheses. Note that the teacher would be more concerned with correcting the *hypothesis* underlying the deviant sentence than with inducing the student to correct the particular *sentence.*"[12] Certainly we should give our students abundant opportunities to experiment in spontaneous use of the language, knowing full well that in doing so they will produce some ungrammatical sentences. Such opportunities should be provided as early as possible in the students' language-learning experience, in association with the structured teaching sequence.[13] This type of freewheeling provides the students with opportunities to try what they can do with what they know: making "infinite use of finite means" (to use the oft-quoted phrase of Humboldt). *It is during such interaction episodes that we can see what systematic errors students are making and correct their erroneous hypotheses* about the surface structure of English (or German, or French).

What is interesting here is not so much what is being proposed as its theoretical underpinnings. First of all, linguistically speaking, it cannot be considered an application in teaching practice of Chomskyan theory. The child's hypotheses about which Chomsky is speaking are, as we have noted, at the abstract level of deep structure. Since knowledge of the grammars of possible languages is said to be innate, *children's hypotheses about the nature of the language to which they are attending cannot really be deviant and in need of correction*, if our interpretation of the theory is consistent. Chomsky says that "various formal and substantive universals are intrinsic properties of the language-acquisition system, these providing a schema that is applied to data and that determines in a highly restricted way the general form and, in part, even the substantive features of the grammar that may emerge upon presentation of appropriate data."[14] In this sense the utterances of children learning their first language are no longer considered "errors" by developmental psychologists who base their interpretations on the innateness theory, but rather exemplars of basic structural relations.[15] Extrapolating directly from linguistic theory to classroom practice is not as simple as the quotation from Cooper would make it appear. As Cook observes in his 1969 article, "It remains to be seen whether..., in fact, the analogy of first- and second-language learning is sound."[16]

The hypotheses of the adult learner: how we can help

In a laudable enthusiasm for keeping language-teaching practice congruent with the latest theories in other disciplines, there is a tendency among some to brush aside what the older learner brings to the second-language learning experience.[17] In the classroom situation that Cooper is describing, the deviations that are "ungrammatical from the point of view of the target language" are at the surface structure level and do not reflect "implicit hypotheses as to the nature of the language being learned" in the sense in which Chomsky has used these terms. We are clearly talking about a different type of hypothesis. As every experienced teacher knows, one of the hypotheses underlying the deviant utterances of an older student learning a second language is that, *until otherwise demonstrated, rules determining the surface structure of the new language will closely parallel those determining the surface relationships of the first language.* (In the case of third or fourth languages, students seem to fall back rather on expectations based on their weakest foreign language, as though they were subconsciously applying the principle: "This is foreign, so speak foreign."[18]) First-language learners who hear only surface realizations of the underlying rules of the particular language they are learning (interspersed with some performance errors), and who are surrounded during their waking hours by the language they are trying to acquire, do not have this conflict in their natural language-learning situation. They detect logical relations and begin in a basic fashion to express these relations. It is these relations, as Lakoff has observed,[19] that are a part of universal grammar. This explains why young children learning different languages seem to pass through similar developmental phases, producing similar early grammars that represent the same basic relations, before they reach the stage of differentiation of the details of the surface structure of the particular language they are acquiring. Even young children, however, who are learning a second language in a natural, untutored fashion, seem to suffer for a while from the interference of the surface features of one language with the surface features of the other.[20]

The adult learner, on discovering that many features of the two surface structures are not comparable in their functioning, frequently *overcompensates by overgeneralizing* divergent features of the new language to instances where the two systems do in fact coincide. (Having learned that a French adjective normally follows the noun, as in *une pomme rouge*, an English speaker will frequently overgeneralize to *un crayon long*, where the order paralleling the English order, *un long crayon*, would have been appropriate.) Research in error analysis reported by Richards[21] shows over half the errors he cites to be interference errors, whereas among the remaining overgeneralization errors many are overcompensatory. Learning the limits of generalization of specific rules in a new language is a problem that can often be handled better by clear explanations which highlight differences in the surface structures of the native and target languages, than by "encouraging" students to produce deviant utterances according to their current hypotheses until they have had sufficient experience to correct themselves.

In free interaction we cannot ensure that sufficient opportunities of miscomprehension will occur at particular points of overgeneralization to provide the student with adequate data for the correction of these hypotheses. Both *context and the teacher's long experience of deviant utterances in this particular language reduce the number of occasions when there is blank incomprehension*, so deviant utterances may be reinforced, rather than brought to the awareness of the student. Nor can we ignore the factor of attention. The student attending specifically to problems of comprehending and expressing meaning comprehensibly may well not have sufficient cognitive processing capacity available to note and store at the same time subtle signals of the deviancy of certain surface structure features. Furthermore, it is not true that young children correct their developing speech when faced with incomprehension; instead, they fight for comprehension by repeating the deviant form over and over until the adult listener recognizes their intent. Consequently, the procedure recommended by Cooper can hardly be considered a replication of child language-learning strategies.

Inconvenient facts like these seem to be easily forgotten as soon as we begin to explore again the attractive hypothesis that procedures for teaching a second language should derive from the premise that the processes of learning a second language are identical with those for learning a first language. As Stern has put it so aptly, "Once language development has taken place, it produces a lasting structural change. If a new language is learned in later years, it is filtered through the language acquisition device of the individual, modified by his first language."[22] Or, in the terms of cognitive psychology, *new learning draws on previous learning, with which it forms a synthesis, thus modifying the knowledge store.*

How much is innate?

Unfortunately for the L_1 learning $=$ L_2 learning argument, recent research has left it far from clear how children do acquire their first language, and some assumptions reflected in writings on second-language teaching appear now to have a very problematic status. Reputable linguists,[23] philosophers,[24] and psychologists have sharply criticized Chomsky's theory of an innate linguistic faculty that enables children to identify the form of the grammar of the language with which they are surrounded. In Schlesinger's view, "there can be no question, of course, that the organism comes to any learning task with some innate equipment; the question is only how much is innate. The soundest approach seems to be to make as few assumptions as possible, and to try to explain with these as much as possible."[25] Bruner says, "I am prepared to believe that in the linguistic domain the capacities for categorization and hierarchical organization are innate, and so, too, are predication, causation, and modification."[26] Braine would accept as innate the mechanisms that permit us to perceive temporal position and co-occurrence relations.[27] Ervin-Tripp observes that "order relations seem very apparent to children.... Order is almost always accurately reproduced in imitations."[28] Bever maintains that "there is not as much innate structure to language as we had thought, if the 'universal grammar' is stripped of those aspects that draw on other psychological systems" (notably, mechanisms of perception, learning, and cognition).[29] The present consensus appears to be that it is the logical structures basic to various intellectual processes that are innate and that distinguish man as a species, not language-specific structures, and that these logical structures make it possible for man to acquire and use language as well as to perform other cognitive operations. In this sense the concepts of "noun phrase," "verb phrase," or "sentence" would not be innate, as McNeill had earlier suggested,[30] but rather the capacity to categorize, to establish hierarchies of categories and relations between categories, the categories themselves being derived from the common experiences of human beings in a natural environment. In this sense, second-language teachers have always exploited the innate language-related capacities of the students by taking for granted that *they can apprehend basic relationships of temporal order, co-occurrence, category, and hierarchy, and such operative relations as agent-action, action-object, causation, and modification.*

Even the Chomskyan concept of the child acquiring a language system by hypothesis testing is by no means uncontested. Braine argues convincingly that the child cannot be proceeding by the testing of hypotheses, because *real hypothesis testing is dependent on the reception of both positive information (acceptance) and negative information (rejection or correction).*[31] Without negative information a child cannot test hypotheses about grammaticality. Yet, strong evidence exists that children do learn language from positive information only, even though some of this information is inaccurate (for example, in cases where the child's deviant utterance is accepted by the adult). Whether children are corrected or not, they acquire the language of the community in which they are growing up, and busy parents notoriously miss many opportunities to correct their children's speech, even adopting the children's own forms on occasion, forms these children are often hearing also from others of their own age.[32] It seems, in fact, that mothers and other caregivers tend to correct the truth value of children's utterances, rather than their deviant syntax.[33] To complicate matters, young children do not adjust their utterances when negative information is provided (even when this is done in an insistent fashion, as with Braine's child at the beginning of this chapter [34]), but they continue to operate within their own structural system until it has evolved to the stage where the particular adjustment indicated by the correction becomes functionally warranted. It is, therefore, far from proven that children acquire their first language by a process of hypothesis testing. We may like to use this technique in our classes for motivational reasons, or to add variety to our approach, but we cannot claim at present that it is more than a heuristic on our part. If we do use it, then both positive and negative information (acceptance and rejection of utterances) must be provided.

Linguistic input

We are also frequently told that children do not learn language from a limited and structured corpus, that children hear language of all levels of complexity, and that it is because of this constant exposure to a full array of language structure and vocabulary from the beginning that children are able to discover for themselves the complete grammar of the language. Some people have asserted on the basis of this presumably scientific information that second-language students should not be presented in the early stages with a simplified form of the language (that is, with basic patterns and a limited vocabulary[35]), but should be exposed from the beginning to the full range of language.[36] Child language acquisition studies have shown, however, that it is not the case that children learn from a wide variety of complicated structures and vocabulary. Actually, children tune out much of what they do not understand in language that is not addressed to them. Attention and memory play essential roles in comprehension. What the child is not attending to is processed minimally, if at all, and the child's memory span initially is very short. *The sentences to which children are directly exposed tend to be short, repetitive, and quite limited in range of structures and vocabulary.* This we know from the investigations of Ervin-Tripp and her associates at Berkeley. Ervin-Tripp quotes a sample of adult speech to a two-year-old child which runs as follows: "Come play a game wit' me. Come play a game with me. Wanna play a game with me? You wanna play a game with me...? Come look at Mamma's colorin' book. You wanna see my coloring book? Look at my coloring book. Lookit, that's an Indian, huh? Is that an Indian? Can you say Indian?"[37] (The same mother was using with adult friends sentences like the following: "It gives me a certain amount of consolation which allows me to relax my mind and start thinking intelligently an' putting my efforts all in one y'know force goin' in one direction rather than jus' y'know continually feeling sorry for yourself."[38]) As for the child's own use of language, Weir has given examples of the speech of her child, David, at 3 years of age, talking into the microphone with which he had become familiar: "Here's de place. Bad boy bad boy Dave. Bad boy bad boy Dave. Dave is not a bad boy. Mike is a bad boy. Dave is OK but Mike is not."[39] Here we have the child saying over to himself simple noun phrases with modifiers and affirmative and negative declarative sentences with occasional ellipsis.

Which theoretical studies have the most to offer?

We must be extremely wary of basing what we do in the second-language classroom on presumed definitive statements about language learning from either linguistics or psychology. As Schlesinger has put it so aptly, "Psychological theorizing about language learning is in its infancy, and generative grammar is not yet fast frozen."[40] Generative grammar is in fact in such a state of evolution at the moment[41] that we bystanders would do well to wait until the dust settles before attempting to shape our classroom practice in any radical way according to principles and models that tomorrow may be passé. Lamendella has concluded that "theories of linguistic description are relevant to language teaching only to the extent that they form part of the data which psycholinguists may use in constructing a cognitive theory of language. It is this theory which may properly be utilized as the theoretical basis for second-language pedagogy."[42] Such a theory of language stemming from psycholinguistics is gradually being elaborated, but a final form is not yet in sight. In 1970, Bever observed: "I have said little about the effects of general principles of learning on linguistic structure because I do not know anything about how language (or anything else) is learned, while I do have some initial understanding of the mechanisms of perception."[43] Today, he would not claim more. Problems of first-language acquisition aside, we can gain insights from certain important discoveries in the area of perception, both auditory and visual, that will enable us to help our students learn more efficiently and that can give us firmer bases for the designing of learning materials. A little later we shall see what light these throw on particular learning problems with which we are all familiar.

What is "cognitive"?

At this stage, a word of warning is indicated. At times we hear about a "cognitive" approach to second-language teaching, and its proponents speak as though the techniques they propose in some way exemplify the principles of cognitive psychology. When we examine what they are saying a little more closely, we sometimes find that they are merely proposing a return to the deductive presentation of grammar rules before practice to make what is practiced presumably more "meaningful," and that this is considered a more "cognitive" way to proceed. I do not intend to consider here the pros and cons of a deductive versus an inductive approach. Kelly traces this controversy back at least to St. Augustine, and quotes Lubinus as writing in 1550: "Now what and how monstrous an absurdity is it...to bid them give an account, why they speake Latine right, before they can in any wise speake properly."[44] *In a teaching situation both induction and deduction may be very effective*, depending on the way they are integrated into the total teaching-learning situation. In fact, most teachers use one approach or the other at different times, depending on the age and ability of the learners and the nature of the problem under consideration. I am merely concerned here with the very meager interpretation of cognition that identifies it with a deductive presentation of grammar rules and an emphasis on analysis of structure, useful as these may be at the right place and time. Psychologically speaking, analysis is a cognitive process but so, most definitely, is analogy, which requires the prior recognition of a pattern – the realization that there is something common between two otherwise different events – which is a process of abstraction. Learning rules is a cognitive process, but so is inferencing. We cannot imitate without activating a cognitive process.[45] It is noteworthy that small children find it difficult to imitate an utterance: They either interpret and rephrase it, or they answer a question or perform an action.[46]

Cognitive psychologists make no attempt to establish a value hierarchy for these processes. They try to find out what takes place when we perform any of them. They are interested in different strategies of learning and the stages of maturation at which each becomes dominant, or is, in Piaget's system, a possible operation for the child.[47] They are interested in how we recognize phonic or graphic patterns and the interpretations we impose upon them.[48] They conduct much research into short- and long-term memory, semantic memory networks, and processes of recognition, rehearsal, recoding, storage, and retrieval of information. They try to determine what makes any object of learning or any situation meaningful to a particular student. Essentially they are interested in what goes on *inside* the organism: how we observe, interpret, interrelate and comprehend, and reorganize and use *any* material for learning, because all living is learning. From what they discover, they are able to make suggestions for improving institutionalized learning (that is, in-school tasks), and for making the most of incidental, informal learning, while recognizing that no process or procedure is appropriate for all types and conditions of learning.

For the cognitive psychologist, then, cognition "refers to all the processes by which the sensory input is transformed, reduced, elaborated, stored, recovered, and used.... Given such a sweeping definition, it is apparent that cognition is involved in everything a human being might possibly do; that every psychological phenomenon is a cognitive phenomenon."[49] This processing of input and preprocessing of output is what we need to understand if we are to teach a second language.

The psychology of perception

The experimental findings of the psychology of perception, which has made great strides in recent years, have much to contribute to our understanding of language learning. Psychology is not an alien science coming to strange conclusions that contradict what we ourselves observe. Much of what psychologists discover appears to us to be "common sense," because they are describing the operations of the human organism. Thus, recent psychological studies in perception help us to understand experiences enshrined in such familiar expressions as "He was only listening with half an ear";[50] "It was just on the tip of my tongue";[51] "You took the words right out of my mouth";[52] and "OK! OK! I get the picture!"[53]

I shall now take some common problems of second-language learning and show how recent theories of perceptual processing can help us to analyze and deal with them.

We sometimes hear a teacher complaining: *"My students rattle off drills (or write out paradigms; or whip through packets of assignments) all right, but they never seem to remember anything from one day to the next."*

How familiar this sounds! These students are relying on *short-term memory* for their answers, particularly in drills and exercises where all the elements are supplied. In aural-oral drills particularly, the rhythm of the cues helps the students to produce the answers with a minimum of cognitive processing. Because they are not personally identifying the salient regularities in the material they are "rattling off," they are not forming concepts they can relate to other information in the long-term memory store. Each utterance is a relatively unrelated new experience. Once the students have developed a concept of the crucial relationship being practiced, *each utterance in a series becomes a variation on a theme, which permits rehearsal and recirculation of the concept for recoding in long-term memory.* Sentences in most drills and exercises are semantically empty for the student in the sense that they have no personal reality as a reflection of present experience. Consequently, they become exercises in manipulation of language segments, which is purposeful only as manipulation. Mechanical, nonmeaningful activity does not use up a great deal of processing capacity – just enough to mimic, more or less accurately, and make minor adjustments, which are discarded as rapidly as they are produced. As a result, a process of *time-sharing* takes place on the following pattern:

– *he's coming today...*
[That boy with the red hair looks interesting.]
– *they're coming today...*
[He's drumming rhythmically with his fingers.]
– *she's working today...*
[I wonder if he likes dancing.]
– *I'm working today...*
[Ah! he prefers cinnamon gum. I must remember that.]

It is no wonder, then, that the point of the drill never reaches the long-term store, from which it might have been retrieved the next day or a week or two later.

For our second problem, we apply information drawn from Neisser's three stages of perceptual processing.

A teacher may ask: "*If listening is a passive or receptive skill, why do students have such problems answering questions on what they heard? The tape is very clear. How can I help them to be better listeners?*"

Studies in perception make it clear that listening is far from being a passive skill (and the same may be said of reading, which shares with listening certain processes in a different sense modality).[54] Listening involves active cognitive processing. Far from being an act of reception, it involves the construction of a message from phonic material, with the result that the message we construct may sometimes be different from the message the speaker intended, as we shall see later.

Students need to understand that there are *three stages in the aural reception of a message*,[55] and changes in the original message can occur at each stage. First of all, listeners must recognize in phonic substance sound patterns in bounded segments related to phrase structure (here we are helped by the rhythm of speech). At this stage we are dependent on echoic memory, which is very fleeting. Unless we interrelate meaningfully the segments we detect, we lose them as echoic memory fades. To extract a message, then, we must immediately begin processing, identifying the groupings we have detected according to the content of our central information system, that is, according to knowledge we have already stored. (This store of knowledge is limited at first in the second language, but expands as we continue to learn.) We recirculate the material we have organized through our immediate memory, thus building up an auditory memory of it that helps us retain the segments we are processing. It is valuable, then, for language learners to recapitulate mentally what they are hearing as they process its meaning (this is a form of subvocal matching). Much of this processing of incoming information takes place during the *pauses in speech*; thus, speech that has been speeded up within segments is still comprehensible if the pauses are slightly lengthened, so that the overall presentation rate remains the same. There are implications here for presentation of listening comprehension materials on tape, especially in view of the modern emphasis on normal rate of speech from the early stages and the use of authentic listening materials. Students should learn to use the pauses in natural speech to gain processing time.

It should not surprise us that, when we are listening to a language with which we are not very familiar, we often lose whole segments here and there, even though we comprehended them when they were uttered. At this stage we must interrelate incoming segments with those we have retained and hold some in immediate memory to interrelate them with what follows, so that we can construct a sequential meaning for the utterance and for the sequence of utterances. We are then, by our organization, anticipating the full form of the message, and this explains why we often supply a completion when the speaker hesitates. *The more we can gather the incoming information into meaningful chunks, the more we can retain.*[56] It is therefore important to train students in the perceiving of syntactic groupings of words as units. To achieve this we should encourage our students to repeat what they hear in meaningful segments, and we should ask questions that require meaningful segments, rather than single words, as answers. It is also important to train students to hold longer and longer segments in their memory to improve comprehension.

Having constructed *our* meaning from what we are receiving, we recode this for long-term storage, that is, *we reduce it to the gist, and this is what we recall when asked about it.* When we ask students questions about what they have been hearing, we should always encourage them to give the answers in their own words in the second language, rather than expecting them to repeat exactly what they heard. This encourages real processing rather than superficial "playback" and gives practice in retrieval of the coded material.

It is clear from this analysis that *attention plays an important role* in comprehension. If attention wavers, we identify the wrong segments, we skip some segments, and we construct a different, idiosyncratic message. Sometimes students will begin by drawing inferences from the wrong cues, thus misinterpreting the import of what they are hearing, their attention being now focused on any elements that seem to support their erroneous interpretation of what they are hearing. Students should be warned to pay close attention to any preparatory discussion, titles, or pictures that will give them clues to the central theme. In normal communication the context (the situation, the time of day, the persons interacting) helps us in interpreting a message. If we miss a segment or two, or if some of what we have heard "slips our mind," we fill in the gaps from expectations based on previous experiences in such situations. This is why listening comprehension is facilitated when there is a visual or situational element or even some background noises on the tape to indicate that the speakers are in a railroad station or at the seaside.

Emotion also affects our cognitive processing. Personal thoughts and apprehensions take up some of the limited processing capacity, interfering with interpretation and retention of what is being perceived. It is natural, then, that nervous or embarrassed students cannot "hear" well, or "hear" what was never said. The more disconcerted they become, the more they grab at sounds here and there, as they attempt to process some kind of message. It is also *natural for students to forget what they heard and understood, and thus be unable to recount it.* Material that is relatively unfamiliar cannot be gathered into large enough chunks, processing capacity is overstrained, and there is not enough cognitive energy left for the listener to rehearse and recode for storage what is being interpreted. In this case students understand as they hear each segment but cannot store a sequential message.

Since reinforcement plays a role in maintaining attention, *listening should be accompanied by some activity* through which students can demonstrate their comprehension and experience the pleasure of success. If they can do this through some form of personal expression in speech or writing, they learn at the same time that comprehension of a message is part of a communicative act. Activity is also important in testing listening comprehension, because then we are not testing something vague we may be calling "the listening skill." We are testing the results of listening — something students have learned or something they can do as a result of what they have heard. For instance, students may fill in maps or diagrams as they listen, or make notes of information they will need to complete a project, to solve a mystery, or to act out a role in a dramatic activity. This approach makes a listening exercise more purposeful and maintains attention.

Let us now look at the problems of listening from another point of view, drawing on other areas of cognitive research, notably artificial intelligence (AI) studies.

After a talk by a native speaker (or a listening comprehension test), a student may protest: *"But that's what she said! I heard it!"*

Many teachers do not realize that listening is a *creative process*. We are receiving linguistic and extralinguistic input as we listen, but, from what we extract from the stream of sound and from the situation, we are creating a message. The speaker has a meaning to convey that is expressed in a certain arrangement of words, uttered with an intentional intensity and rise and fall of the voice. What the listener understands the meaning to be, however, is influenced by other factors than these. The listener has expectations about the message that derive from knowledge of the world, knowledge of the speaker's world, and previous experiences with the speaker or other people similar in some ways to the speaker. When the communication is across cultures, students' expectations of the message may be awry because of certain stereotypes in which they believe or because of ignorance of culture-related attitudes.

When students are unfamiliar with a speaker's intentions, beliefs, or attitude toward the listener, *interactional content* is low. Experimentation has shown that we recall much more accurately the actual words spoken when interactional content is high, that is, when we know the speaker well.[57] In this case, the message we create from what we are hearing is much closer to that intended by the speaker because we have much more knowledge of the kinds of messages this speaker usually encodes and how this speaker is likely to interpret the situation. When these expectations are not realized, we respond with: "Hey! Wait a minute! I didn't expect you to say that!" or "Stop! Say that again!"

The student who uttered the remark at the beginning of this section apparently did not share the same "script" as the speaker. *Much of comprehension is drawing inferences.* Since all the information we need is not in the linguistic output, we draw on our knowledge of ways of living, behaving, and reacting to help us create a meaning. AI research has made us aware of this fact. In trying to program computers to comprehend human messages, AI researchers have had to build in to computer programs all the little details of life we take for granted that our listeners know. ("I bought it yesterday." "Oh! you were downtown!" is a coherent sequence because "bought" in our society implies shops, the usual location of shops, and a number of details like entering, looking, finding, picking up, interacting with sales personnel, packaging, paying, exchanging remarks, and so on. These elements of the script are not mentioned in the above exchange because they represent information shared by both speaker and inter-locutor.[58]) Lack of knowledge of many details of the background and habits of speakers of another language can lead to our "hearing" (creating and storing) what was never said.

Similarly, we may hear all of the linguistic output and still say: "*I heard what he said, but it's all double Dutch [or Greek] to me!*" This is another variant of the situation just discussed. Since the listener does not share the same script as the speaker, a message may be created from the output that does not make sense to its creator. Wrong inferences have been drawn and, since the auditory material itself has now faded from memory, the listener is left with the incomprehensible message extracted. If further discussion elicits information that was lacking, or activates some aspect of our knowledge of the world to which we were not previously attending, the stored interpretation will be dusted off and reviewed in the light of the new information. The listener will then exclaim: "Oh! that's what you meant! Then why didn't you say so?" to the astonishment of the speaker who feels that this is exactly what he did say in the first place.

The problem with creation of messages that were never uttered, as in "But that's what she said! I heard it!" is that *we store the message we have created*, not the original linguistic output. Later, it is our interpretation of what we heard that we recall, not the speaker's original message. (This is a common problem in courts of law and explains why two witnesses will give quite different versions of what was said by a third person.) This phenomenon, called false recognition memory, has implications for *testing listening comprehension*. Students will select incorrect multiple-choice or true-false items and swear that these represent what was said. Carefully constructed multiple-choice and true-false items can pinpoint genuine misinterpretations on the part of students. Effective distractors provide interpretations of the speaker's intention that are plausible for the student who has not assimilated all the information provided or has not understood the cultural significance of relationships, situation, or attitudes.

Other problems it would be interesting to analyze in similar fashion, with insights from cognitive psychology, are the following:

— *We've practiced and practiced that structure but they still get it wrong when they try to say something on their own.*
— *Mary's the first to recognize when something is wrongly pronounced, yet her own pronunciation is nothing to write home about.*[59]
— *You can tell she's French by her accent!*[60]

Analyses of problems like these show the types of useful indications we as teachers can gain from an understanding of cognitive processes – information that will help us to understand the problems of individual students and to design materials and activities with which they will be successful because we are not demanding of them responses beyond their processing capacities at a particular stage. If teachers are to be required more and more to prepare or adapt materials themselves, they will need to think carefully about how students learn, and how they retain and use what they have learned. To quote a famous poet: They "must be taught as if you taught them not."[61] This will become a possibility when we understand natural processes of language acquisition and use, selecting and refining practices in accordance with theory and experience.

Let's discuss

1 Gather together the various arguments (from this chapter, chap. 12, and other readings) for and against the identity of processes for first- and second-language learning. Discuss these in your group. What conclusion have you yourself come to on this perennial issue? Which methodologies are based on these two processes' being the same, and which on their being different?

2 Analyze the problems you still have in the foreign or second language you know best. Can any of these problems be attributed to interference from features of your first language? (Consider phonology, as well as morphology, syntax, semantics, and pragmatics.) Can you trace the sources of those problems you do not think come from interference? See also L. Selinker, "Interlanguage," in *IRAL* 10 (1972): 209–31.[62]

3 What kind of linguistic input do second-language learners normally receive in class? How does this differ from the input they receive out of class? Some people believe that second-language learners should hear and read only authentic language materials from the beginning. How do you feel about this approach? What kinds of authentic materials would be accessible to beginners?

4 Consult the references in notes 50–53 for the experiences reflected in the idiomatic expressions to which they refer. Then discuss with your group the insights you have gained into the processes to which they allude.

5 Make a list, with descriptions, of possible listening exercises based on recommendations in this chapter. (Try to be innovative in thinking out new ways for students to practice listening.)

6 Take a listening passage for the level you are teaching. Work out some true-false items, basing the incorrect items on false recogni-

tion memory. Try the passage out on a class and check the success or otherwise of your false items as distractors. What did you learn from this experience?

7 From your reading of this chapter and other chapters in this book, what answers would you give to teachers who raised such problems as those at the bottom of p. 101?

8 Draw up, as a cooperative class exercise, a list of activities that test the results of listening.

8 The natural and the normal in language learning

I have just completed the index of a book – a tedious task that must be performed methodically, but a *normal* enough activity for a writer or an editor. Is it a *natural* activity? That depends on our definition of "natural." According to the American Heritage Dictionary (AHD), one definition of "natural" is "pertaining to...the expected order of things." Once having signed a contract that said I had to make my own index, it was natural that at some stage I should be spending several weeks in this way.

One of my early index cards was headed "Natural language use," which was clearly an important category. As I drew to the end of my indexing and began cutting down on redundant entries and cross-referencing, I found this card redundant. So I cross-referenced it: "*See* Normal purposes of language." My entry "Normal purposes of language" also has a cross-reference, "*See also* Macro-language use,"[1] which completes the circle with a cross-reference: "*See also* Normal purposes of language." It seems, then, that these terms may bear looking into, in their interrelationships. They are not to be confused with "Creative language use," which, in my index, is cross-referenced "*See also* Communication (interaction)," which has the subentry "autonomous." ("Communication" is also cross-referenced to "Emotional factors," and, via that route, to "Personality of the student," and "Teacher-student relations," a set of interconnections whose importance we will discuss later.)

Let us look then at *the natural, the normal*, and *the macro*, and see what we can learn from the investigation.

Normal purposes of language

On looking back at "Talking off the Tops of Their Heads," which I wrote in 1971,[2] I see that I speak there about situations where the

Revised version of an article originally published as "The Natural and the Normal in Language Learning" in H. D. Brown, ed., *Papers in Second Language Acquisition, Language Learning* Special Issue 4 (1976), pp. 1–8; and as "The Natural and the Normal in Language Teaching: Where's the Difference?" in R. A. Schulz, ed., *Personalizing Foreign Language Instruction: Learning Styles and Teaching Options* (Skokie, Ill.: National Textbook Co., 1977), pp. 101–8.

students are on their own, "trying to use language for the normal purposes of language," and these normal purposes I have listed as: establishing and maintaining social relations, expressing one's reactions, hiding one's intentions, talking one's way out of trouble, seeking and giving information, learning or teaching how to do or make something, conversing over the telephone, problem solving, discussing ideas, playing with language, acting out social roles, entertaining others, displaying one's achievements, and sharing leisure activities.[3] Later in the same article, I talk about "natural uses of language in interaction." Somehow, between 1971 and 1975, I seem to have moved over to a preference for the term "normal purposes of language." I wonder why.

Returning to the AHD, we find "normal" means "conforming, adhering to, or constituting a usual or typical pattern, level, or type;...the usual or expected...form," and in the discussion of synonyms under this rubric we read: "Normal stresses adherence to an established level or pattern that is associated with well-being, although based on group tendencies rather than on an arbitrary ideal."

As we teach another language, or help someone learn another language, *who are we to say what is a "natural" use of language for particular individuals in particular situations?* How are we to know what, for them, is the "expected order of things" at a deeper, nonapparent level, since this depends on such elusive factors as personal assessment of the situation and perceived relationships? Expectations are particularly difficult for us to divine when our student comes from a culture with which we are not intimately familiar. We must recognize that what to one person is "natural" may well be "unnatural" to another, or even disconcerting or distasteful.

We can, however, present to a person from another culture what are, in specific contexts and in certain relationships, the "established patterns of behavior" based on "group tendencies." If our students are to function in a new culture freely and without embarrassing misunderstandings on both sides, that is, maintaining a sense of "well-being" for themselves and those with whom they are interacting, they must learn to conform to the "normal" in that culture, even if it is not their own "natural." They must be able to use readily and in an unconstrained way the usual or expected forms.

Children acquiring their mother tongue learn what is "normal," rather than what is "natural" in interaction with others. As they explore the potential of the language system, their output is pruned and shaped by such indications as, "Don't you dare talk to your mother like that!", or "I'll give it to you when you ask nicely," or "Run away, you rude little girl!" The child practices the established levels and patterns in simulated situations: in games, for instance, where one child says, "I'll be the doctor," and another says, "I'll be the mamma," or "I'll be the teacher." (The teacher in this game is always a very authoritarian figure – "real mean" – which makes it great fun to act out.)

In our second-language class, then, we seek the normal. We try to create, or simulate, likely situations in which our students may wish to use the language, and we prepare them to choose confidently from the many possibilities within the language for expressing their intentions. (The challenge for the teacher is to make these situations seem as natural as possible.) We also prepare them to produce the expected (or normal) responses the unfamiliar culture requires. These do not come "naturally."

"Natural" construed as "not normal"

Paulston, who grew up in Sweden, tells how, on a return visit after a number of years abroad, her "natural" was construed as "not normal." At a gathering in her home in Stockholm to celebrate an American Thanksgiving, she asked her sister-in-law politely, "Do you know everyone?" to which her sister-in-law replied sourly, "I don't know everyone, but if you are asking me if I have greeted everyone, I have." The sister-in-law had behaved in the normal Swedish fashion by going around the room shaking hands with everyone and saying her name aloud to those whom she had not previously met. Paulston's remark, natural enough in an American setting, had been interpreted as a reflection on her sister-in-law's knowledge of the usual or expected forms of behavior in a Swedish setting.[4] If Paulston, returning to her own native culture and speaking the language perfectly, could violate the social norms in this way after a period of immersion in another culture, then it is quite apparent what what will appear to be natural language use on the part of the learner of Swedish as a second language will be the result of much careful preparation at some stage along the way.

Halliday's functions of language

At this point, we may turn for a moment to some work of Halliday on the functions language fulfills for children learning the mother tongue.[5] Halliday lists seven such functions: the instrumental, the regulatory, the interactional, the personal, the heuristic, the imaginative, and the representational. We will consider each of these in turn.

106

1. The *instrumental* (manipulating and controlling the environment). Halliday calls this the "I want" function. When babies first produce one-word utterances like "Nan!" for "banana," they begin to discover the amazing power of language.

2. The *regulatory* (exercising control over others: the language of rules and instructions). This is the "Do as I tell you" function. "Go 'way!", "Gimme dat!" and other simple orders prove to be very effective in imposing a small person's will on parents and baby-sitters.

3. The *interactional* (language defining and consolidating the group). This is the "Me and you" function, as the child savors the warmth of personal relations with utterances like "Love Dacky!"

4. The *personal* (language enabling the users to identify and realize their own personality). Halliday calls this the "Here I come" function, and we recognize it in "Me! Me!" or "Dacky cry!"

5. The *heuristic* (language as a means of learning about things). This, the "Tell me why" function, becomes a very persistent one. The writer remembers a little immigrant child who learned a great deal of English by frequent use of two questions: "Whazat?" and "Whazifor?"

6. The *imaginative* (using language to create one's own environment). We are all familiar with this "Let's pretend" function: the living companionship of the security blanket ("Blanky") and the elephant in the bedroom when it is time for lights to go out.

7. The *representational* or *informative* (language used to convey messages about the real world). Halliday considers this "I've got something to tell you" function to be a minor one for the child, whereas adults tend to think of it as the most important language function. Certainly, in our language classrooms we tend to overemphasize the informative function, to the neglect of the six preceding functions, without which there is little depth of communication.

To these functions of language use by children, as outlined by Halliday, I would like to add:

8. The *play* function (rhyming and making up nonsense words – trying out the possibilities of the language system being acquired). This I will call the "Billy pilly" function. Through it, children enjoy their newly developed instrument and toy for quite a long while. Some never outgrow it, and become poets, creative writers, and memorable lecturers.

For the learners of a new language, we must not forget:

9. The "*ritual*" function (language defining the social group, language as good manners). Halliday says this "How do you do" function seems a needless complication to the child. It must certainly concern older language learners, however, if they are to experience "well-being" with members of a different culture from that to which

they are accustomed. (This is the function that tripped Paulston up on her return to Sweden.)

These, then, are the learning functions in the child's development of language, according to Halliday, and they deserve some reflection on our part as teachers of another language. Through these functions, language takes on meaning and value for children *because of its uses*. At first their language is functionally simple, that is, they are expressing only one function at any one time. With maturity, the use of language becomes functionally complex,[6] with its internal organization reduced to a small set of functional components or *macro-functions*: the *ideational* (the potential for expressing a content in terms of the speaker's experience and that of the speech community), the *interpersonal* (all use of language to express social and personal relations), and the *textual* (the operationally relevant in contexts of situation).[7]

Macro-language use and micro-language learning

All of this is very applicable to our work in second-language teaching. When we talk, as some do, of plunging students directly from the outset into macro-language use, in sink-or-swim style, in the hopes that they will somehow discover what they need, we ignore the fact that, *in the mother tongue, children first acquire the mechanisms for the simple functions*, and that it is just as much a part of normal language use to say: "Open it," "I'm tired," or "She's a doctor," as it is to say, "Sh! If I were you, I wouldn't be telling everyone I was working on that new, secret weapon system in underground storage!" As children gain experience in expressing themselves for the various simple functions they put it all together in the macro-functions.

Elsewhere, I have used the term "micro-language learning"[8] for acquiring the basic mechanisms for the simple functions: expressing desires and needs (the instrumental); giving and taking orders (the regulatory); including, excluding, persuading, refusing (the interactional); expressing pleasure, dissatisfaction, enjoyment, anger (the personal); asking when, where, why, and how (the heuristic); pretending, supposing, wishing – the "ifs and ans" (the imaginative); describing, narrating, explaining (the representational or informative); greeting, apologizing, asking socially acceptable questions (the ritual); and playing language games. *Such learning is essential if efforts at macro-language use are to be rich and expressive* rather than searching and impoverished. While encouraging our students to perform on the macro level, we need to provide ample opportunity for them to acquire the means at the micro level, never forgetting that the micro is an essential part of the macro, although insufficient of itself.

The answer to our problems is not, then, to throw aside our years of experience in helping students acquire the means, but to develop more fully, and more immediately, their *confidence in experimentation* in the expression and comprehension of a multiplicity of meanings through these means. For this experimentation to be fruitful and to carry over into confident, autonomous, and purposeful communication, we need to ensure that everything we do in language learning is related to normal purposes of language, whether we are dealing with the spoken or the written language.[9]

Natural language use

Let us now reconsider natural language use. *Natural language use presupposes natural relationships.* To return to the AHD: "natural" means "free from affectation or artificiality; spontaneous; not altered, treated, or disguised; present in or produced by nature." Much as we teachers may strive for healthy, understanding relationships with our students, these relationships can be only as "natural" as the student wants them to be or is willing for them to be. Our students have the right to choose their friends and confidants and a right to privacy in their thoughts and associations. *Many who pride themselves on being libertarian are authoritarian in their relations with people.* They insist that others be open and relate to them, whether they want to or not, and even refuse to accept the possibility that an approach to people that is different from their own may be more natural for others. In this delicate area, we must never impose, but always be open to initiatives and sensitive to approaches, however diffident.

Gardner speaks of *anxiety in the language class* as one of the hindrances to motivation and achievement.[10] Anxiety can result from an overzealous attempt by the teacher to develop natural communication where it is not welcome, or before the student is ready for any such relationship. Why should the teacher know that the student's father is an alcoholic, unless the student chooses to share this problem? Why should another have to declare publicly that she hates all music, or can't water-ski for sour apples, unless her relationships with the teacher and the class warrant such personal disclosures? In real life, the student's natural use of language may be for sudden displays of emotion, or for hustling, bragging, and bullying, all of

109

which may run counter to the teacher's culturally acquired sense of social deportment and morality. In any case, *how natural is the situation where the teacher is always right?* (He or she knows the expressive options the language offers and the intonation and gestures for maintaining superiority, whereas the student is struggling and insecure.)

Language in and out of the classroom

If we wish to develop natural language use, we take the language out of the classroom. We establish language clubs or accompany the students on trips; we invite them home or to weekend camps or day picnics; we visit their homes; we establish telephone contacts through which they can speak the language; or we involve them in some community effort. ("Community" here, as before, refers to the school community or the wider community surrounding the school, as appropriate.) If these more ambitious projects are not feasible, we resort to simpler ones: We take them into the local park to look for as many different kinds of weeds as possible; we get them to prepare a meal together in the cafeteria kitchen; we set up language tables so that they can talk in the language over lunch; or we join with them in making posters for an international day to which they can invite people from the surrounding community – all while using the language they are learning. We bring the community into the classroom itself by inviting native speakers to chat informally about their occupations and interests. In no matter what way, we break up the traditional classroom relationships and *build a different interactional structure* of working and learning together. Let us look more closely at these possibilities.

The most natural way to learn a new language is to use it in some form of involvement with community life: within the school community itself or in the wider community outside the school. In a bilingual situation, this means becoming involved ourselves in the other-language community in which our students' real lives are lived. Natural second-language use without self-consciousness can be attained through service to the community, which earns the esteem of the community. This has been the immigrant way since time immemorial – the little children who learned the new language acted as interpreters for their parents (at the bank, in the shops, in relations with the teacher), and in this way parents and the children themselves felt pride in their skills.

For older learners, a language can be practiced perfectly well while working with immigrant or migrant children in an after-school club, or while helping smaller children adjust to kindergarten life in a strange environment. Little children may find that their helper "talks funny," but they adjust rapidly to this phenomenon. Consequently, many an adult or adolescent language learner has found the tolerance and acceptance of the very young, when absorbed in mutual tasks, a low-anxiety situation for practicing natural language use. Little children are uninhibited teachers who correct and supply the appropriate word in a perfectly friendly and egalitarian way. Older people or adolescents find this easier to accept; it is not so threatening to their self-esteem, or to their picture of themselves as seen by others, as it is when the correction comes from a peer or an authority figure.

The problem of the inhibited speaker (or writer) is not new. The teacher of language arts in the mother tongue has had to face it too, and many students have been labeled inarticulate or almost illiterate for years, until they found, or were found by, a teacher who cared enough to pause and listen to (or read) what they had to say (or write). Innovative teachers of the native language who have paused, and waited, have sometimes found, to their surprise, that all kinds of students can speak (and write) expressively when they have something to communicate that they themselves consider significant, and someone who cares enough to pay attention to what they have to say. Guidry and Jones report a course in "Cowboy English" for the "dumb goat-ropers" or "kickers" from the small towns and rural schools of East Texas, who were considered quite hopeless in expressing themselves in their native English. When their energies, enthusiasm, and depth of experiential knowledge were given expression in a pictorial essay on the East Texas State University rodeo (and for one student in a self-initiated account of "How to Build a Five Strand Barbed Wire Fence in Blackland Soil") it seemed they had many expressive means at their disposal. One of the students identified their real problem quite succinctly when he said, "This is the first time that anybody in a course like this ever asked me to tell them what I know."[11]

Our second-language students also know many things about which we know little. Do we care? Too many teachers are too busy "teaching students to express themselves," or even "organizing natural language activities" (a contradiction in terms), to ever discover what *their students' real interests and preoccupations* are. For them, student-initiated or student-centered activities are too untidy and too "time-consuming." In this way, they forever bypass really purposeful and significant (that is, natural) language use.

Here, then, in the students' personal interests and real preoccupations we find the source, secret until willingly revealed, of natural use of language by the student. But discovery of this wellhead is not, of itself, sufficient.

Teacher-student relations

For natural language use of any authenticity, the old, time-honored authority structure of teacher and student relations has to be broken down, and *a relationship of acceptance and equality* established for which many teachers are not emotionally ready. Natural language use will come only when barriers are broken down – pride in status and superior knowledge on the one hand and, on the other, defensive attempts to please, to succeed by giving what the authority figure wants, and to hide one's weaknesses and one's real feelings. *One cannot mandate the breakthrough in trust and confidence that permits genuine progress in communication* in any language. It may come with one group; it may never come with another. Teachers who seek natural language use in their language classes must decide whether they are ready or willing for such an experience.

When we speak of natural language use or using language for the normal purposes of language, let us fully comprehend the difference. We can all promote normal uses of language in our language classes, and this of itself is a challenge. Some of us, with some classes, will see the flowering of natural language use if we are psychologically willing and prepared for the change in relationships it will bring. At least, let us recognize the difference and the value to our students of each experience.

Let's discuss

1 Reread the normal purposes of language listed at the beginning of this chapter. What other normal purposes can you identify? Within the categories listed, what subcategories seem to you to be most important?
2 List the activities you commonly engage in in the classroom. In the light of what you have read in this chapter, which of these activities do you now consider useful for second-language learners? How could you convert them into more normal, or more natural, activities?
3 How can you take the language out of the classroom in your present teaching situation?

4 What problems did you yourself have in learning to speak a language naturally? From what you now know, what advice would you like to give your former teacher?

5 What kinds of practice would you suggest for the nine functions of language discussed in this chapter. Are these normal types of activities? If not, how can you make them more normal (or natural)?

9 Apples of gold in pictures of silver: where have all the words gone?

> *I love smooth words, like gold-enameled fish*
> *Which circle slowly with a silken swish...*
> Eleanor Wylie, "Pretty Words," *Collected Poems*

Having stated my bias, let me range myself with much of human-kind: my fellow word lovers. Riddles, word puzzles, acrostics, and puns fascinate and delight. Slips of the tongue (malapropisms or spoonerisms) are a pleasure; at most, they provoke mirth and gentle teasing. "Redundable" (for redundant and replaceable) pleases, rather than irritates. Intuitively, we feel it is a word we needed. The comic, the professional word manipulator, is always sure of an audience. Language, the possession and preoccupation of us all, is not dry bones. It is a living, growing entity, clothed in the flesh of words: flexible words that, chameleonlike, change and blend to create new meanings.

Why then have we, who love words, whether linguists or language teachers, seemed, more recently, to eschew them, to ignore their essential role in communication through another tongue, claiming that structure, syntax, grammar (whatever we may prefer to call it) is what must be learned first, and well, before we bother our students with too many words?

Comenius and labeled pictures

This emphasis, it seems, is of recent mintage. Comenius, the influential language teacher and materials developer of the seventeenth century, was not afraid of words. His *Vestibulum*, with materials for a child's conversation, contained a few hundred words arranged in sentences, whereas his *Janua linguarum reserata* was to contain all the common words in the language, about 8,000 in number, grouped

Revised version of an article originally published in B. Sigurd and J. Svartvik, eds., *AILA 81 Proceedings II, Lectures, Studia Linguistica 35*, 1–2 (1981): 114–29.

according to centers of interest in labeled pictures. "A *Janua* should remain a *Janua*," he said, criticizing some overzealous contemporaries; it should not be stuffed with uncommon words.[1] The sentences in the *Janua* explained the nature of the objects depicted, of which the children were to be shown actual examples. Thus, in Comenius's method, children learning another language were, at the same time, finding out about new and interesting things (not just their names but also their functions) through examination of objects, descriptions, and labeled pictures, which the language learners would be encouraged to copy and label for themselves. In his *Orbis Sensualium Pictus* (1658), this approach was used for simultaneous presentation of Latin, German, Hungarian, and the vernacular, Czech.[2]

Pestalozzi and the object lesson

Comenius's labeled pictures remind us of the object lesson emphasis of an equally influential educator, whose work straddled the eighteenth and nineteenth centuries, the Swiss, Pestalozzi. Though not usually cited for his ideas on the learning of languages, Pestalozzi stated unequivocally that "the natural method of learning the mother tongue or any other language" was "connected with the knowledge acquired through observation and the natural procedure in the learning of both must be in harmony with the course of nature according to which the impressions derived from observation pass over into knowledge."[3] Maximilian Berlitz, one of the early direct method exponents, also advocated object lessons in the initial stages. "The expressions of the foreign language are taught in direct association with perception," he said. "The student thus forms the habit of using the foreign language spontaneously and easily, as he does his mother tongue, and not in the roundabout way of translation."[4] To supplement the concrete vocabulary available in the classroom, Berlitz, like Comenius, used labeled pictures.[5] (This technique of gathering together collocations of words in a semantic area is reminiscent of the lexical fields of Gouin and the vocabulary of centers of interest used in establishing *le français fondamental*, both discussed in the next section.)

As an example of the object lessons that began appearing in language-teaching textbooks, we may cite Meadmore's *Object-Lesson Handbook* (1905), a second conversation book for teaching English to children in France. Here again, *informative content was learned along with the foreign language*, the author intentionally introducing "en très grand nombre les termes correspondant aux objets et aux gestes esquissés dans [les] petits tableaux" that they were to accompany.[6] The readings and detailed pictures were intended to provide material for oral discussion, as in Meadmore's lesson on "The Bakery":

> In the making of good bread, three things are absolutely requisite: flour or meal, yeast or leaven, and water containing salt.... The *baker* mixes these ingredients together and kneads them into a spongy mass called *dough*. This *dough* swells considerably and is weighed out into lumps which are shaped into *loaves*.[7]

Going back 250 years before Meadmore, we may compare this passage with a section on the *Panificium* (Bread-Baking) in Comenius's *Orbis Sensualium Pictus*, which is in English and Latin (with numbers following the nouns for easy reference to the equivalent objects in the picture accompanying the lesson):

> The Baker 1. sifteth the Meal in a Rindge 2. and putteth it into the Kneading-trough 3. Then he poureth water to it, and maketh Dough 4. and kneadeth it with a wooden Slice 5. Then he maketh Loaves 6. Cakes 7. Cimnels 8. Rolls 9. &.[8]

Meadmore speaks of the need to teach children "une foule de termes concrets d'un emploi journalier dans la conversation" (that is, a great number of *concrete terms in daily use in conversation*).[9]

Gouin and vocabulary in lexical fields

The same emphasis on a great number of specific terms is found in the writings of the Frenchman Gouin, the learning-through-physical-response exponent of the end of the nineteenth century, whose method achieved its greatest success in Germany. Like Comenius and Meadmore, Gouin emphasized *the acquisition of a great number of specific terms* in the new language (particularly verbs, action words that could be physically performed as they were used). His series introduced 8,000 words in lexical fields: topics and situations like *the home*, subtopic *the kitchen*; or *occupations*, subtopic, *the carpenter*. Within these situations, students would act out very detailed sequences of appropriate actions in relation to objects, stating aloud exactly what they were doing with what. Thus *the situational vocabulary was acquired along with the verb*.[10] "The specific substantives are more important than the general substantives," Gouin maintained. "The general terms are, so to speak, terms of luxury, which the language can upon necessity do without."[11] As Gouin saw it, we are more likely to want to use the words *bus* or *taxi* than *vehicle*; *hamburger* or *bread* than *food*.

116

Frequency counts

As the grammar-translation approach took over at the end of the nineteenth century, interminable lists of very specific words appeared at the beginning of every lesson; these were to be memorized. They were also worked into complicated sentences for translation, which skipped in desultory fashion from semantic area to semantic area. These words were never seen again after the lesson was completed. The ultimate in this use of vocabulary as the slave of grammatical ingenuity was inflicted on Sweet in his Greek class, when his master concocted the unforgettable sentence: "The philosopher pulled the lower jaw of the hen."[12]

Reaction against the increasing load of very specific words was manifested in the frequency count movement. Scholars tried to find out from analysis of a body of language material (a written corpus at first, but later recorded speech) which were *the most useful words for language users*, on the assumption that these should be learned first, and that elementary materials should be restricted to certain levels of the count.[13] The most thorough proposal for reducing the word-learning burden was Ogden and Richards's *Basic English* (1930), with a total vocabulary of 850 words, which, skillfully combined, could express practically any concept.[14] "What is the difference," ask the creators of Basic English, "between visiting a man and going to see him, extracting a tooth and taking it out, forbidding a person solid food and saying he may not have it. . . . What we do is the same whether we bestow ten dollars upon a man or give it to him. The difference is a purely verbal one. We give an account in different words of the same thing. The second way [of expressing these notions] keeps to the vocabulary and rules of the system of Basic English."[15] This kind of vocabulary limitation was possible for the production of utterances by language learners, but it did not prepare them to comprehend the full flood of authentic speech or writing. Furthermore, since language learners had to analyze each concept to keep within the 850 words, this sometimes led to awkward combinations and paraphrases that were more difficult for the non-native to construct than it would have been to learn the more precise terms in the first place.

Frequency count developers took into consideration such important questions as *range of use* (in various domains and registers) and *coverage of lexical area*. It soon became apparent that frequency lists could not be taken at face value for teaching purposes, however, since the 200 most frequent words were, for the most part, articles, pronouns, prepositions, conjunctions, some adverbs, and a few common content words like *take, put,* and *tell; time, name,* and *home* (that is, function words with a few general-purpose nouns and verbs).

117

Beyond these indispensable items, the needs of the language learner in the area of vocabulary become very personal, depending on individual interests and objectives, and the situations and topics associated with these. The researchers on *le français fondamental* tried to meet this need by taking into account *disponibilité (the ready availability of words to the native speaker)*. The paucity of obviously well-known nouns in the higher ranks of frequency (those specific content words that Gouin had emphasized) was rectified in intuitive fashion in the French count by the inclusion of words associated with *centers of interest* such as parts of the body, clothes, furnishings, food and drink, transport, occupations, or city and country. As Michéa put it: "En présence d'une *situation donnée*, les mots qui viennent les premiers à l'esprit sont ceux qui sont liés spécialement à cette situation et la caractérisent, c'est-à-dire les noms."[16] In other words, many nouns that are available to us when we need them do not necessarily show up as high-frequency items. Yet these are the ones we think of first when we reflect on a situation, and these are the words we feel lost without. Textbook writers try to add vocabulary of this kind, using their own judgment. It is clear, however, that *learners must eventually develop their own vocabularies* if they are to be able to use the language freely in the types of situations into which their personal or career interests will propel them. As the discrepancy between frequency of items in counts and the needs of learners became more obvious, the intense interest such counts had generated began to dissipate.

Structures or lexical items?

The decline in emphasis on vocabulary learning was accelerated by movements in linguistics that concentrated on phonology, morphology, or syntax, with a corresponding neglect of semantics. With the growing popularity of audiolingual and similar structurally based materials, students were encouraged to concentrate on grammatical structures for expressing their meaning, on the presumption that these structural frames could be fleshed out with words at a later stage when students were more certain of their lexical needs in particular situations. Unfortunately, for many that time never came. Many students discontinued their study of the language at the stage when they were able to shape utterances, but not to give them living meaning through judicious selection of lexical elements and collocations.

Functional-notional materials

Hope seemed to dawn with the advocacy of notional syllabuses: Notions, topics, and settings seemed to promise new life for the word. A perusal of *Threshold Level English*[17] and *The Threshold Level for Modern Language Learning in Schools*[18] reveals, however, a predominant emphasis on structures, or syntactic formations, as exemplars (with a certain amount of concrete vocabulary to flesh these out), even though the presentation of the syntactic structures does not adhere to any traditional sequence. (For the Threshold Level, 1,000 words for recognition and production and an extra 500 for recognition were considered sufficient.)

The same impression emerges from a close study of *Un niveau-seuil*.[19] In the statements of purpose and procedure, the authors affirm their deliberate decision *to elaborate the linguistic devices needed by learners in communicative exchanges in specific situations of use.* "Un niveau-seuil," they state, "ne saurait satisfaire à tous les besoins sémantiques d'expression. Il ne permet pas de tout dire, mais simplement de communiquer adéquatement...dans des situations simples de la vie courante."[20] (In other words, a threshold level cannot meet all the semantic needs of the speaker, but it provides enough material for adequate communication in the simple situations of daily life.) For such situations, the authors supply useful formulas like *je peux le faire, il s'est corrigé,* and *il bat sa femme.*

Vocabulary returns with interest in semantics

Some recent approaches to language learning and teaching do bring back an emphasis on vocabulary, notably Suggestopaedia[21] and Natural Language Learning.[22] This parallels the renewed interest in semantics in linguistic, sociolinguistic, and psycholinguistic theory. Attempts to program computers to understand and produce linguistic communications have led to a flurry of research on semantic memory, where meaning is stored in networks of relations between concepts, whence it may be retrieved in the form of words, as context and collocation require.

As early as 1966, Hymes had protested against the "Garden of Eden" view of much theoretical linguistics, with its *overemphasis on the ideal, rather than the earthy reality of language use.* "Human life," he said, "seems divided between grammatical competence, an ideal innately-derived sort of power, and performance, an exigency rather like the eating of the apple, thrusting the perfect speaker-hearer out into a fallen world. Of this world, where meanings may be won by the sweat of the brow, and communication achieved in labor..., little is said. The controlling image is of an abstract, isolated individual, almost an unmotivated cognitive mechanism, not, except individually, a person in a social world,"[23] the very person who needs words, as we have already observed. This abstract individual, in the Chomskyan system of which Hymes is speaking, has an innate *faculté de langage*, whose chief characteristic is a knowledge of the grammar of a possible language, which seems eventually to acquire an uninteresting surface structure of words, almost as an irrelevant distraction from the central preoccupation with what we might think of as "pure language."

Hymes's "person in a social world" needs to be able to communicate, even if not in "all and only grammatical sentences of the language." Studies of second-language acquisition by adults have shown how *functional communication can take place through an ordered series of lexical elements* – Zoila's "big words." Zoila was a 25-year-old Spanish native speaker who was working as a housekeeper in English-speaking homes in the United States. Zoila managed to communicate fluently, for the satisfaction of her own communicative needs, without bothering too much about structural or morphological accuracy. "Zoila," we are told, "seems to focus her attention on those elements in speech which convey content. She ignores noninformative elements."[24] Her own description of her communicative method is instructive. "I never listen," she says, "you know the...the words little, uh, small words for continue my conversation....In the sentence I never using this little, little words [function words]. ...I'm...hear and put more attention the big words....I know "house" is the *casa* for me."[25]

Of course, we would want our language learners to progress beyond the level of language control of Zoila. "A word fitly spoken is like apples of gold in pictures of silver," as a wise man once expressed it (Proverbs 25:11). More prosaically, "an idea well-expressed is like a design of gold, set in silver."[26] Nevertheless, in her practical way, Zoila may be pointing out to us something that from our intellectual stratosphere we have been missing on the earth below. "A thought may be compared to a cloud shedding a shower of words," said Vygotsky.[27] Surely the time has come for us to pay attention to this "shower of words" and consider carefully how we can provide even our elementary learners, and much more so our advanced learners, with the means to "get across meaning," even before they can express discriminatingly fifteen ways to ask that the door be opened.

120

The network of relations

To return to the "shower of words" metaphor, Vygotsky makes it clear that "thought does not have its automatic counterpart in words"; consequently, "the transition from thought to word leads through meaning,"[28] and this muddies the waters. If we go back over theories of meaning in linguistics, philosophy, and psychology, we find *a common notion underlying vastly different approaches,* from Saussure to Quillian, that of the *network.* For Saussure, "initially the concept is nothing, that is only a value determined by its relations with other similar values, and...without [these relations among values] the signification would not exist."[29] In a strikingly parallel statement, the cognitive psychologists Collins and Quillian, who are struggling with the problems of programming computers to comprehend and converse with people, assert that, in the structure of memory, "*a concept would be a set of relationships among other concepts....* An interesting aspect of such a network is that within the system there are no primitive...terms..., everything is defined in terms of everything else."[30] Saussure saw meaning as being defined by oppositions and contrasts, that is, by "everything that exists outside of it."[31] Wittgenstein's view of a concept, materialized in language in use, is the mirror image of Saussure's concept. Instead of oppositions and contrasts, Wittgenstein emphasizes "a complicated network of similarities overlapping and criss-crossing: sometimes overall similarities, sometimes similarities of detail": *ein kompliziertes Netz von Ähnlichkeiten, die einander übergreifen und kreuzen. Ähnlichkeiten im Grossen und Kleinen.*[32] There is, then, diversity within the concept, as well as among concepts.

It is through words, for the most part, that concepts find expression in language use. *Elusive as the full meaning of concepts is, conveying their meaning through words adds to the difficulty.* The delimitation of the word fails to capture the elasticity of the concept. (When, for example, does a *stone* become a *boulder* or a *rock,* and when is it a *pebble?*) Words also straddle concepts, and they develop new meanings as they enter into different combinations and relationships. Words also play with meanings, as in idiom and metaphor. As Miller and Johnson-Laird have pointed out: "There is no such thing as the literal meaning of a sentence, only the literal meaning that a given listener places on a given utterance of it."[33] With the elusiveness of the concept paired with the unpredictable behavior of the word, it is small wonder that human beings fail to make themselves understood. The *mot juste* is indubitably an apple of gold, to be savored and treasured.

Halliday's term, "meaning potential," is well chosen as a description for language: This he defines as "sets of options, or alternatives in meaning, that are available to the speaker-hearer."[34] Halliday emphasizes what Malinowski has called "the dependence of the meaning of each word upon practical experience and of the structure of each utterance upon the momentary situation in which it is spoken."[35] *For Halliday, a semantic network is a hypothesis about patterns of meaning*, with three facets: (1) It is a hypothesis about what the speaker can do, linguistically in a given context, that is, about the meanings accessible to him; (2) it is an account of how social meanings (patterns of behavior) are expressed in language; and (3) it forms the bridge between behavior patterns and linguistic forms.[36] This takes us beyond the interrelationships and options the more traditional network of concepts provides to the *contextual features that impinge on the choices of the speaker.* "Contextual" refers in this case to the inner as well as the outer context – not only to situational features, but also to linguistic and emotional factors that are often strongly influenced by the attitudes and values of the speaker's cultural environment.

The cultural component in meaning

Clearly, Halliday's model provides food for thought for the language teacher. "Practical experience" and "patterns of behavior" vary from culture to culture, as well as from individual to individual within a culture. There is some commonality, of course, in the realities of human life everywhere. People eat, sleep, talk, or ride, whether in a jet plane or on an ox cart (yet, even here, the mode of "riding" may have varying connotations, and therefore different meanings, for the members of different cultures, implying to one status, to another weariness, and to yet others haste, necessity, or diversion). *Bever's analysis of the knowledge basic to all concepts expressed through language* is illuminating in this regard. "At any given moment," he says, "part of an individual's potential knowledge is the congeries of associated sensory, perceptual, and conceptual features, each such group associated by a linguistic label."[37] Bever distinguishes four different kinds of knowledge that are components of these linguistically labeled concepts, each of which must be taken into account for full comprehension of utterances: *semantic meaning* (the minimal denotational or referential information, which is shared across cultures because human beings experience a common physical reality); *cultural ideas*, of which *linguistic ideas* are a subset (cultural ideas representing the nonsemantic aspects of a concept that derive from shared life in a culture, and that frequently determine the way the structural forms of the language shape the message conveyed or perceived, as in the use of *tu* or *du* in French or German); and, finally, *personal ideas*, which arise from the individual's own experiences (these ideas are culture-independent and may even conflict with cultural ideas).[38]

Of linguistic ideas, Lyons observes that "the meanings of words (their sense and denotation) are internal to the language to which they belong.... Each language has its own semantic structure, just as it has its own grammatical and phonological structure."[39] *There is a common reality, yet each language selects and combines elements of meaning idiosyncratically,* as do individual language users (who by temperament, personality, and experiences of life may be culture-bound to a greater or lesser degree). This is what makes "choosing one's words" such a challenging yet satisfying activity, and the choices that are made so revealing that stacks of books crowd library shelves with attempts to explicate them. A declaration like that of Henry James, "Summer afternoon – summer afternoon; to me these have always been the most beautiful words in the English language," is both individualistic and culture-specific. It reflects James's upper-class New England background, as well as his personal predilection.

In view of the complexity of "meaning potential" for communication, whether in the native or in a second or third language, it is unfortunate that the term "communicative language teaching" seems to have been preempted for a somewhat narrow view of basic needs in communication in a restricted set of situations. Johnson speaks of the need for "inventories specifying semantic and pragmatic categories which are arrived at by considering presumed communicative needs" of the students.[40] He acknowledges the dilemma this creates for the language teacher who, faced with preselected, itemized content, is then expected to teach for the kind of global performance that comprehension and production of authentic language for unpredictable personal messages imply. This is not to say that there may not be a genuine need for a "systems approach" to language learning for certain groups with readily identifiable short-term needs. It does seem appropriate, however, to separate special cases (language for specific purposes, a unit-credit system for adult migrants, or specialized training for certain occupations and professions) from language teaching in general worldwide. *Each situation will require its own analysis of needs,* and for many the predominant need will continue to be "language *for* communication" (that is, both comprehension and production), acquired through contact with authentic oral and written materials, and practiced in communication

123

situations – foundational preparation for later specialization when the need arises.

The kinds of materials a "communicative approach" to specific learner needs of a practical nature can generate for large groups of students, under publisher pressure for rapid and economical production, run the risk of presenting the learner with what Robinson has called *hollow language*. As Robinson points out, " 'anything' a native speaker says will not always fulfill the goal of increasing a student's understanding and sensitivity toward people with different cultural values and behaviors"; even authentic language may be "hollow in a cultural sense, hollow in a personal sense, and hollow in a motivational sense,"[41] despite the fact that propositions and illocutionary acts may be situationally and socially appropriate. "Language *for* communication," taught with explicit discussions of how language works to convey meaning, will prepare students to analyze their own meanings, in relation to the linguistic and cultural ideas of their native background, as they select from the options the new language provides. Explicit study of pervasive ideas and preconceptions will sensitize them to the inner meanings of the messages they are receiving and enable them gradually to frame their own in culturally acceptable ways. For this, the various kinds of speech acts the "communicative approach" has brought to the fore[42] are useful, we might say indispensable, but these again are a framework for, rather than the essence of, communication.

Language *as* communication and language *for* communication

Widdowson makes the distinction between items selected for frequency of usage and those selected because "they have a high potential occurrence as instances of use of relevance to the learner's purpose in learning."[43] Insofar as Widdowson approximates usage to Chomsky's competence and use to his concept of performance, items with a "high potential occurrence" are still in the domain of usage, or items to be learned and produced as a demonstration of existing competence. For them to become use, or performance or *parole*, they must be used expressly *to achieve the learner's purposes then and there*. As items being practiced for future use, they are on a level with the widespread practice in *langue* or usage, which they are intended to complement, if not replace. Time spent talking out what one is predicted to need at some future time is just as much practice as is structural practice, situational practice, or practice in communicating. Motivated use where students talk about things they really want to talk about is not being tapped, as it must be if language is to be learned *for* actual communication, rather than *as* communication in the abstract. We may be getting closer to communicative competence, but *we are still in the realm of demonstrations of acquired competence, rather than genuine performance.* "Usage," says Widdowson, "is...that aspect [of performance] which makes evident the extent to which the language user demonstrates his knowledge of linguistic rules. Use is another aspect of performance: that which makes evident the extent to which the language user demonstrates his ability to use his knowledge of linguistic rules for effective communication."[44] Demonstrating the ability to use, no matter how artfully the opportunities for demonstration are contrived (through role playing or simulated situations, or whatever), is not use. *Real use can occur only in episodes of effective communication – student-originated and student-sustained.* Here the idiosyncratic and unpredictable will inevitably intervene, despite the best-laid schemes of materials developers and classroom teachers.[45] This is genuine interaction.

Vocabulary in communication

This discussion on language *as* communication and language *for* communication brings us back to our central topic of "words fitly spoken" (or written). We may use structures or illocutionary acts, but without *an extensive vocabulary from which to select* we can convert neither into comprehensible communication. As Zoila in her practical way realized, "book red table kitchen" is more readily comprehensible than "the *X* is on the *A* in the *B*."[46] Furthermore, inventories of grammatical structures or of speech acts are finite, quite restricted, and therefore learnable. Vocabulary acquisition, on the other hand, continues throughout our lives, even for the native language: at times imperceptibly, at other periods more rapidly as we come into contact with a new area of study, a new professional milieu, or a new dialect or sociolect. Augmentation of vocabulary is the one area of language learning that does not seem to be slowed down by increasing age. It seems rather to become easier as one matures, and as one's knowledge of the world and differentiations in the realm of thought broaden. Even in a foreign language, the first ten words are probably the most difficult one will have to learn. *One's personal vocabulary is an individual achievement and possession, poor or rich though it may be.*

Semantic memory

What then are the psychological mechanisms that account for this extraordinary ability to expand one's means of expression? Psychological experimentation is filling in details of what Quillian has termed "semantic memory." Tulving describes this construct as follows:

> Semantic memory is the memory necessary for the use of language. It is a mental thesaurus, organized knowledge a person possesses about words and other verbal symbols, their meaning and referents, about relations among them, and about rules, formulas, and algorithms for the manipulation of these symbols, concepts, and relations. Semantic memory does not register perceptible properties of inputs, but rather cognitive referents of input signals. The semantic system permits the retrieval of information that was not directly stored in it, and retrieval of information from the system leaves its contents unchanged.[47]

Research into semantic memory is still in a ferment of development, but we can draw interesting implications from those aspects of the model for which there is a reasonable consensus.

Semantic memory is viewed as *a network in which conceptual nodes are linked by inferential relations* that draw on the redundancies within concepts. (A series of inferences like "*dog*: animal with four legs: infer *can run*: infer *can run onto roads*: infer *can be killed on roads*: infer *for safety keep on leash*" enables us to comprehend an utterance like "Her dog shouldn't be over there.") The concepts in semantic memory are independent of the forms of a specific language. Words of the language we are using become linked with interconnections of the conceptual network and proceed to draw on the inferential relations already established for these interconnections.[48] *Thus, new words are absorbed into the organizational structure and become usable.* This is one of the most important aspects of the model. "Organization occurs in memory...to permit inferences in storing and retrieving semantic information. It is by using inference that people can know much more than they can learn," as Collins and Quillian express it.[49] When we encounter words of a new language we can rarely match them in a one-to-one relationship to lexical items of our native language and thus profit from the interconnections already formed (although many, unfortunately, try to do this). *The new forms must be linked up with their own culture-specific inferences.* We must also learn their limitations and expansions in relation to apparently similar meanings of lexical items already familiar to us (their differences in distribution, in collocations, and in syntactic requirements).

Since, as Jenkins puts it, "the mind remembers what the mind *does*, not what the world does,"[50] these new connections become established only *through use in meaningful contexts*. The fallacy for most learners is "looking for meaning as one would look for marbles," as Morris once observed, "a meaning [being] considered as one thing among other things, a definite something located somewhere."[51] As Hardwick points out, "Morris is stressing," as does Wittgenstein, "that the process of semiosis is not something that goes on 'in the mind,' but in the activities by means of which something is taken-into-account by individuals involved in group activity. 'Meaning' is a part of that activity...rooted in the forms of life."[52] The meanings, both semantic and cultural, of the forms of a new language are, therefore, most readily and precisely learned in the milieu where the language is spoken. Failing this, we need to surround the learner with as much authentic speech, writing, kinesics, aspects of the cultural milieu, and contacts with speakers of the language who have been brought up in the target culture as possible. These supports are more readily available to second-language learners than foreign-language learners, although social and psychological distance may impede the students' profiting from them as they might.[53] In a foreign-language situation, taped and videotaped material, films, songs, contacts with native speakers, and visits to areas where the language is spoken are essential, if the outward forms of the language are to be infused with authentic meanings and inferences.

How we store and retrieve

Acquisition, storage, recognition, recall, and retrieval are our next concerns. These we can deal with only briefly here. Basic to effective operation of these functions is organization. *Memory is structured.* Input must be coded according to some organizational scheme, or memory would become overloaded and recognition and recall would become well-nigh impossible. What we actually store is dependent on *attention and motivation*, which are reflections of our purposes in relation to the material impinging on our perceptual system. We take in, we code, and we store what we see as being relevant to our goals. How we organize it for storage is frequently idiosyncratic, but the more we "chunk" items of information into what we perceive as categories and natural groups, the more we retain.[54] *Students have very personal semantic networks into which they process what they find to be useful. Consequently, vocabulary cannot be taught.* It can be presented, explained, included in all kinds of activities, and experienced in all manner of associations (visual, auditory, kinesthetic, tactile, olfactory if one wishes), but ultimately it is learned by the individual. As language teachers, *we must arouse interest in words*

127

and a certain excitement in personal development in this area (that is, motivation to learn ways of expressing meanings that are important to the individual student, even if not to others in the group). We can help our students by giving them ideas on how to learn, but each will finally learn a very personal selection of items, organized into relationships in an individual way. This individuality should be encouraged, since it is a well-attested fact that idiosyncratic organization in memory results in more efficient recall.

It is generally held that we do not store surface forms of language intact. Through inductive processes, *we extract the sense and store meaning.* We also store phonetic features for reconstruction of lexical items as needed. In attempting to retrieve words, we often dredge up items with phonetically similar features, particularly initial and final segments, stress patterns, and number of syllables. For instance, we may produce *extraneous* for *extenuating,* or, in searching for a name, we may go through a series like *Mulligan...Houlihan...hooligan...Goolagong.* This has been called the "tip of the tongue" phenomenon by Brown.[55] Similarly, we tend to store conceptual attributes associated with lexical items, rather than the "meaning" of a word.

It is because of the redundancy of such elements in each lexical item that so many inferential cross-associations can be made. Concepts are associated in memory according to such relations as superset or superordinate (*cat: animal: mammal*); similarity (*knife: dagger*); part (*house: room*); attribute (which often provokes a syntagma like *green: grass*); proximity (*sea: beach*); consequence (*cold: sneeze*); precedence (*indigestion: overeat*); and parent (*baby: mother*).[56] We can test the existence of these cross-associations by writing down rapidly a series of word associations and examining the relationships between adjacent items. In fact, it is when such associations do not fall into the usual categories that we detect the influence of salient personal experiences and touch on the "personal ideas" within the concept.[57]

Helping students to learn vocabulary

Useful vocabulary-oriented activities move from whole to part (*face:* eye, nose), agent or object to function (*oil:* cooking; *barber:* cut), or from superset to subset (*animal:* cat, dog). Games and competitions are easily developed that evoke words demonstrating similarities and differences (*rock:* stone; *stone:* feather); consequences (*cliff:* fall); precedence (*lunch:* breakfast; *relax:* come home); proximity (*shop:* bus). Although *single* words and expressions are listed in the preceding discussion, the types of activities developed should, whenever possible, involve *using the words in the context of a meaningful utterance* or series of utterances in a communicative exchange.

Valuable also, because they establish relationships among groups of words or parts of words, are the processes of compounding; dividing off prefixes and suffixes in such ways as to demonstrate their contributions to meaning in many combinations (the same process revealing the meaning nucleus between prefix and suffix); and the creation of new meanings with different arrangements of word segments. Exercises for these processes should emphasize *creativity*, even if some of the new words created are not in actual use, but are nevertheless possible words of the language (e.g., compounding: *egg-scooper*; applying meanings conveyed by prefixes and suffixes, or "topping and tailing": to underwhelm). Students need to acquire linguistic flexibility and confidence in drawing freely from their networks elements that facilitate both interpretation and production.

Free associations, practice with collocations, and chaining words in syntagmas (*down* the street, *down* the stream, *down*hill; *never*: again, *never*more) also enable students to activate and reuse all kinds of routes within their semantic networks (both those that are conventional within the language and those that arouse idiosyncratic connections). Cloze exercises, word puzzles, and word games[58] all help to establish and confirm relations among items of the new language, the activated processes of recall and retrieval providing further opportunities for the rehearsal that is so essential if material is to remain available in long-term memory.

Pattern matching and pattern completion

Recognition and recall (which is basic to retrieval) are different processes. Kintsch calls recognition "pattern matching" and recall "pattern completion." He considers pattern completion (recall) to be "one of the most important human information processing operations."[59] *We can recognize much more than we can retrieve; in other words, we know much more than we can actively recall.* The great amount of material we can match (or recognize) facilitates listening and reading. Both recall and retrieval are, of course, necessary for production. The more associations and interconnections we have developed, the more efficiently we can recall and retrieve. Since we exert active control over production processes we can paraphrase, circumlocute, and avoid when we cannot retrieve the words for which we are searching. In listening and reading, however, the selection is not ours. It is fortunate indeed that pattern matching is less demanding than pattern completion. Because of this difference between recognition and recall, we must not require students to be able to use actively all the vocabulary they encounter. They must be encouraged to develop as broad and far-reaching a *recognition vocabulary*[60] as they can, in areas of special interest to them, while *settling for less in production vocabulary*. This will be achieved largely through frequent experiences of listening to and reading authentic language material that attracts and focuses the students' attention (a prerequisite for retention of new words and expressions).

The individual's personal acquisition of vocabulary

It is clear that if semantic networks are of an individual character, vocabulary cannot be taught (in the sense of "inculcated"). It can be presented in interesting, attention-focusing activities and in materials where information the students wish to extract can be obtained only through knowledge of or inferring the meanings of words and expressions in context, but *ultimately selection for storage is an individual act of the learner*. So that what has been selected may be committed to long-term storage, the students' desire to retain these items must be aroused by continually reentering them in activities in which they enjoy participating, but in which they must demonstrate what they know in order for the activity to continue. Constant use, which is dependent on interest and focused attention, will facilitate recognition or retrieval (as required) and ensure the maintenance of the item in a readily reactivated semantic network.

Students must learn how to learn vocabulary, in this sense, for themselves.[61] They need experience in discriminating variations within the areas of meaning the language allows: learning limitations and potential expansions of meaning in comparison with the distribution and coverage in languages they already know. Diagrammatic demonstrations of coverage and range are frequently useful, encouraging adjustments within individual semantic networks. These may be purely illustrative of the ways in which the new language divides up semantic space, or they may be comparative, highlighting both similarities and differences in relation to the native language or other languages with which the learners are familiar. Such schematic presentations add salience and vividness that focus attention, but as with all areas of language knowledge, control in language use (that is, empirical respecting of boundaries and limits) comes through frequent *communicative interaction in activities and interludes that have significance for the learner* and in which meaning is successfully apprehended and conveyed.

Where students are acquiring a cognate language, learning to penetrate the orthographic or phonological disguises well-known words have assumed multiplies the possibilities for recognition and for creative production. Even with noncognate languages the same process makes available to the learner an extensive "international vocabulary" (*jet*; *stress*; *diesel*; *satellite*) that reflects common experiences in an interdependent modern world.

Since one's vocabulary is a very personal possession and one's ability to exploit its elasticity in acceptable and comprehensible ways is equally individual, *students should be encouraged to seek the ways they find most helpful* for expanding and maintaining their knowledge of the lexicon and the semantic potential of the new language. Some make lists and memorize them; some read a great deal and mark with an asterisk a word they do not understand each time they meet it, thus creating their own frequency counts; some note down words in a short context, repeatedly writing down the same words until their meaning and use are assimilated; some make associations with words that sound or look similar in their native language, even though the meaning may be different; some practice using new words as they talk to themselves, in order to commit them to long-term memory; some read dictionaries.[62] Above all, students should not be forced to learn in ways they find unappealing or personally unsatisfying if the ultimate goal for each student of developing autonomous long-term learning strategies is to be achieved.

Lest this discussion of detail should distract us from *the unity of language performance in context*, we cannot do better than reaffirm, in conclusion, that words are but surface manifestations of meanings that are personal and communicable. As Jenkins puts it: "Recall is not just a function of what the outside world presents to you but also...a function of what you do with the events as you experience them."[63] Potential meanings are provided by a new language, but these are realized by motivated individuals. Teaching a new language involves not just providing opportunities for acquisition of forms, but also encouraging active communication of ideas and expression of individuality through these new forms. Ben Jonson once said: "Neither can his mind be thought in tune, whose words do jarre; nor his reason in frame, whose sentence is preposterous." We can serve our students best by helping them to use effectively well-chosen words that can express subtleties and to understand the messages of others in an intercultural context. "A word," as Vygotsky so perceptively observed, "is a microcosm of human consciousness."[64]

Let's discuss

1 Discuss the various ways vocabulary was presented in your early and later language classes and in your textbooks. How did you

feel about this type of presentation and practice? From what you have read in this chapter, what do you now think of these procedures?

2 Study the Threshold Level (or the *niveau-seuil*) and compare it with a well-known frequency count. What are the similarities and differences in the vocabulary selected?

3 Discuss the implications for vocabulary acquisition of Halliday's semantic network and Hymes's "person in a social world." What changes do these suggest for vocabulary study in class?

4 Discuss ways of drawing on stored relationships in semantic memory for vocabulary acquisition without passing through the native language.

5 Study the vocabulary and the way it is presented in a recent textbook. Can you detect any signs of "hollow language"? How could this have been avoided?

6 Can you devise activities or procedures for vocabulary acquisition (other than those in this chapter) that are congruent with what is known about memory? Work several of these out in detail and exchange your proposals with others in your group.

10 Language learners as individuals: discovering their needs and wants

In a recent novel, a landowner gives his foster son the following advice as a guiding light in times of change: "There are times," he says, "when you must sit down, and take note, count the animals, find out what the harvest will be, and go clearly into time, never blindly, always ready to change course, as a good navigator must, when he finds the map wrong."[1] The area of language teaching and learning is not static, set in some mold that represents an unchanging model of how things ought to be. The rapid shifts, vehement controversies, even recriminations, of the past fifty years make this quite clear (see chap. 1). From time to time, we need to sit down, ponder the possibilities for the harvest, and change course if we find our present direction is not leading us where we need to go.

Providing for consumer needs

Consideration of the harvest in modern terms implies market research, and market research presumes that there are consumers. Who are the consumers of what we have to offer in language teaching and what will they be wanting from us in the next decade? Our consumers are not only students, but also the society of which they are a part. As in all marketing research, we must not merely identify what we think our consumers need, but also what they want (that is, what they feel they need). As educators we must provide for a balance between these two if students are to be motivated to learn what we offer.

What our students need depends on political situations, societal demands, and the career opportunities these create; what our students want derives from their or their parents' perceptions of these community factors, their final choices being influenced also by per-

Revised version of an article originally published with B. J. Melvin as "Language Learners as Individuals: Discovering Their Needs, Wants, and Learning Styles," in J. E. Alatis, H. B. Altman, and P. M. Alatis, eds., *The Second Language Classroom: Directions for the 1980's*, Essays in honor of Mary Finocchiaro (New York: Oxford University Press, 1981), pp. 81–93. Used by arrangement with the publisher.

sonal preferences. *The decisions that determine educational programs are rarely made by earnest language-acquisition researchers, teacher trainers, or theoreticians of language-teaching methodology.* This in-group may have some effect on language learning through materials production, but even then the final word will come from the consumers, since books are accepted by publishers and flourish or fade according to their degree of response to the currently perceived needs of the wider society.

In support of this position we may consider the first tangible result of the 1979 Report of the President's Commission on Foreign Language and International Studies: the creation of a *National Council on Foreign Language and International Studies* "to focus public attention on the nation's declining competence in foreign languages and the urgent need for improved understanding of international affairs" (*Chronicle of Higher Education*, June 2, 1980). Funded by private foundations and federal agency funds,[2] the council, which will be expected to make specific recommendations on such issues as "how many people should know what languages, where they should learn them, and how the learning should be made possible," has only one member who is an expert on language teaching. These policy decisions will be made by community representatives in response to an analysis of the needs of the nation in its relationships with other nations. Their recommendations, enhanced by the lure of possible funding and high-level support, will no doubt have a major impact on the direction second-language study will take in the future, as their analyses and recommendations define career opportunities. As good navigators, we must be ready to change course if we find our map is wrong.

Meeting the needs of adult migrants in Europe

The most striking example in recent times of the implementation of high-level decisions of a political entity that has perceived the need for the learning of languages by a segment of the population within its jurisdiction has been the work of the Group of Experts called together in 1971 by the Committee for Out-of-School Education and Cultural Development of the Council for Cultural Co-operation of the Council of Europe. This group of highly respected applied linguists and language teachers[3] was charged with creating "the conditions for the establishment of a suitable *structural framework for the development, through international co-operation, of a coherent and progressive European policy in the field of adult language learning.*"[4]

134

The political and social need was created by the number of adult workers who were moving from their homelands (Portugal, Turkey, and other economically depressed areas) to the more prosperous countries of the European Economic Community, without speaking the languages of their host countries. In 1977, the Parliamentary Assembly of the Council of Europe accepted the recommendation that:

The Committee of Ministers:
  a. call on the governments of the member states...to develop the teaching of modern languages, taking account of:
     i.   the particular needs of less privileged groups, particularly migrants;
     ii. the need to diversify the languages taught;
     iii. the cultural advantages of maintaining language minorities in Europe;
     iv. the pedagogical aspects of language learning;
  b. encourage, with regard to the teaching of languages, the adoption of co-ordinated educational policies based on proposals drawn up at the European level.[5]

In this way, they consecrated the efforts of the Group of Experts and their collaborators and opened the way for the application on a wide scale of their work as set out in *Systems Development in Adult Language Learning* (Trim et al., for the CCC of the Council of Europe, 1973), *The Threshold Level in a European Unit/Credit System for Modern Language Learning by Adults* (Van Ek, 1975), *Un niveau-seuil* (Coste et al., 1976), and *Waystage* (Van Ek, 1977).

The European unit/credit system was developed on the basis of an analysis of the linguistic needs of adults in forty-four occupational categories. In the analysis, the actual activities in which persons of these specific occupations would need to use another language were studied and estimates made of the degree of proficiency they would require in each of the linguistic skills of understanding, speaking, reading, and writing. Some materials along functional-notional lines have been developed to meet these needs and more are in production.[6]

The functional-notional materials of the Council of Europe were developed to meet the specific needs of adult guest workers in the European context. They are not necessarily transferable to other areas where needs may be quite different. The American program for adult workers that draws closest to that of the Council of Europe is Occupational English as a Second Language (also called Manpower ESL), a component of bilingual-bicultural education that has been part of the training and technical assistance provided by the Area Manpower Institutes for the Development of Staff (AMIDS), a federal program begun in 1968. AMIDS deals with the educational

135

needs of disadvantaged groups. It teaches Survival English (cf. Waystage) and such specialized ESL programs as English for Auto Mechanics or for Japanese workers in clothing factories.[7]

Although the program and materials prepared for the Council of Europe may not provide exactly what is needed in other places with different problems, the amount of energy and hard work generated by this high-level decision to promote the learning of languages is exemplary. The European experience foreshadows the need for our language-teaching profession to prepare to adapt to a noteworthy change of direction when national policies are elaborated as a result of the work of the National Council.

Language learning linked with international studies

One fact already evident in the name of the National Council (and earlier in the name of the President's Commission) is the close link that is assumed between language learning and international studies. This association has not been strong in the past, so it behooves us to begin now to study the implications of this linkage for second-language and foreign-language programs of the future by building bridges of discussion and cooperation with our colleagues in international and global education and in the less commonly taught languages of Asia and Africa.

All decisions, however, will not be made by experts or teachers. We must discover what students feel they need from us, if their study of a language is to serve the purpose of developing their understanding of the ways of thinking and valuing of persons of a different culture as well as language, and some appreciation of their achievements, problems, and aspirations, so that along with learning the language they may develop the tolerance and sympathy that bridge gaps between persons of different backgrounds. This will be a new and untraveled path for many of our language teachers, who will themselves need reeducation if they are to be successful in *building cooperative programs* in this area, which combines language teaching with the study of other disciplines. We are approaching a new frontier that will require of us the flexibility and the innovative, untrammeled thinking of the frontier.

What do our students feel they need?

Leaving aside the broader political and social determinants of student needs, we come to the personal. Many students will have other interests than those of international affairs or even international trade. We must avoid the attitude of the past, which has tended to see one response to a multifaceted problem at any particular moment. In the days to come, we will have to accept the fact that *there is no single pedagogical answer, only the answers of many individuals.* Language teachers must learn humility. They will have to abandon the authoritarian approach of "*designing* the program to meet their students' needs" as they see them, in favor of discovering first how the students perceive their needs, and then considering what contribution they can make, as teachers and course designers, to meeting these needs. We must stop thinking we know and start finding out.

We begin by studying seriously who our language learners really are. What age are they? Are they from a minority culture? Are they visitors or do they intend to stay in this country? Are they refugees? Are they literate in their own language? Are they learning a foreign or a second language (in the now generally accepted meaning of that term[8])? Are they learning this language for everyday intercourse? for job requirements? for personal enrichment and broadening of their educational experience? for reasons of ethnic curiosity or attachment? in order to understand and interact with a coexistent community? to fulfill school or college requirements? as a tool for study purposes (particularly through listening or reading materials)? as an additional skill to enhance a professional career? just for curiosity or love of language? because of a personal relationship? because they want to travel (for pleasure or business)? as a necessity for research? In this last sentence alone, we have touched on twelve possible motivations, each indicating a somewhat different orientation to the learning task. How can we continue to think in terms of one approach and one prototype set of courses in the curriculum?

How then do we proceed? A questionnaire on students' perceived needs is a good start, but it cannot supply all the answers, since the questionnaire constructor begins with certain assumptions that determine the questions the students will address.[9] Even a section for free response may not provide sufficient information, because not all students have a clear idea they can articulate of what they would like the language course to provide. There are many possibilities that do not occur to them. *A questionnaire needs to be supplemented by teacher observation and attentive listening to students and community.*

Student needs as the basis for course design

Sensitive teacher interpretation indicates many directions in which course design may develop, as indicated by the extreme diversity of

137

the following responses from teachers in a 1978 survey of foreign language learners' goals in fifty countries and the fifty states of the United States.[10]

> To gain an appreciative understanding of different modes of thought and to develop the ability to communicate within this framework. (Holland)

> To read – particularly scientific and technical English – so as to be able to extract information relevant to the practice of the students' profession and important to the development of the country as a whole. (Mexico)

> To be able to communicate with persons from other countries; to be able to read and understand newspapers; to be able to understand what is said on TV and radio. (Sweden)

> To form a harmony between academic learning and professional training or career education as contributing to the goals of liberal education, e.g., to combine linguistic skills with a professional speciality – law, accounting, chemistry, etc., for a practical or utilitarian value. (Thailand)

> At a time when students are capable of understanding the global gestalt, are studying the intricate balances of nature and mankind in courses ranging through history through literature and beyond, are firming up their philosophies of life, the foreign language class can – and should – center attention on the role of the human being in an interdependent collection of land/sea masses. Language is the vehicle that carries us down the multilaned routes connecting people, all of whom are in motion. Language study can make the collisions on these byways meaningful rather than disastrous. (United States)

Perceptive interpretation of the articulated and implicit messages of students, parents, and community representatives can then be expressed in *experimental course design*.[11] The response of students to experimental courses will reveal clearly enough whether their needs are being met and enable them to express more concretely what they feel is still missing. Slowly, extra courses will be added and others modified to meet these needs. The proof of the pudding being in the eating, this more indirect approach will gradually lead to a viable diversified curriculum that allows for much student choice, without the chaos of individual offerings for each student.

What all of these motivations require, if the students are to feel their needs are fulfilled, is *a solid, flexible basic course* on which the student can later develop diversifications of language use for specific purposes.[12] Without a serious general-purpose foundation, students can become locked into an approach that subsequent language experience causes them to realize they do not really want. The basic course must, however, provide for both the aurally and the visually oriented and introduce students to the various possible benefits of language study, interpersonal, cultural, expressive, global, professional, and humanistic, in such a way that each student is prepared to make a real choice of the direction in which to continue.[13]

After the basic course, there should be choice, that is, *courses with differing orientations that provide clear-cut options*, even if these options go against the teacher's personal predilections. Even in a one-class situation, options can be included and tests can be constructed that allow students a choice in how they will be tested (Altman and Politzer, 1971). Until teachers are trained or retrained, or retrain themselves through thoughtful reading and observation, to recognize these potentialities, the promise of the present time will fade rapidly. Unless the students, with their needs and wants, become central to our planning and implementation, we will continue to reecho the old adage: *plus ça change, plus c'est la même chose.*

Let's discuss

Read the following quotations from responses to the Rivers *Questionnaire on Foreign Language Learners' Goals*, 1978.[14] Consider the situation indicated by the attribution in parentheses. What approach would you take to course development to provide for the interests and needs expressed in each quotation?

1 Our students do not want to *only* learn how to order meals in London, but how to understand the cultural, political, social, literary, and economic problems and issues of the Anglo-Saxon world. They do not want to listen to tapes about tourists in New York; rather, they would prefer tapes in the target language from the Voice of America or the BBC dealing with issues of importance. Our students want content not frills. (Brazil, college, English)

2 To learn a considerable amount of vocabulary and structures that enable the learners to understand lectures and take notes, to understand what they read in their specialization (engineering), to make notes and write reports on what they read or see in the laboratory/workshop. (Kuwait, junior college, Arabic, English, and French)

3 To learn how to understand lengthy, highly technical articles written in English and intended for native readers, i.e., to learn the conventions for making grammatical cohesion, discoursal functions (hypotheses, classifications, etc.) and author's attitude. To learn how to read quickly in order to cover lengthy bibliographies. (Israel, college, English)

4 Since I have detected an opposite trend in the current talk of "communicative skills," I must state that I am strongly against setting up "Englishness" as a goal for English teaching. A Swede will always remain a Swede, and whether he can mutter the right words at the bar of a London pub is of little importance. What does matter, however, is whether he is able to express his – inevitably Swedish – views and has such a knowledge of the interlocutor's – English, American, African, or other – national background that he is prepared for an exchange based on goodwill and understanding. (Sweden, junior college, English and French)

5 The objectives are not very clear at the secondary-school level. Yet, they do become clear as soon as one leaves school or accedes to the university. Hence the shift nowadays toward English for Special Purposes:

a) English for secretaries: final year of Technical School;
b) English for Science students: final year of Lycée;
c) Special English for students of the Facultés des Sciences et Techniques de Gestion, de Médecine;
d) English for hotel people.

The goals are becoming clearer here, as the secondary-school *responsables* now have accepted to consider the needs of the prospective clerks, technologists, and graduate and undergraduate students. All the skills have to be developed, but ultimately the main skill should be *the reading skill*. The other goal is to belong to an international community whose language is obviously English. French is still as important as Arabic, Tunisia's mother tongue. (Tunisia, Ministry of Education, English)

6 To form a harmony between academic learning and professional training or career education as contributing to the goals of liberal education, e.g., to combine linguistic skills with a professional speciality – law, accounting, chemistry, etc., for a practical or utilitarian value. To develop the student's intellectual powers through foreign-language learning. To use foreign language as a tool for advanced studies in different disciplines – not limited only to literary works. To develop communicative competence for either instrumental or integrative orientation. (Thailand, undergraduate, English)

7 To know and use the worldwide language (English) efficiently; to negotiate with foreigners fluently; not to be one-track mind; to work diligently and efficiently. (Thailand, senior high school, English)

8 The overseas students with whom I work come to the UK for post-graduate studies. Their most important goal is to cope, from

the beginning of the academic year, with the various demands
of their academic studies (seminars, lab work, lectures, reading,
reports, etc.) Successful study is also dependent on the students'
psychological well-being. Thus the other important goal is
improving their ability (and confidence in their ability) to communicate orally with those around them – both native speakers
and foreign students – and to cope with the practical problems
of settling down in a new environment (linguistic and non-lin-
guistic). (England, graduate, English)

9 The most important goal for my students, most of whom are
teaching training candidates, is to give them the opportunity to
USE the language in situations which offer them the chance
to say what they think, believe. It could be in a guided discussion
or in a simulation game. The important thing is to break down
barriers and build up confidence. (West Germany, undergraduate
and adult classes, English)

10 It seems likely that the Western European countries rapidly
develop into bilingual communities as recommended by the
Council of Europe and the EC summit. To me this means a more
subtle approach to language teaching objectives and practices
and definitely a de-schooling of language instruction, i.e., foreign
language learning should and will be excluded from the syllabus of "academic" subjects and rather become a natural culture
skill comparable to sports, games and music. (West Germany,
graduate and undergraduate, English)

11 In the educational situation in which I work I consider *advanced
reading skills* the main objective for my teaching. Students leaving
our school often go to college where they should be able to
read scientific/technical books/periodicals. Insufficient knowledge
of English may seriously limit their academic performances.
Listening Comprehension should receive more attention than it
presently does. *Advanced speaking* and *Advanced writing* skills
seem to me to be of less importance. *The Threshold Level* (Council of Europe Publication) seems to be sufficient. (Netherlands,
senior high school, English)

12 To gain an appreciative understanding of different modes of
thought and to develop the ability to communicate within this
framework. To gain insight into the phenomena of language
(in and out of context). N.B. These aims are not necessarily (of
course!) those of all my students. Some do English as a vaguely
useful subject when they can think of nothing else, some need
it for strictly career purposes – to be an English teacher (fairly
well paid here!). (Netherlands, graduate, undergraduate,
English)

13 The country in which I have been working (Finland) is particularly isolated, geographically, historically, culturally, and linguistically. For students, learning another European language is
often principally a means towards securing a better job. From
the teacher's point of view, it should, I think, be largely an attempt to extend the horizons of the students, giving them a
deeper appreciation of their own culture. At the same time, the
students very much need to acquire confidence when encountering people from other countries, especially when they, the Finns,
travel abroad. The point I want to stress in the case of the
Finns, whose own language is understood virtually nowhere else
in the world, not even in Hungary, is that by learning, say,
English, they will be able to communicate with all speakers of
that language, whether or not it is those speakers' mother
tongue. This is vital for this group of learners as well as the more
obvious educational objectives. (Finland, undergraduate,
English)

14 They should be able to read and understand science and technology literature, ranging from college/university level textbooks to
advanced research papers, available through English. They
should also be able to write English competently because the medium of examining is English. Because of the academic pressures of their educational situation, they should ideally achieve
near native-speaker competence in reading, understanding, and
writing English. At the spoken level, the aim need not be so exact-
ing because face-to-face examination in English is limited in
scope and largely confined to the geographical boundary of their
country. (India, undergraduate, English)

15 English is the medium of instruction at the university but it has
no role outside the university. Students need to comprehend
lectures and references written in English. The comprehension
of spoken and written language represents the essential goal
of the students. (Sudan, undergraduate, English)

16 To be able to communicate with persons from other countries;
to be able to read and understand newspapers; to be able to
understand what is said on TV and radio. (Sweden, grammar
school, English)

17 Knowledge of English broadens opportunities of work in all fields
be it science, technology, mass media, etc. Moreover it is needed
for any graduate work since translation of any specialized matter is a slow and expensive process. The fluency required varies
according to the fields of work or types of jobs. For graduate
work reading comprehension and translation is most needed. For
clerical work reading and writing knowledge is essential. For

hotelry and touristic jobs fluency in speaking is a requirement. In politics, literature and mass media, knowledge of variations in meaning according to structures is a crucial matter; this is where sensitivity to what is said and how it is said become the main task of the language teacher. This is one of the reasons why I stopped teaching literature in the department and decided to work for a Ph.D. in Linguistics. (Egypt, graduate and undergraduate, English)

18 These goals are to broaden young people's work opportunities, to enable them to learn about another culture thereby enriching their lives and to facilitate international understanding between different peoples hence promoting the cause of peace. (Egypt, intermediate school, English)

19 To read – particularly scientific and technical English – so as to be able to extract information relevant to the practice of the student's profession and important to the development of the country as a whole. Also, to be able to understand and analyze the socio-political, economic and philosophical context in which the information or viewpoints are presented so as to better determine their applicability to the student's own environment. (Mexico, graduate and undergraduate, English)

20 Graduate and undergraduate students of the science and technology departments throughout the country increasingly need English in order to carry out the following activities (in decreasing order of importance): (a) a capacity to read (for different purposes, according to level) the literature of their specialty and related areas of interest, and (b) capacity to communicate orally on own subject with English-speaking specialists they may come into contact with during the undergraduate course or during their later professional careers in their home country or at international conferences. Other activities are also needed but these do not necessarily apply to all students. The needs of the Technical or Vocational School student seem (as far as is known for Chile) to be somewhat more restricted – though varied – according to the particular work that is concerned, as, after all, it is only a selection of the whole of the language that is actually used in any one vocation in order to enable the people to carry out their jobs efficiently. (Chile, graduate, undergraduate and technical, English)

21 Developing communicative confidence (as well as competence) freeing students from inhibitions caused by mistake-oriented teaching. (New Zealand, adult classes, English)

22 Being able to converse in English in their work, contacts with native speakers, and with their English-speaking children or

143

grandchildren; being able to read all signs and advertisements, contracts, ads, etc., they are likely to be confronted with; being able to write notes, application forms, want-ads; being able to understand most of the oral English they are exposed to. (Canada, adult immigrant classes, English)

23 The most important goal I have is to develop the children's listening, reading, speaking, and writing skills to the point where they can fit comfortably into the academic mainstream closest to their chronological age and developmental level. (Canada, elementary school, immigrant children, English)

24 They should be able to express *their* ideas as fluently as possible. (Canada, adult classes, English)

25 My present work experience is teaching English as a second language and teaching Spanish literacy skills to native speakers of Spanish in a language maintenance bilingual program. Our goals are first of all survival skills for a new culture and then the literacy skills which will enable them to function near grade level with their peers as quickly as possible. (New York, Spanish bilingual program)

26 The most important goals for foreign-language learners in Hong Kong are as follows: 1) to find well-paid jobs 2) to secure promotions 3) to lead a highly materialistic life. (Hong Kong, junior college, English)

27 Because of the increase of non-English speaking migrants to Australia, foreign languages should be taught to English-speaking Australians to help them to understand and tolerate their new neighbours. Migrants, on the other hand, need to learn English in order to live more easily in Australia and in order to keep in touch with members of their family growing up as native speakers of English. Migrant children should be given every opportunity to continue studies in their mother tongue. Studies in Aboriginal languages and culture should be made available to all Australians to promote a) understanding of Aboriginals by White Australians b) pride in their own heritage on the part of Aborigines. (Australia, immigrant and adult classes, English)

28 For children in Israel I believe that knowing English is essential as a window on the world. (Israel, undergraduate, English)

29 To foster regional understanding and good will. This can of course be done via the languages in the region, but the use of a foreign language, e.g., English, has a certain neutrality and thus helps to decrease national and regional parochialism. (Singapore, graduate, English)

30 Both English and French have a role to play in combating parochialism, but so have the major Nigerian languages within the

country and they cultivate a national identity better than English in many respects. (Nigeria, graduate and undergraduate, English)

31 To have a medium which bypasses the linguistic problem in Belgium between Dutch/French speakers, with English having less negative emotional connotations. (Belgium, undergraduate, English)

32 Learning a foreign language is not only acquiring a new mode of communication; it is also being able to develop two sets of symbols and concepts, thus developing abstraction, generalization, and flexibility of mind. Moreover, it means for the learner to open his mind to a new culture, a new way of thinking, a new way of living. "He who knows better, understands better, thus loves better." In this respect, an important goal for foreign language learners is the development of adaptability and respect for others. It becomes then a question of attitudes and behavior (less prejudiced, less biased...). (France, undergraduate, English)

33 Sweden being linguistically peripheral, students consider languages to be a must. Languages, especially English, are the key to an academic career and opportunities in the outside world. (Sweden, senior high school, English)

34 Learning the FL for fun or personal enjoyment. (Brazil, language institutes, English)

35 Gain self-confidence and get a broader understanding of other nations' culture. Be able to talk with immigrants in a common language (English) from whichever part of the world they come. (Sweden, adult classes, English)

36 To develop a sense of caring and responsibility for others in the learning situation and also for the activities there. From this perspective I think, everything else falls into place. (Canada, short intensive courses, English)

37 The most important goal of a student learning English as a second language in the United States is mastery of the language and the contexts in which it is used so that they may better realize personal, educational, social, and economic aspirations. (USA, graduate, undergraduate, ESL education)

38 Help narrow the gap between the "have's" and the "have-not's" by allowing Third World countries access to modern technology *and* encouraging them to adopt *selectively*. (Vermont, graduate, ESL Teacher Training)

39 To develop a functional control of a second-language system as a means for understanding and partaking in the culture of those who speak that language as well as a means for better

understanding one's own language and culture. (Washington, D.C., undergraduate, EFL and FL)

40 In the bilingual border situation, I believe that it is of utmost importance for as many people as possible, and certainly for everyone who claims to be educated, to be fluent in both the languages of the area, including standard and non-standard forms. (Texas, bilingual English/Spanish)

11 Motivation in bilingual programs

Life today is programmed. We are each fighting our individual battles against the impersonalization of daily transactions and the phony concern for our well-being of those who wish to organize us, sell us a bill of goods, or use us in some way to advance their causes. Strangely enough, some of us do not feel particularly motivated to cooperate with them and are strongly tempted to bend, fold, staple, and mutilate every card they send us. Is it possible that some of our students feel the same way? The interest some of us manifest in ways of motivating our students has its counterpart in the concern of those businesses that engage in market research purely to increase profits. We have a product, we are sure it is a good product, and we want an increasing number of consumers to like it, so that we may have an outstanding program that will increase our self-esteem and add luster to our reputation. Where does our consumer, our student, fit into all of this?

Motivation is individual

It is important to consider the question of motivation from the point of view of the student in the bilingual program from the start.[1] We must remember that motivation is the private domain of the learner. As educators, it is not for us to attempt to manipulate it, even for what we see as the good of the consumer. Our role is to seek to understand it. We then try to meet the needs and wants of our students with the best we can provide, thus channeling their motivation in directions that are satisfying to them. It is true that our consumers are not always consciously aware of what they need and may have only vague glimmerings of what they really want. We can help them clarify these two, so that *their natural motivation – that energizing force each living entity possesses –* may carry them

Revised version of paper originally published in R. C. Troike and N. Modiano, eds., *The Proceedings of the First Inter-American Conference on Bilingual Education* (Arlington, Va.: Center for Applied Linguistics, 1975).

forward to joyful and satisfying learning under our care and nurture. Note that I say "nurture," not direction. What we seek to stimulate is self-directed learning, which results from self-realizing motivation.

The student's hierarchy of needs

There are many ways to look at motivation.[2] If we turn to Maslow, we learn that all human beings have a hierarchy of needs[3] that must be satisfied before they can reach the stage where the achievement of their potential as individuals becomes their chief concern – the stage where they seek to develop their powers and increase their knowledge and experience. The universal needs in the hierarchy stimulate motivation, the higher ones coming into play only when lower-level needs have been gratified.

First, *physiological needs* must be satisfied: The hungry and the cold cannot be expected to feel an urgent need to acquire another language. Next comes the *need for safety, for security and stability*, for freedom from the threat of unpleasant and unwelcome change. This level satisfied, students need to feel that they are *accepted by teachers and peers* and that people care about them as persons. Only when they are respected for what they are and feel that what they can contribute is welcome (that is, when they rise in their own esteem) can their energies be devoted to *efforts to realize their potential* through educational programs that reach out and beyond the immediate, the present, and the known.

The implications of this hierarchy of needs are very real for many of our bilingual programs. Are we concerned with our students' basic needs? Are they well fed and sheltered? Do they feel secure and welcome in the culture of the town and the school? *Are they respected as individuals, so that they may respect themselves?* Are they encouraged to become the types of persons valued by their own culture, or is the school in a well-meaning but insensitive way trying to turn them into pale imitations of an ideal from a dominant but alien culture? If our students are not learning a language as we would like them to, the reasons may well be traceable to unsatisfied lower levels of Maslow's hierarchy of needs. If we are trying to fit them into our pattern, a pattern that will alienate them from those with whom they feel their primary identification, resistance (not necessarily conscious, but nonetheless real) or anomie will prevent them from satisfactorily learning the language.[4] *Anomie is a feeling of uncertainty about one's place and one's loyalties* in a new situation. Attracted by the new but with emotional ties to the old, the individual suffers conflicts. Children becoming bilingual may find themselves distanced from their own culture and gradually becoming absorbed in the pervasive new culture. As a result, they may feel very confused, unhappy, and somewhat fearful of too deep an involvement with the second culture in case it should lead to alienation from the familiar ways of their own community.

Instrumental or integrative motivation or both?

At this point, we need to examine more closely the frequently cited distinction between instrumental motivation (a person learns a language as a tool for some pragmatic purpose) and integrative motivation (the person is interested in the other language community to the point of being willing to adopt distinctive characteristics of their behavior, linguistic and nonlinguistic).[5] According to Gardner and Lambert, integrative motivation leads to the most effective language learning, yet *it is the ultimate demands of just such an integrative impulse*[6] *that many students in bilingual programs must reject,*[7] if they are to retain their place in and usefully serve the communities from which they come. Instrumental motivation they may have, as in many developing countries and emerging communities, where the future good of all depends on a certain number becoming thoroughly proficient in the use of another tongue and being able to move freely within another culture. *In such situations, instrumental motivation can provide a strong drive for language mastery.* Efforts to behave in ways acceptable to the majority community and to speak as like them as possible may, in such circumstances, also indicate a pragmatic desire to ensure social mobility and economic rewards equal to those that accrue to the representatives of the majority culture, which is surely an instrumental motive. As persons with instrumental motivation of this kind experience success in language learning, their sense of achievement and the enhancement of their ego further channel and direct their motivation. We must not violate the private and deeply emotional identification of our students by insisting that they value what we value and share our culturally acquired attitudes. *Understanding and appreciation of a second culture and ability to cope effectively with its demands* are sufficient to ensure interpersonal and communal harmony without our requiring such a wrenching emotional switch.

149

Relaxing tensions in the classroom

A compromise may be reached through the valuable activity of *role playing*. Situations are described or set up in which students act like persons of the other culture, identifying with them completely in characteristic behavior, language, social attitudes, and implicit values, as good actors do. Such acting out will increase their understanding of the other culture and the way the language operates for communication within the culture, while the students themselves are protected psychologically from an identification that threatens their sense of belonging and their deep-seated loyalty to their own community. Puppet plays, similarly, protect the participants and provide, in the legitimate world of make-believe, an outlet for behavior through which they experience identification with the other culture. *Masks have performed a protective function for children at play* throughout the world, and these also may be used. The inhibited, who cannot bring themselves to act before others and are not adept with puppets, will often speak through the characters in picture stories, as little children do when they are experimenting with social behavior. These various forms of vicarious identification protect children from much emotional conflict, embarrassment, or possible public failure, because it is not they but the pictured or modeled characters who are responsible for what is being expressed or performed (and they can even scold them if anything goes wrong).

Apart from the question of conflicting identifications, there are other ways in which language teaching can threaten minority students at the levels of security and belonging. Too often in our classes we are so busy teaching our syllabus or completing lesson units that we really *do not allow our students time to learn in their own way.* Alschuler and co-workers conclude that, from the point of view of motivation, structure and process may be more important than content.[8] The basic aims of our language programs are to enable students to communicate freely and without inhibitions, not only in speech, but, in most bilingual situations, in writing as well. Communication is always a two-way process in whichever modality. Genuine communication requires a revealing of the self, which leaves one vulnerable to humiliation, ridicule, or searing embarrassment. In an authoritarian situation where there is a "right" answer that must correspond in all particulars to what is in the teacher's mind, the student is even more in jeopardy. Recognized achievement in this case comes through compliance and repression of one's own inspirations and reactions. To encourage authentic language activity, the teacher needs to create a structure and develop a process wherein individual students feel safe in venturing their own contributions in interaction. *There should be a warmth that welcomes what they have to contribute* and gives it serious consideration, which builds them up in their own esteem and in that of their fellow students.

A change in structure: small-group work

For these reasons, it is important to break up the second-language or bilingual class as often as possible into small groups. Full individualization as a structure may not be possible for many reasons, and if it is taken to mean largely independent study it will not be desirable for more than a small percentage of language-learning activities where communication is to be developed.[9] On the other hand, many opportunities for interaction are provided by a small-group structure where groups are self-selected and have purposeful activities in which to engage together. Some will object that in the ensuing unsupervised production of language there is a danger of errors becoming established. *Learning activities for the improvement of accuracy in language use should be separate from opportunities to use the language for communicative interaction.* Studies of spontaneous speech reveal that native speakers do not produce the perfect structures of an ideal grammar when talking about things that matter to them. Sentence structure changes direction while one is speaking; mistakes in subject-verb agreement occur; verb endings are omitted; incorrect prepositions slip in; hesitation and fill-in expressions are frequent. Many sentences are not "complete." (We may ask, what is a complete sentence? "Not what she said anyway." Is this utterance more or less expressive than "The words she spoke do not form a complete sentence"?) If uninhibited speech (or writing) is our final goal, then much practice in speaking (or writing) without the censorious figure of the teacher looming large is essential.

Achievement motivation reflects individual concerns

Once lower-level needs of safety, belonging, and esteem are satisfied our students' strong drives will be channeled into "self-actualization, self-fulfillment, self-realization."[10] In order to understand this phase, we may draw ideas from the studies of achievement motivation – *the inherent desire of all human beings "to achieve something of excellence."*[11] If such a desire is natural in our students, why do so many of them seem uninterested in high achievement in their language classes? The answer often lies in the discrepancy between what the teacher perceives as a worthy vehicle for the student's intensive effort and the student's own perceptions. Each child is naturally curious and active, but not necessarily curious or excited about the things that seem of such importance to the teacher. Our students may well be striving for excellence in many activities among their peers in their natural environment, while *the teacher remains completely ignorant of the things that matter to them most.*

As language teachers we are fortunate. Language is a vehicle of expression, not an end in itself, and its use is interwoven in life with a multiplicity of activities. If students do not appear to be interested in practicing language use in the ways we have designed, it is the ways we should try to change, not the students.

Here, we may look at the apparent success of *total immersion programs,* like the St. Lambert experiment,[12] in stimulating confidence and fluency in speaking another language. What elements of these programs, we may ask ourselves, can be transferred to a traditional school language-learning situation? The difference is not merely a matter of time spent on the language, but, more importantly, the role the language plays during this time. In an immersion program, *the language is integrally interwoven with all the daily activities of the children* – their work, their play, the supplying of their wants, the satisfying of their curiosity. This contrasts with many conventional bilingual classes where "language practice" still consists of pattern drills and paradigms. For a second language to be acquired so that it becomes a part of the child's natural repertoire, it must be used in normal activities. Things spoken are intended to be understood – to convey greetings, information, requests, or jests to which others will react, either verbally or through action or emotion. Things written are intended to be read by someone who might find the information interesting, helpful, or provocative of further activity, not merely so that they may be corrected, graded, and returned to the writer.

If we keep in mind the basic principle, namely, *language for the normal purposes of language,*[13] we may be surprised by a resurgence of energy in its use and curiosity about its operation. We have much to learn from innovative teachers of the native language as well as the second language, who sometimes find, to their surprise, that all kinds of students can speak and write expressively, when they have something to communicate that they themselves consider significant and someone who cares enough to pay attention to what they have to say.[14]

What does each of us know about *our students' real interests and preoccupations?* In a thought-provoking article on creativity Birkmaier proposes that we take inventories of the activities in which students engage on their own, of their reading interests and habits, and of the experiences they have had during their short life-span, and that we use these in developing teaching and learning strategies.[15] This is not merely the suggestion of an "expert who has never been in a class-room," but is an approach that has been implemented with gratifying results by many practicing teachers. Unfortunately, too many teachers are too busy, too well organized, too successful at eliciting the perfect response, to tolerate the "shavings on the floor" that inevitably accompany a program evolving from student-initiated and student-centered activity. With language learning, they are thus excluding the very essence of what their program should be seeking, namely, really *purposeful and significant language use.*

The bilingual program and the community

Once we recognize the importance of natural use of language and a program based on the students' active concerns, we find ourselves involved in the community in which the students' deepest concerns are rooted. Bilingual programs cannot, and must not, be conducted apart from the communities represented by the two languages. Self-actualization and self-fulfillment can be realized in a satisfying way through *service to the community, which earns the esteem of the community.* Bilingual programs should be so closely linked with their communities that students learning the two languages readily go back into their communities to help those who need their newly acquired skills. If learning English, as well as Spanish, Korean, or Greek, makes it possible for bilingual students to act as interpreters in their parents' hardware store, pharmacy, or restaurant, to assist in filling out medical benefit or income tax forms, or to write letters to grandmothers in the old country, students will see indisputable worth in what they are learning. A language can be practiced perfectly well while working with young people in an after-school club or while helping smaller children adjust to kindergarten life in a strange environment. The bilingual class must go out into the community; it must always consider itself part of the community, learning from the community while giving to the community and serving its needs. *Bilingual teachers must know the minority-language community they serve, in its rich diversity,* so that they can involve the community in developing a program that reflects its real preoccupations and concerns, while bringing its distinctive achievements to the notice of the majority-language speakers by whom they are surrounded.

We talk a great deal about motivation. We worry about motivation. In a program where students are actively learning in a real-life context and actively engaged in using what they are learning in ways they recognize as worthwhile, the question of motivation becomes academic. Both teacher and students are too deeply involved in what they are doing to ask its meaning.

Let's discuss

1 In the district in which you are teaching, do you see the need for a bilingual program? What form should it take (see note 1, this chapter)? What restrictions does your state, province, or local district impose? What can you do about the situation? (Work out a detailed plan of action, including a model of the type of program you feel is needed.)
2 Discuss Maslow's hierarchy of needs in relation to a bilingual program with which you are familiar. What changes should be made to ensure that the various levels of needs are met in this program?
3 You feel that some students in your bilingual class are experiencing anomie. What factors do you think are contributing to this situation? What changes can you make to eliminate the causes and alleviate the effects of this anomie?
4 Discuss instrumental and integrative motivation in relation to particular students in your bilingual class. Do your observations support Gardner and Lambert's view? What other motivations seem to you to be at work? How would you refine or replace the integrative-instrumental dichotomy?
5 What projects would you propose to bring together minority and majority language communities?

12 Foreign-language acquisition: where the real problems lie

In the last twenty years we have seen a shift of emphasis in linguistics from the predominant interest of the structuralists in phonology and morphology to the preoccupation of the transformational-generativists with syntax and, following that, a lively concern with semantics and pragmatics. This has been paralleled in psychology by a move from the consideration of language as an accumulation of discrete elements in associative chains to the study of human conceptual and perceptual systems, and a growing interest in the pragmatics of language in situations of use.

First-language acquisition studies

This direction of change can be observed in first-language acquisition studies, too. We see the move from the view of such psychologists as Skinner (1957), Mowrer (1960), and Staats[1] that the acquisition of a language is a matter of conditioned habit formation (a position easier to demonstrate with examples drawn from phonology and morphology), to the interest of McNeill (1970) in an innate language acquisition device programmed to identify the form of the grammar to which it is attending. Bever has turned our attention to the perceptual and semantic strategies that facilitate language acquisition;[2] and the later work of Brown (1973) has concentrated on *semantic as well as grammatical relations*. Semantic complexity has now become an important consideration in studying the order of acquisition of linguistic forms in the early stages.

As early as 1970, Bloom drew attention to *the intersections of cognitive-perceptual development, linguistic experience, and nonlinguistic experience in the language development of children*. "Induction of underlying structure," she says, "is intimately related to the development of cognition," and further, "Children's speech is very much tied to context and behavior.... It appears that children learn

Revised version of an article originally published in *Applied Linguistics* 1 (1980): 48–59.

to identify certain grammatical relationships and syntactic structures with the environmental and behavioral contexts in which they are perceived and then progress to reproducing approximations of heard structures in similar, recurring contexts. In order to use a structure in a new situation, the child must be able to perceive critical aspects of the context of the situation."[3]

With a similar appreciation of the importance of context, Bruner and Halliday have sought to identify the communicative needs of infants as revealed in their prelinguistic and early linguistic behavior. In this behavior they already find indications of the *functions of language in use in speech acts.*[4] "Use," as Bruner has said, "is a powerful determinant of rule structure."[5] Bruner prefers to turn his attention to the role played in the development of syntactic competence by the uses to which language is put in different contexts. "Initial language at least," he says, "has a pragmatic base structure."[6] As infants grow in experience in social interaction, they gain insight into linguistic ways of expressing ideas they previously held by other than linguistic means; in other words, they learn "who is doing what with what object toward whom in whose possession and in what location and often by what instrumentality."[7]

Semantically based relations such as these, which derive from the work of Fillmore[8] and Chafe (1970), have been found useful in the study of child language by researchers other than Bruner. Brown (1973) and Schlesinger (1977) have also found them more descriptive of what the child is acquiring than the syntactic relations basic to the Chomskyan model of generative grammar. Once the notion that the child's first linguistic task is the identification of an abstract system of syntactic relations is rejected in favor of an acquisition based on the functions of language in use, the theoretical assumptions are more easily aligned with *the stages of cognitive development from infancy to maturity* postulated by Inhelder and Piaget (1958)[9] and with Piaget's emphasis on the operative aspect of the symbol, which acts on and transforms existing reality.[10] Giving orders, asking for things, stating who does what to whom, and expressing needs and wishes are all possible at the stage when language is being acquired, whereas ability to recognize and express abstract relations comes nearer puberty.

Comparing first- and second-language acquisition

Research in first-language acquisition has always held great appeal for second-language teachers. Parents are bemused as they watch their young children acquire with ease and rapidity a level of operation in a language they themselves took years to achieve in a formal setting. Teachers become wistful as they compare this apparently effortless learning with the struggles of their adolescent or adult students. It is inevitable, then, that we yearn to find immediate answers to our own problems in this fascinating first-language acquisition research.

Here we touch on the most ancient and vigorous controversy in the whole area of language-related studies. *Is the process of learning a second language similar to or even the same process as learning a first language?* In discussing this question, people become dogmatic on what is for the most part anecdotal evidence or analogizing. The apparent insolubility of the controversy can, to some extent, be traced to the differing levels of generality at which the various disputants are developing their arguments. Do they mean, for instance, that older students of English learn to use the copula "is" in English in exactly the same progression, making the same errors along the way, as do children growing up in English-speaking families? Or, on the other hand, are they maintaining that adolescent or adult students learn to use a new language through practice in its use in the normal functions of communication, as do young children, rather than through detailed explanations of the rule system? That the acquisition of precise structures runs parallel in first- and second-language learning has yet to be conclusively demonstrated. The second position, that we learn a language by using it, rather than by studying it, is oversimplified and dichotomous. To some extent a further extension of the old educational adage "we learn what we do," it ignores the varying linguistic capabilities and experiences, the learning preferences, and the individual motives and goals of mature students in widely diverse circumstances. Unfortunately, the "language-learning situation" at all levels and in all circumstances cannot be simplified and unified to this degree, as all experienced teachers are aware.

Until we can agree on what is meant by the similarity or identity of first- and second-language learning processes, we shall probably continue quite happily to extrapolate or to refuse to extrapolate from first-language acquisition studies. The answer must be found elsewhere. *Research into the process of acquiring or learning a second language is urgent and important.*[11] But again, we must be cautious. Much of the second-language acquisition research reported has been directed to the understanding of the process of acquisition of a second language by young children in informal settings or bilingual classes. The same caveat applies here. Should we expect these findings to cast much light on the learning of new languages by adolescent and adult students in formal instructional settings, the most usual settings for such learning? We need more studies of adult language learners, like the avoidance studies of Schachter.[12] These provide a useful complement, if not corrective, to the general preoccupations of much contemporary second-language acquisition research.

Interference or hypothesis testing?

The earliest second-language acquisition studies of the seventies focused to a great extent on the plausibility of the notion of transfer, particularly negative transfer or interference, from what was learned in the first language. This was to some extent a reaction to the overoptimistic emphasis on transfer in the preceding decades that had led to, or paralleled, a plethora of contrastive studies of pairs of languages, which in some cases attempted to predict problem areas for the learners of these languages. Controversy raged as to *whether errors made by second-language learners represented negative transfer (interference) from first-language habits of use or were really developmental errors of a universal character*, since they often seemed similar to those made by first-language learners at a comparable stage in their control of a language.[13] Even errors that seemed to provide clear evidence of the use of first-language grammatical rules in the second language were taken by some writers to be the result of the active process of testing the hypothesis that the second language operates on similar principles to the first language, rather than as the transfer of first-language habits.[14] This paralleled the theoretical position, derived from Chomsky, that first-language learners were testing hypotheses as to the nature of the language they were learning.[15]

Corder's hypothesis-testing assumption attempts to provide an alternative explanation for the same observable phenomenon that others have been calling transfer, but it is an explanation based on a different theoretical orientation. It is of interest, before we reject one view and accept another, to look more closely at the basic theory (in this case, hypothesis testing in general) in relation to those aspects of second-language learning and use that the supporters of transfer theory were trying to explain, to see whether the hypothesis-testing view can deal more convincingly with the empirical data.

One important fact about hypothesis testing is relevant in this regard. *When one is testing a hypothesis, a serious disconfirmation makes one immediately seek another hypothesis that seems to fit the facts.* In using a second language, however, one often continues to make the same error, even when one knows that the second and first languages operate differently for expressing this particular meaning. The notion that repeated errors of this type can result from the learner's testing the hypothesis that the two languages operate in a parallel fashion at this point (the usual explanation of the hypothesis-testing theorist) is difficult to sustain in light of the fact, frequently observed and experienced, that *one is constantly repeating the same error and then immediately correcting oneself*, often with a sense of mortification and exasperation at one's inability to perform according to second-language rules one has studied and feels one "knows." These types of persistent deviations from the L_2 norm are called "fossilized" errors. (Transfer theorists, of course, have no problem with this phenomenon, since they consider it to be due to interference from the habits of use of another language or from earlier imperfect learning, based sometimes on defective materials.) For those interested in second-language learning and teaching, this is a most persistent problem and one that must be adequately accounted for in any theory purporting to explain second-language learning and use.

Krashen's Monitor Model

Krashen considers this phenomenon to be indicative of the operation of two separate systems: language acquisition and language learning. Language *acquisition* is considered to be implicit, subconscious learning that develops from natural communication; it follows a fairly stable order of acquisition of structures. This acquired system is the initiator of performance, which may be self-corrected on the basis of "feel" for grammaticality. Language *learning* is explicit, conscious learning that is helped by error correction and the presentation of explicit rules. It does not contribute directly to acquisition of the language or to performance, since utterances are initiated by the acquired system. Conscious learning is available to the learner only through *a Monitor that operates to improve accuracy through self-correction*. Conscious learning of this type, according to Krashen, is possibly unnecessary for most language acquirers, except for certain aspects of language use, such as formal speaking or writing, since operation of the Monitor requires time that is not available in normal communication, which is focused on meaning, not form.[16]

Personally, despite my years of fluency in French and my many close personal and informal relationships, I find myself conducting a rapid monitoring during normal communicative speech in that language (and I speak fast). I become conscious of this monitoring especially at problem points where I know the rules are tricky for me as a native speaker of English. I find myself, at these choice points, running through the rules, even lengthening a syllable ever so slightly as I select the correct morphological segment or syntactic arrangement (for a gender agreement, for instance, or the position of an adverb in a multisegment verbal group). According to Krashen, I am, as an individual, presumably "focussed on form or correctness"; my French friends, however, consider me "completely involved" with my message.[17]

The Monitor Model, at this stage of its development, provides a novel attempt at describing what language learners experience and language teachers observe, but it cannot be considered explanatory. Explanations given by Krashen are tied directly to the developmental, "creative construction" position theoretically, a position still to be satisfactorily validated empirically.[18]

From the psychological point of view it is difficult to distinguish between self-correction by "feel" and self-correction by "rule," in the sense in which Krashen uses these terms. McLaughlin points out that at least some of the students in the Krashen et al. study[19] who claimed to be self-correcting by "feel" rather than "rule" may have felt uncertain about how to verbalize the "rule" satisfactorily, as they were required to do if they admitted to "rule" as their self-correction device.[20] It is difficult to take this introspective report of acting by "feel" or by "rule" as indicative of the kind of difference Krashen makes basic to his model, until we are sure of the psychological difference between the two. This problem is reminiscent of Carroll's discussion of the distinction between "habits" and the "internalized rules" of "rule-governed" behavior. Carroll maintained that a "rule" was a construct independent of actual behavior, whereas a "habit" was what the person had actually learned, that is, the behavioral manifestation of the internalization of the rule.[21] An extension of Carroll's approach might well apply to Krashen's "feel" and "rule."

From the psychological point of view it also seems *highly improbable that acquisition and conscious learning, as Krashen describes them, could be noninteractive, totally separate systems*, separate not only from each other but apparently from any previous learning.[22] Such a model simply does not tally with the great body of recent research in cognitive processing. Until we can find psychological support for these basic elements of the theory, it remains an interesting, carefully elaborated metaphor of limited scope.[23]

McLaughlin proposes that we substitute for conscious learning and acquisition the terms (and concepts) of "controlled and automatic processes," which have been developed in recent information-processing theories, with the changes in implications these require, since "a model that focuses on behavioral acts is falsifiable – a property that is unfortunately lacking in models that depend on appeals to conscious experience."[24] Furthermore, we do have considerable knowledge of the operation of these processes. Carroll quotes Schneider and Shiffrin as defining a "controlled process" as one that is "activated under control of, and through attention by, the subject." On the other hand an "automatic process" is one that "(nearly) always becomes active in response to a particular input configuration, where the inputs may be externally or internally generated and include the general situational context"; it is "activated automatically without the necessity of active control or attention by the subject." Further, "any new automatic process requires an appreciable amount of consistent training."[25] Clearly, "automatic processes," as defined by Schneider and Shiffrin, cannot be equated with Krashen's "acquisition," which is implicit, subconscious learning, not susceptible to training. Automated and controlled processes parallel much more closely Rivers's *two levels of language behavior* for which students need to be prepared: a higher level of selection, where the student is conscious of the implications and ramifications of the changes to be made, the decision at this level setting in motion operations at lower levels that are interdependent, but operate within closed systems that can be mastered to a point of automatic production.[26]

In 1968, Chomsky claimed for the study of language a central place in general psychology.[27] Since then, language-related studies by psychologists have proliferated. This is hardly the moment for second-language acquisition researchers to cut themselves off from the intense research into cognitive processes, which are surely highly relevant to any consideration of language acquisition and use.

Interference at the morphological or conceptual levels?

Continuing our search for enlightenment with regard to the persistent problems foreign-language learners face, we may question the level at which evidence for "interference" or transfer is sought by investigators in error analysis studies. ("Transfer" is the preferable term, since it includes positive, or facilitative, transfer as well as negative transfer, or interference. Without including positive transfer in the examination of data, any conclusions as to the amount of transfer rest moot.)

The investigator may be looking for *evidence of transfer at the morphological level*, as some have done. Let us consider the situation of an English speaker learning a Romance language. In the subject's first language, in this case English, the third person singular of the present tense of most verbs takes an ending that is not used for the other persons for which an unmarked form is used. In the second language, the student does not attempt to add an ending to the third person of the verb while continuing to use the unmarked form for the other persons. As a result, it may be asserted by some that there is no evidence of transfer from first-language habits of use.

The discussion may, however, be conducted at a higher level of conceptualization. The subject, we may say, is not accustomed to using, in the first language, forms of the verb that are marked for person, number, and tense, except in one or two very frequent positions that have been learned through constant use as exceptions to the general rule. In a new language, therefore, the student finds it difficult to develop an awareness of the necessity to attach a variety of endings to verb stems to make these semantic distinctions. As a result, when trying to communicate in the new language, the student tends to use unmarked forms as he or she would most frequently do in the native language, leaving it to other unbound morphemes in the sentence to convey the semantic distinctions. (This tendency is regarded in many current studies as simplification of the type used by children learning their first language, whereas it may be coincidental that the resulting utterances are similar in the two cases.)

To take a further example, other second-language learners, while learning their first language, may have developed the concept that gender makes a clear and identifiable semantic distinction, with rare exceptions, as in English. When these learners find that grammatical gender distinctions, apparently unmotivated, pervade the second language, they may find it hard to conceive of these distinctions as important enough to affect practically every part of speech – nouns, adjectives, articles, pronouns, and even some forms of the verb. Although this has been explained to them, they still have to make a conscious mental effort to keep this all-pervading concept in mind when applying lower-level inflectional rules in all kinds of positions and relationships. Specific errors these learners make in omitting the morphemes indicating these agreements may be interpreted as intralingual, as simplification, or as overgeneralization errors, whereas the basic problem is *an interlingual conceptual contrast*.[28]

Much more attention should be paid in classroom teaching to the comprehension and thorough assimilation of these fundamental conceptual differences between languages, so that students are *learning to operate within the total language system*, rather than picking up minor skills in its application. In the same vein, it is essential that the student acquire an understanding of the different way a new language sees and expresses temporal relationships across the language system, rather than concentrating exclusively on particular uses of specific tenses and the correct forms for these uses.[29] Without a conceptual grasp of such overriding interlingual contrasts, the second-language learner will be unable to use effectively the lower-level knowledge of paradigms and rules that have strictly limited application.

A similar psychological problem is demonstrated in the common phenomenon of English-speaking students of French who find it hard to comprehend what the use of the subjunctive, rather than the indicative, conveys to a native speaker of French. They have never internalized the overriding concept that the subjunctive mood in French usage conveys a subjective view of the situation (that is, a personal opinion) as opposed to the objective view of the indicative. Thus, *Je ne pense pas qu'il soit parti* ("I don't think he's left") implies that I am not giving factual information, but my own assessment of the situation, whereas *Je pense qu'il est déjà parti* ("I think he's already gone") is based on some objective clues and may well be followed by an explanation like *Parce que la porte de son bureau est fermée* ("Because his office door is shut"). Because they lack this conceptual understanding of its use, English-speaking students of French tend to spatter subjunctive forms everywhere in the hope that some will stick in the right places. This insecurity and uncertainty about the extent of applicability of new rules, because of a lack of knowledge of how they fit into the meaning system of the new language, is *a distinctly different psychological phenomenon from that of overgeneralization*, which is described by Selinker as the extension of a newly acquired second-language rule "to an environment in which, to the learner, it could logically apply, but just does not."[30] (Selinker would categorize as overgeneralization the extension of the use of the past tense of *walk/walked*, to *go/goed*, an error commonly made by English-speaking children, even though they may previously have known and used *went*.) Psychologically, the phenomenon I am discussing seems to share some of the features of the native-language phenomenon of hypercorrection and may perhaps be better described as *overcompensation*, an attitude of better more than less. The reader will think of many other cross-linguistic conceptual problems like those of aspect in Chinese and Russian, and the problems Japanese speakers have with the use of the definite and indefinite articles in English (although the actual forms in this case are simple).

Experimentation conducted at this level of conceptualization, rather than at the level of the morpheme, might produce more interesting insights into the problems of adolescent and adult second-language learners. It is difficult to say whether one is referring here to habits of thought and approach to language use developed through using the first language or to hypotheses the second-language learner is making about the new language. Perhaps we should ask them, the learners themselves, as has been done in some psychological experiments with mature subjects. (Schachter, Tyson, and Diffley, for instance, drew on grammaticality judgments by adult learners of English in a study of the interlanguages of speakers of Arabic, Chinese, Japanese, Persian, and Spanish.[31]) Until errors can be identified as interlingual (due to transfer from the first to the second language) or intralingual (deriving from elements within the second language itself) by some more clearly demonstrable psychological criteria, interpretation of research in this area will remain somewhat hazy. Once we can clarify what we are dealing with, we may find, as Hakuta and Cancino maintain, that "interference errors in second-language learning are fine examples of language transfer and...strongly point to areas of *dynamic interplay between the two languages.*"[32]

Psychological support for problems of conceptualization

Do we have any psychological justification for viewing the problems in this way? In other words, what can be the meaning of "conceptualization"? Several recent directions in cognitive research hint at an answer.

Schlesinger has hypothesized a model of speech comprehension and a model of speech production, both of which comprise three essential components: cognitive structures, semantic structures, and surface structures. Children develop cognitive structures, which consist largely of relations between aspects of the environment, through their experiences and also through the categorizations they acquire as they learn a language. *They learn to categorize relations and concepts semantically as they learn a specific language.* Through this language they learn to express their intentions in accordance with the restrictions, or realization rules, the language imposes. This implies that persons speaking different languages may share cognitive structures or notions, yet "for the purposes of speaking, a given situation may be perceived differently by speakers of two languages."[33] That is, they adopt a different point of view. *This different point of view is expressed in the surface structure realization their language requires.* According to Schlesinger, "each language prescribes which relations have to be mastered by the child."[34] Nonlinguistic concepts also occur in cognitive structure and to express these may involve a clumsy circumlocution.

In Schlesinger's model, then, learning another language means acquiring new categorizations of semantic relations in accordance with the realization rules of the new language. This can result in the development of new cognitive structures (new ways of perceiving relations) or the opportunity to express relations dimly perceived, which could not be put into words in the native language.

Although the concepts are not identical with those of Schlesinger, work in *semantic memory* also lends support to the notion that it is conceptual differences that have to be mastered if one is to become fluent in expressing one's meaning in another language. According to artificial intelligence theorists, no word or group of words has a discrete meaning that can be attached like a label one can learn to use. Neither do specific grammatical forms always convey one identifiable meaning. Words and grammatical structures all acquire meaning within *networks of conceptual relations* that have been built up through the experiences of life, including linguistic experiences, and these constitute our long-term memory. The networks consist of primitive meanings connected by relations, and language forms become associated with these networks so that the use of words in context activates interrelated concepts to produce the intended meaning.[35]

In this paradigm, the problem of learning to operate within the system of a new language is one of *developing new networks, or extensions and modifications of existing networks, to express the interrelationships represented by the grammar and lexicon of the new language.* These interrelationships will not at first be independent of the conceptual networks already established. Some of the latter will be facilitative where the conceptualization of the two languages is reasonably similar (this constitutes positive transfer). When sufficient interconnections are established for the new language system, it may be expected to operate autonomously, although associations with the old system will remain, so that we are able to say: "Of course, in my first language the conceptualization of this set of meanings is different. It would be expressed thus and so."

Interconnections also remain for other languages we have learned and, until the new system is firmly established, these can be activated and expressed at unexpected times and in unexpected ways. The writer can remember producing on one occasion, when learning Spanish, the conglomeration "mais, aber, sed, pero" to the mystification of the listeners.

Adult awareness of differences between language systems

Adult learners are particularly conscious of deviations from the established networks and will seek to understand the nature of the system within which they should operate. If the teacher or teaching materials do not make this clear, the adult learner will seek a systematic explanation elsewhere – in an old textbook or from another person.[36]

Experimental evidence that adolescent and adult learners are very conscious of the points where the rule system of the second language diverges from that of the first language is provided by Schachter's avoidance studies. In an interesting investigation using written compositions in English, Schachter found that, although it appeared in

165

quantitative data that a group with a contrasting relative pronoun rule system in their first language (in this case, Chinese and Japanese learners of English) made fewer errors than a group whose first-language relative pronoun rule system was similar to that of English (Persian and Arabic students), another approach to the data revealed that subjects in the first group were avoiding or approaching very cautiously the use of rules to which they were not accustomed, and which they therefore found difficult. Ipso facto, fewer uses of relative pronouns by the Chinese and Japanese subjects yielded fewer errors in their use. Schachter concluded that if students find particular constructions in the target language difficult to comprehend, it is very likely that they will find ways to avoid producing them.[37] Clearly we need to analyze much more comprehensively what may be considered evidence of transfer from first-language learning and use to second-language learning and use.

Strategies of language use

It is interesting to note that, as with first-language acquisition studies, second-language acquisition research has been moving from an almost single-minded emphasis on the acquisition of the syntactic and morphological rules of the second language to *strategies of language-in-use to meet the needs of communication*. It is here that we can place Hakuta's prefabricated utterances, which are learned as units to be plugged into speech acts,[38] and Hatch's discourse analysis,[39] which examines in second-language situations communicative exchanges that recall the joint "action dialogue" of Bruner's studies,[40] and what Brown calls "episodes."

It must be emphasized that studies with very young children in bilingual situations do not produce particularly relevant insights into the strategies employed by linguistically and conceptually mature adolescent and adult foreign-language learners.[41] The linguistic input the latter receive is primarily from textbooks and other learning materials, and they have well-established patterns of interaction from much experience in communication in their first language. Research into strategies of language use within the corpus with which the student has become acquainted at a particular stage of classroom learning would be very interesting and enlightening for hard-pressed classroom teachers. A full-time teacher carrying the typical school course load and teaching the usual large group is far too busy interacting with many students during class hours to study the linguistic and pragmatic reactions of individuals analytically. What I am proposing here is not study of the "interlanguage" of particular students at specific points in their acquisition of the target language (although this can be enlightening). I am referring rather to strategies foreign-language learner-users employ to make "infinite use of finite means."[42] When these strategies have been identified and described, they may be encouraged, or even taught, and incorporated into teaching materials.[43]

The value of second-language acquisition research for the teacher

This rapid survey demonstrates the interest of second-language acquisition studies for those who teach languages, yet far too little is known about them by language teachers, program designers, and materials writers. Certainly this is a burgeoning field, and much has been but sketchily researched at present; positions are taken and abandoned somewhat rapidly as experimental data are reexamined and reinterpreted. Yesterday's dogma may be devalued currency before it can receive serious applied consideration. Yet, as with all psychological research, much that is fundamental will be retained and recombined in the evolution of theory. As Neisser has expressed it: "the cognitive theorist...cannot make assumptions casually, for they must conform to the results of 100 years of experimentation."[44]

It is from solid research in this area, and in related fields of cognition, that we may hope to develop criteria by which to evaluate the appropriateness and potential effectiveness of the many techniques of language teaching, which seem to rise and recede like the tide at regular intervals – serving their purpose of refreshing the scene, but often carrying away with them indiscriminately both useful and dispensable practices.

As teachers of second and third languages, we seek to provide for everyone who seeks such knowledge the most effective learning situation we can devise. For this, *we need knowledge, not hunches*. As in every other field of endeavor, nothing comes without effort, and helping another person to acquire another language will never be easy.

Let's discuss

1 How would you develop a second-language course based on the hypothesis-testing theory? How would this differ from a course

based on the theory of controlled and automatic processes in language use?

2 What kinds of problems at the conceptual level do you find among the students you teach? What seems to you to be the best way to help them overcome these problems?

3 If you were to develop a course based on functions of language, which functions would you emphasize? How would you ensure that these functions were learned through use? How would this course differ from one based on syntactic structures?

4 From what you have read in this chapter and other chapters in this book, how do you think the teaching of a second language to young children should differ from the teaching of a second language to adults?

5 In this chapter we read that "words and grammatical structures all acquire meaning within networks of conceptual relations that have been built up through the experiences of life, including linguistic experiences." What implications does this have for the teaching of a second language? How would it affect the usual teaching that goes on in most classrooms?

13 Learning a sixth language: an adult learner's daily diary

I recently had the opportunity to begin learning another language, the fifth non-native language I had studied. For five weeks I kept a day-by-day diary of my language learning and using experiences. I present it here, just as I wrote it, as case-study material on non-native language learning processes, strategies, and affective reactions. My observations are admittedly those of a sophisticated language learner. The experience, however, made me much more sensitive to the problems a person encounters in learning another language. I hope that reading this diary will have a similar effect upon my readers.

The following background information is essential for the interpretation of the diary entries.

In January 1978, I spent a little over five weeks in Spanish-speaking areas of South America. My aim was to begin the study of Spanish. I had already learned five languages. I had learned English as a native language and French, which I now speak with bilingual confidence and fluency. I studied Latin for three years in high school and for one more year at the advanced level as an undergraduate. I studied Italian during my senior year in high school and have largely forgotten it; I do, however, listen to it at times on ethnic radio programs in Boston, and I hear it spoken around me in the Department of Romance Languages and Literatures at Harvard. I studied German on three occasions, separated by four- and ten-year intervals (the last about eighteen years ago); I consider German a language I can read, but I speak it only in simple, informal sentences when situations abroad demand it.

I took with me to South America an elementary textbook for Spanish, with a few accompanying tapes, and a Berlitz phrasebook. I was given six two-hour lessons by a university faculty member and his assistant, who taught me as a team. I supplemented assignments they gave with information from my private textbook. I listened to radio and television programs and conversations on social visits. I read the newspaper. (My hostess E, an American living in VM, was a close friend and spoke English with me.) After two weeks in VM, I

Slightly revised version of an article originally published in *Canadian Modern Language Review* 36 (1979): 67–82. By permission of the editor, Anthony S. Mollica.

went on an eight-day tour to a beautiful but distant area of the country with twelve Spanish-speaking tourists (all inhabitants of a neighboring city and all previously unknown to me), a guide, and later four university students (*las lolas*). After my return from the tour I had opportunities for one more week to use the language on social visits in VM. I continued to study by myself with my private textbook and occasional work with tapes. I listened to television. I then spent five days on my own in another Spanish-speaking country and talked with people I met on buses and planes, in airports, on trains, in the hotel, and in streets and shops. I listened to my transistor radio and continued to read newspapers and guidebooks in Spanish.

For cross-comparisons I have given each day a week and day reference number; for example, 1.1 means Week 1, Day 1; 3.5 means Week 3, Day 5.

Language learning diary

January 10 (1.1)

[On the plane to South America, I began to study a Berlitz phrasebook.]

1. I find myself making as many associations as possible with what I know: *sed* – sedative; *treinta* – trente; and also negative associations (*tardes, not* tardy).
2. I repeat things over and try using them in some sentence context, putting them together in little phrases.
3. I was not embarrassed to try out little phrases as soon as I knew them (e.g., with the Brazilians on the plane, who were sympathetic non-native speakers and strangers and so posed no threat). I tended to try them out as soon as I saw an appropriate opportunity – either aloud or mentally.
4. I found looking over a short pronunciation guide or a rapid overview of grammar helpful, before actually learning piecemeal.

January 11. In VM. (1.2)

1. I am feeling the need for function words (adverbs, prepositions), and for exclamations, fill-in expressions, polite responses, and words like *ayer-hoy-mañana*.
2. I look up conjugations – how to express past and future.
3. I look for shortcuts based on previous knowledge of languages: *once* = Fr. onze; *lluvia* = pluie, therefore *llena* = pleine.
4. I feel the need for common words – bread, fruit, etc.

170

5. I notice a tendency to use German with the Spanish-speaking maid – *sehr gut*, etc.

6. I need to understand how things work, e.g., *ser/estar*.

January 12 (1.3)

1. I am listening hard to try to segment and recognize some of the segments or words within segments; I try to identify English, French, or Latin cognates.

2. I am still forming conscious associations for memory: *estoy* (était), *ser* (sera).

3. In my first class: I find it very tiring and demanding to make continual and prompt responses to questions and still remember the material. I find it easy to respond to a question, but harder to remember the question form and ask the question.

It is worthwhile, and more interesting, to make up one's own additions (to sentences proposed) with extra information or real information – one begins to think in the language in this way.

4. I am seeking for rejoinders and adverbial expansions – *Lo lamento, Desculpeme* (?) (I should have copied it down!) *Perdóneme*.

5. I spent half an hour in the language lab and found it demanding and tiring, requiring much concentration. I don't think it's true you can just parrot utterances.

6. Assignments are becoming more difficult and certainly unreal. You *cease to think in the language* when the exercises make you say things which are contradictory and do not apply to you, e.g., *Yo soy norteamericana; Yo soy chileno. Soy estudiante, soy profesor.*

7. I feel a need to find out as many things as possible as soon as possible, so I am constantly looking up the textbook I brought with me for extra information beyond the loose-leaf assignments I am given.

8. I realize the value of practicing saying things over to develop fluency and to keep thinking in the language.

9. I feel an early need for some sound-symbol correspondences if I am to practice from written examples.

10. In the Vocabulary section of my private textbook, it would be useful to have the page numbers of the places where the item may be seen in context.

11. I found I misinterpreted *tengo que aprender* as "I want to" from French *Je tiens à*, and I keep thinking this meaning instead of *have to*. This shows the pitfalls of a purely direct method.

January 13 (1.4)

1. I am finding model examples useful to memorize as guides to rules – Yo *estoy* enferma/ yo *soy* simpática.

2. I check on special deviations from or correspondences with French rules, e.g., position of adjectives.

3. I feel the need for models for strange sounds. Descriptions are definitely not enough.

4. I feel a continual need to understand the larger picture into which the bits fit, so I realize the usefulness (indispensability to me) of the index to grammatical and other details in my textbook. Life without it would be most frustrating.

5. I use mnemonic associations: *sesenta* /swasãt/; *setenta*, se(p)tante; *noventa*, novena.

6. I continually need reference tables for pronunciation of sound/ symbol correspondences or paradigms of verbs, lists of numerals, etc.

January 14 (1.5)

1. I ask directions to church. I come out with my little Spanish phrases quite confidently but cannot understand the replies. I finally get to the reception office at the Hotel Europa and they find an English speaker to help me.

2. In the hymns and prayers, I experience interference from practice in reading other languages as I try to read the Spanish script rapidly.

3. I try out my "Lesson 1" sentences on sympathetic people at E's party, as a party joke, with no embarrassment.

4. When I begin to say a Spanish sentence I tend to think in German (*ich...*, *aber*) that is, in my fourth, less-fluent foreign language. Amusingly enough, I am told that I speak my little sentences with a German accent! (Perhaps I am unvoicing the voiced consonants?) This is interesting because I am deliberately avoiding what I recognize as interference from French: /y/ for /u/, etc.; and also what I see to be interference from English /ɪ/ for /i/; /ɛ/ for /e/, palatal /t/ and /d/, diphthongs. Perhaps I am subconsciously slipping into German features, or perhaps it is the absence of the English and French ones which leaves the accent unidentifiable as these?

5. In listening, I am beginning to segment what I hear and recognize cognates with French and English. I feel the need for the adverbs and other function words and also fill-in words. I recognize the cognate ones and a few I have learned.

6. I am observing and recognizing pronunciation features: Mouth position as distinct from French and English; pronunciation of *j* and /b/, and becoming accustomed to the intonation of fluent speech.

January 15 (1.6)

1. I think the alleged German accent is because I am distinguishing two phonemes /b/ and /v/ instead of using /b/ or /ƀ/ for both *Viña del Mar, beber*, etc. [I have been told since that it was probably because of my vowels, after all. By avoiding French and English vowels, I must have fallen back on other "foreign" vowels I had learned.]

January 16 (1.7)

1. I still think German! *Danke schön, ja, und so weiter.* Ridiculous since I am so unfluent in German and rarely, rarely use it.

2. I still can't understand, although I can put together new sentences (elementary ones) and write what I can say. I wrote two pages of biographical notes in class today. (My teacher used these as the basis for a notice in the newspaper about the lecture I was to give.)

3. Pronunciation drilling today revealed continued influence of French of which I had no idea – use of /y/ for /u/ and French stress on last syllable (háblo as habló), and an occasional uvular *r*. These are all things I had had to work hard to acquire in French as differences from English.

4. There is also occasional influence of Italian, which I thought was 90 percent forgotten, in the pronunciation of *ciento* as "chiento," for instance.

5. I find *intense* concentration is required (as well as careful attention to find phonetic distinctions) in order to imitate correctly the models given, particularly as no articulatory help is supplied. It becomes a process of successive approximations. One does not hear one's own mistakes or misimitations unless they are the ones on which one is expressly concentrating one's intellectual attention. Personal and immediate correction and remodeling are essential before one has lost the auditory image of the sound one has made and, quite clearly, one cannot imitate correctly what one has not discriminated correctly at first. Therefore there is need for a clear model and a patient one who is willing to repeat and listen over and over again. I have two – a man and a woman who take turns at modeling and remodeling until I reach a satisfactory approximation. The encouragement of their pleasure when I come near the target is also a help, as is their devoted interest in helping me reach it. Many mistakes in pronunciation come from misconceptions on which I had worked hard and which came from rough approximations (expressed in English spelling) in the Berlitz book.

6. I found applying learned numbers to random figures, dates, and

times of day required much more concentration than I had realized, and I fell into traps (confusing *sesenta* and *setenta*, for instance).

7. I find I *need* to ask questions, to ask for clarifications and to get them at the moment I need them if I am to progress. I do not feel at ease if they are left hanging.

8. I do make mental translations and these give me a feeling of security, yet I do find myself thinking directly in the language when I read, or go over an assignment, or create utterances in class.

9. I find practice exercises where one applies and reapplies new rules in variant situations to be useful and important to my learning. I do not find that they involve "parroting." Instead they require active mental participation because, even if only one element has to be substituted, one has to recreate the complete sentence. This is where I find myself definitely recreating, because if the element to be varied is near the beginning I sometimes complete the sentence meaningfully, although not with the vocabulary supplied by the model, but a related word instead, e.g., "history" for "chemistry."

10. I like to try to say my own little things and usually begin by telling my teachers something about what I have been doing. These creative efforts come out rather slowly and gropingly, but seem to be understood and appreciated. I also add my own flourishes to exercise sentences, thus creating my own meaning, and even adding my own humor at times.

11. In listening, I do not hear it all yet, but grasp what my teacher is saying from a word here and there and the context (what element are we working with at the moment? so what is he probably saying?). I feel myself taking the plunge on surmise and hoping that I am plunging into the right spot in the right way. Mostly my surmise is correct, so perhaps I am putting together more elements than I realize *or* we do not need too many elements when context makes clear what is probably being said.

12. I feel I am "hearing" a few more segments on TV. Certainly my major problem in listening is a meager vocabulary.

January 19 (2.3)

1. I begin to construct short sentences in *English* like my Spanish sentences and to speak with my "foreign voice" with people who know only a little English, or even some English.

2. I learn a great deal from advertisements and street signs. I am constantly reading them and pronouncing them over to myself, and then continuing to repeat over nice sentences from them which contain useful turns of expression. I learn fruits, vegetables, meats, kinds

of drinks, sweets, ices, and recognize useful expressions in insurance, cigarette, or housing ads, shop signs for sales, etc.

January 20 (2.4)

On the way to S, I talk with a young man on the bus, a former Naval College cadet now working in the railways. His English is about equal to my Spanish, and we communicate quite well about ourselves and the problems of the blacks in the USA.

January 21 (2.5)

1. Listening to TV. The frustration of feeling on the brink of comprehension in the sense of being able to segment and recognize phrasings, and hear words here and there, but just not having the vocabulary to know exactly what it is all about. I can guess from a word here and there, from expressions and from actions. Presumably when I know *words* I'll be able to understand. I can recognize numbers now. The same problems arise as I listen to conversations around me. But here I can get a better idea of or guess better what is being said because of the context in which I am myself involved and the situation (e.g., at table eating crabs: the *jaivas* at A).

2. I feel a desperate need for common verbs – going, coming back, putting, looking for, trying – many of which are irregular. I will have to settle down and learn them. I also need past tenses, and the verb "to go" for immediate future. I must learn *on, under*, etc.

3. I also feel the need for *Oh, Ah, Really, Of course* kinds of sounds – it's hard to know where to turn to find them.

4. I am very frustrated by the lack of an English-Spanish glossary in my private textbook and other books. I will have to buy a small pocket English-Spanish, Spanish-English dictionary.

5. I notice the local dropping of "s" at the end of words, which is mentioned in the *Practical Guide to the Teaching of Spanish*, Ch. 4, and which my teacher tells me is "very bad." However, even my well-educated friends do it in conversation. I am glad I knew about it.

6. I amuse people by wrong pronunciations which produce incongruous words – I try to say "beans" and end up with "sissy." My teacher roars with laughter when I say I saw a Japanese prostitute down by the wharf, instead of a Japanese boat.

7. I find I can read the newspaper and other informational reading material quite fluently already and feel I am reading directly in the language.

January 23 (2.7)

1. Verbs are a terrible trial. All those endings for all those tenses and persons! I make associations with French: je parl*ai*: *yo hablé*, to try to remember, also j'ai/*yo he*, il a/*el ha*. I have to pause to make this connection in order to produce the correct form in speech, yet it seems more reliable and more reassuring than having to remember in the void.

2. The problem of the illogicality or unassociatability of irregular forms which are so common. Why should *es* belong to *ser*, not *estar*? It will not stay in place. *Ser* seems to be an amalgam of 3 verbs – the *soy, era*, and *fui* stems, then *fui* also belongs to *ir*, which has the *ir* (*ido, iba*), *va* and *fui* stems. A terrible pest for everyone. Oh for Esperanto and its regularities!

3. I can read fluently now, except for the odd word here and there and can *recognize* the tenses (of course, they are in context).

4. My teacher laughs because I sometimes jump the gun pedagogically, as I did this morning. He asked me the day I was born. I replied and immediately asked him the day he was born: a question which he was just about to ask me to ask! I still add extra information to practice sentences, which my teachers find amusing. Teachers should encourage this. The numbers are beginning to come without reflection.

5. I still have problems *hearing* what is said, with a normal intonation at a normal pace, even when my teacher is only asking questions using things we have learned. I often guess (correctly) from the element or elements I do hear. Clearly students need a great deal of practice *hearing* the language. It isn't at all easy.

6. It is annoying that the textbook has only the irregular parts of the irregular verbs and not the regular parts. I suppose it makes you think, but I find it irritating and you miss out on the many opportunities of *seeing* the regular parts along with the irregular.

7. I find writing out lots of mixed verbs as they come to mind helps.

January 24. At the hotel in S. (3.1)

I felt I could understand the advertisements on the radio tonight.

January 25. The beginning of the tour to the south with a Spanish-speaking group. (3.2)

1. I find I am understood. This gives me confidence. I talk to taxi drivers and find I can amuse them. All that I learned in my six lessons

was useful. It shows the value of learning a number of tenses at the beginning, as well as useful patterns into which one can build sentences.

2. I can understand members of the group when they speak to me and they understand me (what I can say at present). I am learning words hard. I check everything I want in the Sp/Eng, Eng/Sp dictionary which T. lent me, and in my textbook, and the Berlitz book (which I find is very well constructed and most useful).

3. I find myself saying "Buon giorno" to people instead of "Buenos días." Why the Italian now?

4. Half-understanding means one needs luck. The guide asks how many cases we have. I think he's asking how many we are for room allocation. I say "Una," which fortunately is right for both!

5. I became very upset this afternoon, after a day with the group, because the guide had stopped telling me in his weak English what happened next, and I felt stupid asking every time to make sure. (Finally I understood quite well that we were to eat at 8:30 p.m. but not that we were going out, instead of staying in the hotel, so I didn't bring my coat down.) I understand some of his explanations but listening to guides standing in the middle of moving buses is always difficult, even in English. A very nice Swiss and his wife (he is a budding linguist) came to my rescue and asked me to have a drink with them. He is quadrilingual (Irish mother, German father, grew up in Alexandria, married a French-speaking Swiss and has now been three years in South America). I settled down after the drink with my Swiss friends had relaxed me, and regained my courage. During the dinner with the group, I recounted funny stories in French which some understood, and was able to make some conversation in Spanish with the help of a *vaino* with cinnamon and some white wine. I found I sometimes thought the Swiss was talking French when he was speaking Spanish, and I followed his Spanish quite well. Does this mean he has a French accent (or intonation) in his Spanish? At least he translated mutually for me and the Spanish speakers at crucial moments.

January 26 (3.3)

1. I understood at least *what was being talked about* on the radio this morning and can definitely segment, but there is still the problem of the vocabulary I don't know.

2. I feel sure now that in an immersion situation, at least for adults on their own, it is important to have someone to whom one may have recourse in one's own language (that is, in a non-teaching situation and in isolation) because one feels such an idiot when one cannot

express one's own personality at least from time to time. It can be quite traumatic.

January 27 (3.4)

1. It was very reassuring that today I was able to listen in to a long conversation between the Swiss, the architect, and the social worker on the boat, and could follow quite well what it was all about. I did not get the nuances of meaning because of all the words missed, but I definitely felt I was getting the segmentation of the language. (The Swiss explained the really interesting parts later. It was about what the local people thought of the present political situation.)

2. Now that the group knows me they are very helpful, and I am gradually expressing myself more and being more like me. Being able to slip into fluent English or French with my Swiss friends occasionally is a help. (We talk about linguistics and many other interesting subjects.)

January 28 (3.5)

1. I worked on my Spanish in the bus while traveling through parts we had been through twice before. My procedure: (a) reading attentively and learning expressions from the reading; (b) checking in the dictionary on words and expressions I needed immediately; (c) making up sentences based on (a) and (b), repeating these in my head, and where possible trying them out on others in the bus (I think this is the key: continually trying to construct new sentences with anything one is trying to learn); (d) checking in the grammar sections of the textbook I brought for all sorts of things I needed immediately, from demonstratives to reflexives, and particularly *irregular verbs*, and continually referring back to the verb forms of the different tenses. (Quite clearly this is basic, and I am particularly pleased that my teacher in our six rapid lessons did give me past, present, and future, and *I have to* and *I must* forms.) I still feel not having an English-Spanish section in my textbook is a distinct disadvantage and hobbles me in trying to create new sentences.

2. My tour companions are very helpful and look pleased when I produce a bright new sentence out of the blue. Their understanding of my effort and their pleasure at my having made the effort are certainly rewarding (reinforcing?).

3. I was in despair this afternoon because in the bus there were several rapid conversations in my vicinity (one a discussion on religion between the guide and *las lolas* from the Catholic University in S). I could tell what the subject was, but not what the arguments were

at all. On the other hand, I was encouraged when we returned to the hotel and sat around having an apéritif, because I was able to understand individuals, some of whom I had had difficulty understanding before, and was able to contribute to the conversation and make some of them laugh.

4. It was Ricardo's 13th birthday and we had all sorts of fun and games, champagne and birthday cake, singing, etc. I got the general drift of most of it because of actions and an obvious context, but again found around-the-table discussion hard. I do feel it is coming, however, and must keep plunging in.

Having A-M to translate table jokes at times is a help and makes me feel more "in."

5. Our Swiss friends have left us, which is probably a good thing for me, since I'll not have that "out" for the last four days of the tour.

6. German still pops into my mind, and in the morning I have to concentrate on what language I'm to use. I think I can say that the interference comes from the most recent of my two weakest languages. This is hard to judge. Is it because German is the non-Romance language and the Romance languages help as a source of possible positive transfer (admitting that I am well aware that there may not be direct transfer), so I can take a chance adapting the transfer according to rules I already know? Or does using my weakest language make me feel I am "talking foreign" and therefore seem appropriate? Of course, let's admit it, I've forgotten my Italian!

7. The emotional problems in all this are clearly important, as witness my breakdown on the first day. I, of course, benefit from my social and intellectual maturity, determination, and overwhelming desire to get as much out of this month as possible, and my knowledge of how to go about learning a language. How are these transferable to the average L_2 learner?

8. I'm fortunate in knowing (or being forewarned) of such features of local conversational Spanish as the tendency to drop final "s." I have to compensate for this.

9. I am still misled by the *ll* and *j/g* plus *e or i* pronunciations. This shows that I am mentally visualizing unrecognized words in order to make any necessary adjustments to make them guessable from French or Latin, and also so that I can scan the lexicon I have stored. Unfortunately this process takes too long, and the conversation moves on while I'm stuck on an earlier word – which shows the value of practice in rapid recognition of words in oral form.

10. I find I'm thinking in Spanish when I speak my little sentences, although I consciously construct them in my head, with due attention first to any rules I know.

11. I'm also thinking in Spanish when I read, and it's true that

179

reading "in Spanish" what one can read – that is, reading ahead for the complete context – helps enormously in deciphering the words; then, when I come to a block, I begin to go over the surrounding context in English translation to see if I can make it out before referring to the dictionary (which is only a last resort because I'm too lazy anyway). I don't worry too much about the tense forms I haven't learned because they become clear (or else don't matter), but it's those wretched little irregulars again which mess things up.

12. I am still filling in gaps in my knowledge of the *often, everywhere, nearly, perhaps, in front of, behind, inside* types of words. I've picked up rejoinders like *Claro!* and *Exacto!* from listening to others, but need more of the soothing noises for social occasions.

January 29 (3.6)

1. I seem to have given the impression that only German and Italian seem to interfere. This is from the lexical point of view mainly. When I'm seeking a common word, *sehr* pops up instead of *muy* but in the correct word class, so it is really lexical interference. French acts as a guide lexically as does Latin – a guide to word formation; but French structure interferes much more than English structure – in fact I am tempted to use the seeming equivalent of the French *passé composé* for conversational past when the actual form required is much closer to ordinary English past tense. That this effect is because of the close correspondences between French and Spanish that occur elsewhere is very possible. Similarly I had problems at the beginning (and probably still do without knowing it) with transference of French stress (not English, which is more similar) and of French sounds in parallel words *una* as /yna/ for instance, and a French /lj/ for *millón*. I also tend to make participles in compound tenses agree with subjects or objects, which comes from French and is not Spanish.

2. Certainly ways of looking at *being* (*estar/ser*) and ways of expressing time are interesting problems.

3. The gender agreement part is no problem (once you know the gender) because of previous experience with French, Italian, German, and Latin. It's almost expected and it might be more of a problem if it didn't exist, since for me "speaking foreign" implies this.

January 31 (4.1)

1. It is very frustrating that one does not use what one knows in the heat of producing an utterance in a situation which requires it immediately. So I go into a shop and make up some muddled sentence for "Where can I buy films?" and make various peculiar mis-

takes so no one understands until I wave the package of my former film under their noses and wave my arms around saying *Dónde.* Then afterwards I remember I know perfectly well *se vende. Dónde se venden películas*? We should remember this. An oral interview does not always reveal what students know unless the students are feeling relaxed and at ease, and even then they may well be furious with themselves for making silly mistakes and forgetting useful expressions. The SI line, I guess. [See *Practical Guides*, Chap. 2.]

2. When dealing with adult students, and probably bright high school students, we should familiarize them with the book, encourage them to look ahead and find out how certain things are expressed if they find they need them, teaching them how to use the grammatical index and dictionary correctly. I'm continually looking ahead beyond what I am learning to see how it fits into the total picture. Am I exceptional? At least for third-language learners this should be useful.

3. I still have problems with those wretched verbs and vocabulary – common things like *since, again, forget, remember, right away.* Is there a Spanish equivalent for *quand même*?

4. *Listening.* I am still struggling with understanding rapid speech between other speakers. In a one-to-one situation one can control the exchange either by one's own selection of topic, or by lack of comprehension, which results in slower, more careful speech from the other person. For normal rapid speech not addressed to me I am now trying to let it soak in without trying to understand and retain words as they come – like reading for comprehension. I remember what I have written about stages of comprehension and try to apply it. I am understanding better little by little. I understood the guide better yesterday when he was talking about a fort which I had read up beforehand.

5. It is very important to try out in new sentences what you have just learned, if not to others, at least in private talk to yourself.

6. I just came out with *"mais aber sed"* for *pero*!

7. When you don't know a language very well, people you talk to seem to fall into four groups: (a) those who treat you as some kind of idiot and wave their hands at you showing four fingers for 4; (b) those who come close and mouth everything at you in an exaggerated way, distorting syllables and raising their voices; (c) those who avoid you completely so as not to be embarrassed; (d) the helpful ones who continue to speak normally, if simply, and show encouraging understanding, supply a word or two, or quietly correct.

8. Being with the same group of intelligent people for a while is rather inhibiting of attempts at expression, because one feels something of an idiot if one keeps on saying simplistic things, and also

181

because, since you do not completely understand, you realize your simplistic sentences may not hit the right spot, in which case they will be greeted with polite tolerance or explanations of what was really being discussed.

9. Quiet conversations with one person or a couple are best for expression. I've done a lot of concentrated listening in distorted conditions: at long dinner tables in crowded restaurants; shouted conversations in jolting buses (sometimes with the radio blaring); listening to the guide shout in the bus. All of this has been good because I'm beginning now to hear the words in quiet conversation and on the radio, and really people are not using complicated expressions.

10. Now that I can "hear" what they are saying I can see that in the local Spanish they not only drop final "s" as in *Punta Arena(s)*, but also in the middle of words and phrases: "E'paña" and "e'tá." It helps to know these things.

February 1 (4.2)

1. When I go into a post office or shop with a neat little sentence and there are complications, my mind goes a complete blank and I lose all the Spanish I thought I had and become a dumb tourist, not understanding a word and not being able to frame a sentence. (Even now my French deteriorates in similar circumstances.) This is maddening and must be what nervous students undergo when oral exams do not approximate their expectations. This should be kept in mind. Clearly what I am learning must become much more automatic to be useful in such situations. Just now I couldn't frame "I gave it to you" when the mail clerk couldn't find the letter I had just put stamps on and handed her. Well, quite obviously three weeks isn't much, even in a country where the language is spoken.

2. In plane to S: I find I can talk with much less inhibition to strangers in the plane, probably because I can say all the simplistic little things one says on first meeting – information about oneself, comments on the situation. These have already been said when one is with the same people for a while. I also find I can understand now what is being said to me, not necessarily all the words but enough cue words to know what it is all about.

February 2 (4.3)

1. Back in V.M. I listened to a lot of television today. It is frustrating to feel myself on the brink of understanding, yet not understanding more than the general drift. I am now recognizing many words that I've learned. I tried listening and trying to project meaning, and

this helped with the general drift. Of course, the visual elements (facial expressions, dress and bearing of the various characters, and gestures and actions) help, especially in soap operas or "novelas." Then I tried a different training procedure: ignoring the continuing meaning and attempting to train myself to recognize the words rapidly without trying to keep the developing meaning in mind. I am certainly understanding much more than before I went on the tour, but I'm not there yet.

February 3 (4.4)

1. When I'm in France I think in French all the time. Here I think in English and so have to switch consciously to Spanish when I need to speak it. This makes for a slow reaction, then a slow construction of the message, and occasional false starts like coming out with greetings in Italian or German or English. When quick reactions are required ("Yes" or a rejoinder like "Fine" or "OK") I tend to insert English in the Spanish utterance (or French – I tend to say "Oui" rather than "Sí," which is after all similar in sound as well as meaning and seems to fit without clashing).

February 4 (4.5)

1. I was listening to the Minister of Housing giving an economic report to the nation last night. I felt I was following and understanding in Spanish so long as I didn't take up valuable processing time to mentally translate and digest figures (percentages, GNP, balance of payments, etc.), except simple ones like 6%. If I did, I missed the continuing message. The best thing seems to be to listen and try to follow the words at this stage without worrying too much about processing and retaining the meaning over long segments (like stringing on beads without stopping to straighten up the string). Clearly one needs to do a great deal of listening without being required to recapitulate the meaning. There should be much more intensive listening practice provided, if fluent comprehension is to be developed. Without the latter, ability to produce sentences is rather useless.

I feel I am on the brink of a breakthrough in comprehension, but how much more intensive listening is required is not clear. Sometimes closing my eyes helps, because processing all the visual elements on the television screen takes up mental space. So close listening to the sound without the image *is* valuable and this distracting aspect of the visual element should be kept in mind. The visual helps with clues, but also hinders because it must be processed.

2. I have been learning about stem-changing verbs and writing

them down with correct changes but wrong endings (for *ir, er, ar,* etc.). Yet I know these! But I am clearly distracted by the stem changes. I make mistakes which do not reflect lack of knowledge. A note in the book – "Be careful: Note that these verbs are from different conjugations" – would have helped avoid this. Fortunately I picked up on it myself while checking verb paradigms, but will all students?

3. With material on tapes or cassettes, it is a real problem if you don't catch the model sentence properly to begin with. Model sentences should be repeated or, better still, students should have their own tapes or cassettes so they can run the tape back to the sentence they didn't comprehend and hear it over as often as they need to get it.

4. In early learning I like to repeat the correct version of an exercise item after the tape model to get correct intonation and pronunciation (4-phase), so time should be allowed for this. (This goes against something I said in the *Practical Guides.*)

5. More about practice exercises. Students need time to formulate the responses, particularly when the drill requires verb adjustments, stem-changing, and switching in different slots. They also should have the opportunity to go over any particular exercise until they feel comfortable with it (hence the value of individual control of tapes or cassettes). I certainly need this anyway.

6. I had lunch today with Gina Lollabrigida – and about 250 other people. The secret of social (cocktail) communication is to look pleasant, keep a "listening" appearance, and follow facial and kinesic cues, saying *Exacto* and *Claro* at suitable moments. This is especially so when the noise level reaches that of the Concorde. Intonation indicates when you should be responding. These are the dangerous moments when you should keep your ears tuned for a cue word and take off from there, turning it into a question as soon as possible.

February 5 (4.6)

1. I went to a family service in Spanish at the church. I understood some of the sermon from expectations aroused by associations with some key words. Conducting the service and preaching was a young man about 20 years old who spoke Spanish rapidly and naturally.

2. I went to cocktails with E's neighbors in the building. There were five of us: the ophthalmologist and his wife, another neighbor, E, and myself. I managed to conduct a conversation with them and to get the gist of most of what was being said, so the three and a half weeks have led somewhere. Verb endings of tenses in various conjugations are still a problem, naturally, despite my efforts to memorize

a great deal in a short time. They don't come out automatically in the flush of trying to construct interesting sentences. I find I can make people laugh, even in simple sentences. Spanish seems easier to string together than French or German, or perhaps I just don't know any better yet!

3. Clearly for aural comprehension on tapes single sentences require very careful listening and relistening to hear them accurately. Those preparing tapes should use longer contexts from the beginning. I am looking for an opportunity to listen to stretches of the language, but the tapes don't provide these, even though this is what they could most usefully supply to supplement a class lesson.

February 6 (4.7)

Ability to comprehend aurally seems to come and go at this stage, being dependent not only on degree of concentration. When I first begin listening to TV it seems something of a blur and I feel as though I've learned nothing. After a while (10 minutes or a quarter of an hour?) it begins to sort itself out a bit. I have to concentrate hard and consciously; otherwise my mind takes the easy road of receding from the effort and reverting to the blur. In other words, listening with comprehension is hard work and conscious work.

February 7 (5.1)

Four weeks today since my arrival in this country and three and a half weeks since I began learning Spanish. I find I can chat away in Spanish quite freely in unsophisticated conversation but am inhibited by my usually intelligent standard of comments when in sophisticated company. For instance, when we visited the director of the Museum of Fine Arts I couldn't think of how to say a single intelligent thing, although I understood the discussion. The one bright comment I did try to make came out half in French, and the director and E stared, clearly puzzled. On the other hand I chatted quite extensively with the girl from the Institute who accompanied me to a bookshop and the bank, and to her children.

February 9 (5.3)

I got in a hassle at the airport for my departure from the country because some official had never stamped my arrival! Habits are strong, so since the girl at the counter understood some English I continued to talk fast in English (always a mistake with non-native speakers as I should know from my own experiences). When she took me to see the police officer who didn't understand a word of English I suddenly burst into fluent (and flawless?) Spanish, which brought kindly amused smiles to both their faces and everything was smoothed out in the usual way in this culture – "No problems." It is interesting that in a sticky situation it never occurred to me to make use of my newly acquired Spanish (the obvious way to behave), presumably because of deep-rooted emotional convictions that link my native language with "talking my way out of trouble." How insecure one feels in relying on newly acquired skills when "important" outcomes are at stake.

February 10 (5.4)

Visiting a French-speaking family in L, I found my newly-acquired Spanish interfering with my French for the first time, particularly function words like *pero*, as though my mind is now geared to searching my Spanish lexicon for function words, instead of my French lexicon.

February 11 (5.5)

In C, I watched the mime in a "street theater" (children's theater) in the central square. I found I could understand what he was saying when he was explaining his purposes, because he was speaking loudly and distinctly, since it was in the open air in a large area and presumably also because there were so many small children there.

February 12 (5.6)

1. I went to a service in the Cathedral on Sunday morning and by concentrating was able to comprehend the subject matter and general development of the sermon, although not the details, because the semantic area (beginning of Lent and Lenten duties of Christians) was familiar to me and I could anticipate and guess meaning to fill in for lack of knowledge.

2. I went around the Temple of the Sun with a Quechua/Spanish-speaking guide and found I could comprehend on a one-to-one basis. In this situation, the speaker adapts to hesitancies, questioning looks, and incorrect rejoinders by repeating, re-explaining, or elaborating, and there are visual objects being described and explained. I had also read information about Inca customs and practices so, again, the area of discussion was not completely unknown, which clearly helps in leaping gaps of incomprehension and putting together a message.

3. I am improving gradually in following what is being said on the radio. I am still identifying the general subject matter without being sure of the details, but have more moments when I comprehend the details too.

February 13 (5.7)

1. On the way to MP in the train (a trip of three and a half hours each way) I was with a Peruvian girl, a Venezuelan, and an Argentinian. I was able to tell them about myself and conduct general (minor) conversation, with resort to English and French here and there. I was well accepted and included in the group.

2. I could understand the explanations of the Spanish-speaking guides, again aided by the visual element and previous knowledge of the subject.

February 14 (6.1)

My glasses were stolen in the park. I spent about two hours with various policemen in two commissariats, with one officer in particular (a handsome young man!) who took over the case, and I was apparently able to make myself perfectly clear, because I found out later that at least one of the officers actually spoke English very well but he didn't attempt to use it. This was a very good test of my ability to "survive" in the language when I had to and was not able to take the easy way out of asserting my superiority by loudly holding forth in English (thus treating the native as the "foolish foreigner," as I did on my return from MP to C when I found out from the hotel personnel that the airline had no record of me on the list for a twice-reconfirmed flight).

February 15. At the Airport at L. (6.2)

1. I had quite a lengthy conversation with a family group of Spanish speakers who will be emigrating to Australia in March. The importance of the conversation to the Spanish speakers (meeting a real Australian and finding out more about conditions in Melbourne) created a desire to comprehend. I was able to bring out my most practiced sentences (who I was, what I did, where I came from) and construct informative sentences from which the listeners were anxious to extract information (there was plenty of motivation to communicate on both sides). I was able to comprehend their questions and personal explanations which were on a one-to-one or very small

group basis (two or three persons) centered on me. Those who had already spoken with me would urge the others to give me time to put my sentences together.

2. At least from my five weeks' experience with Spanish I have acquired the ability to "survive" orally and in graphic form (since I can now also read the newspapers, information booklets, police reports, and notices without difficulty). The necessity of everyday contact has played a considerable role in forcing me to make an effort which it would have been more comfortable to avoid, and as a result my confidence has been boosted.

Let's discuss

1 In this diary are many references to the problems of listening. Read the diary through again, noting these comments. What was (or is) your own experience with the comprehension of spoken messages in a foreign language?
2 What emotional reactions in foreign-language situations can you recall from your personal experience? Have you observed signs of emotional distress in your classes? How have you dealt with these?
3 What have you learned about developing speaking ability from reading this diary? What would you like to add to this list?
4 There has been much talk about strategies of language learning. What strategies can you identify in Rivers's account? You may like to compare your list with the findings of N. Naiman et al. in *The Good Language Learner* (Toronto: OISE, 1978).
5 What hints for classroom teaching techniques can you draw from this diary?

Appendix: Results of questionnaire on foreign language learners' goals

Varying objectives within the United States

Examination of the data from various areas and languages within the United States revealed no striking regional tendencies across languages. Objectives seemed to be related rather to the situation for a specific language in a particular area, as, for instance, with the emphasis on interpersonal relations and communication for Spanish students in California and for French students in the Deep South, and the desire to understand one's ethnic origin among Italian and Portuguese students in the Northeast. Other traditional influences could be detected, such as the strong liberal-education tradition in French studies in the Northeast. On the other hand, Texans seemed to emphasize the career possibilities of French as well as Spanish. In the Deep South, German put a top priority on communication skills, but this was not so for Spanish in the Southeast, where students and teachers seemed to yearn more for cultural understanding. Midwest high school German gave strong priority to self-expression, whereas high school French in the Midwest emphasized knowledge of how languages work, and Midwest Spanish showed a career orientation. English as a Second Language everywhere was mainly geared toward career concerns, communication, and cultural understanding.

In *French*, there was a difference in emphasis between universities and high schools, irrespective of region. High schools unanimously selected oral communication as their leading priority; universities varied in their emphases, some placing oral fluency first or second (California, Midwest, Northeast, Pacific Northwest, Texas), whereas others placed it last or did not select it at all (Southeast, Deep South). All universities (except for the Pacific Northwest and Texas) rated the study of French literature as important; the rating for literature was lowest wherever the rating for oral communication was highest (except in the Northeast); intellectual development rated highly with most. Except for some universities in the Deep South, French was considered a useful career adjunct by both high schools and colleges. Objectives related to international understanding were not highly rated for French (except for Texas, where seeing the world from a different perspective became important). Travel abroad did not seem to be a major concern of the French respondents. Universities rated cultural understanding more highly

The full account of the survey, with format of the questionnaire, can be found in "Educational Goals: The Foreign-Language Teacher's Response," chap. 2 of Rivers (1983), and in NEC, 1979.

189

than high schools (except in the Pacific Northwest and Southeast). At both levels, the study of French was judged of educational value in introducing students to another mode of learning.

Respondents for *German* rated highly both oral communication and an understanding of how language works, at both high school and university levels, except in the Northeast where another avenue of human knowledge and understanding the values and viewpoints of others were considered more important. Literature was less emphasized by German respondents than French respondents (except in the Pacific Northwest high schools and the universities in California and the Mid-Atlantic states). There was an even split on the value of German as a career tool. Very few of the respondents selected as an objective the reading of scientific or philosophical writings, and those who did gave it a low ranking. Most were more preoccupied with breaking down chauvinistic and ethnocentric attitudes. Only at the university level was the question of travel abroad considered of urgent interest by the Germanists.

For *Spanish*, areas with strong concentrations of Spanish speakers, like Florida, Texas, New Mexico, and California, shared a common concern for developing the ability to communicate orally and to understand the values and viewpoints of their neighbors. They were also concerned about breaking down prejudices due to ethnocentric attitudes. In other areas, more emphasis was placed on intellectual development, a broader educational experience, a different view of the world, and the opportunity to read Spanish literature. Most teachers of Spanish saw the language as a useful career adjunct for their students. The goals for students of Spanish seemed to vary more from region to region than for French, where the differences of viewpoint were greater between levels.

In California the emphasis on the teaching of *Chinese* was on oral communication, understanding of cultural differences, appreciation of one's ethnic origin, and increased opportunities for enjoyment of life, whereas in the Northeast (Chinese and *Japanese*) reading, understanding other cultures, and having opportunities to experience a new mode of learning received the highest rankings.

Idaho (fifteen responses in French, German, Spanish, and English SL) provided an interesting example of situational influences on language-learning goals. In all four languages, preference was shown for oral communication, understanding the values and viewpoints of others, and seeing the world from a different perspective. Spanish, however, put highest priority on experiencing another mode of learning, understanding another culture, and combating ethnocentric attitudes. Spanish teachers in Idaho put a lower priority on oral communication than did the French and German teachers. French respondents laid particular stress on oral communication, possibilities for travel, and the experience of another mode of learning. German respondents saw oral communication, cultural understanding, and seeing the world from a different perspective as most important. On the other hand, English SL teachers emphasized cultural understanding, oral communication, and the development of thought processes and comprehension of underlying meanings, the latter choice reflecting no doubt a realization that non-English speakers in high school and college need to learn to structure their intellectual products in a new way.

National differences in objectives

We shall now consider some very different situations in various parts of the world, in Brazil, Thailand, various countries of the European Economic Community, the Far East, the Middle East, and Australasia.

Teachers in *Brazil* (English FL, French, German, and Spanish: fourteen respondents) identified a strong need for language for career purposes, specifically the reading of technical literature, and for facility in oral communication. They also saw language study as providing an experience of another mode of learning. Teachers in *Thailand* (English FL: five respondents) also emphasized career uses and technical reading, but without the necessity for oral communication. The Thais also felt the need for their students to develop intellectually through the study of English, possibly because of the different thought patterns a noncognate language requires. English, they felt, was necessary to give their students the feeling of belonging to an international community.

Sweden (English FL, French, German: forty-five respondents) has what one Swedish teacher described as a "peripheral language." It is a modern industrialized country, deeply involved in social, political, and economic relations with other European countries. In Sweden, English is required at all levels and is essential for admission to a university. A strong effort is being made to internationalize higher education with exchanges of teachers and students. All languages in Sweden reported emphasis on oral communication, cultural understanding, language as a career tool (requiring particularly the ability to speak, read, and write the language, but with some emphasis on business skills and, to a lesser degree, on translating). The Swedes expected to travel and the students of English, particularly, saw the language as giving them a feeling of belonging to an international community.

Other countries in the *European Economic Community* – the Netherlands, Belgium, France, Germany, Italy, United Kingdom (English FL, French, German: forty-three responses) – clearly cared a great deal about oral fluency in another language for career purposes (to a lesser degree for students of French and German in Britain). They also rated highly the ability to understand the values and viewpoints of others. They stressed the importance of knowing another language for international understanding (meeting other nations halfway, combating chauvinism, feeling that one belongs to an international community). Reading technical literature in another language was judged unimportant by most (except for ESL in Britain). This contrasts with the emphasis on this goal in less highly developed areas and in *Eastern Europe* (Poland, Rumania, the Soviet Union, Yugoslavia: seven respondents) where career goals and technical reading generally rated highly along with oral communication.

The goals of the learners of English in *Japan* (eight respondents) followed a similar pattern to that of the European Common Market countries, with the added emphasis on learning to express one's feelings more freely through a new medium. English teaching in *Israel* (six respondents) seemed more specifically career-oriented with stress on reading all kinds of material, technical and literary, but with a strong emphasis on how language works and on intellectual processes. The Israelis also saw English as a means of broadening their outlook.

The countries responding from the *Middle East* (Egypt, Iran, Iraq, Jordan, Kuwait, Saudi Arabia, Sudan, Turkey: twenty-eight respondents) all showed a strong interest in English for career purposes and technical reading. They looked forward to travel in other countries and broadened opportunities for enjoyment of life. They also considered language important educationally as another mode of learning. Kuwaitis, Iraqis, and Sudanese, in particular, showed a strong interest in understanding the values and viewpoints of the speakers of the language.

Australians and New Zealanders (English SL, French, German, Indonesian, Japanese: forty-five respondents) felt the need to see the world from a different perspective and experience what it is like to belong to another linguistic group. They strongly emphasized oral communication, cultural understanding, and, for Japanese and English SL, the values of those languages as career tools (English being learned mainly by immigrants and foreign students). Australians and New Zealanders also felt the need to combat ethnocentric attitudes in societies that have long been, at least psychologically, monolingual and monocultural, but that are now beginning to recognize their multilingual and multicultural character.

In *Canada* (English SL, French SL, German, Spanish: thirty-eight respondents), there was a common concern in all languages with oral fluency, understanding of the values and viewpoints of others, and the usefulness of another language as a career tool. There was also an emphasis on the need to break down ethnocentric attitudes. Anglophone respondents also stressed the need to experience what it feels like to be a member of another linguistic-cultural group. Anglophones emphasized the need for a bilingual and bicultural country more than francophones, who preferred to work toward meeting others halfway.

For countries responding to the Rivers *Questionnaire 1978*, see chap. 10, n. 14.

Abbreviations used in notes and bibliography

ACTFL	American Council on the Teaching of Foreign Languages (Hastings-on-Hudson, New York)
ADFL	Association of Departments of Foreign Languages (MLA)
AL	*Applied Linguistics* (Oxford: Oxford University Press)
CAL	Center for Applied Linguistics (Washington, D.C.)
CCC	Council for Cultural Cooperation of the Council of Europe (Strasbourg)
CMLR	*Canadian Modern Language Review* (Welland, Ontario)
EFL	English as a Foreign Language
ESL	English as a Second Language
ETF	*English Teaching Forum* (Washington, D.C.)
FL	Foreign language
FLA	*Foreign Language Annals* (Journal of ACTFL)
GURT	Georgetown Round Table on Languages and Linguistics Monograph (Washington, D.C.: Georgetown University Press)
IRAL	*International Review of Applied Linguistics in Language Teaching* (Heidelberg: Julius Gross Verlag)
LL	*Language Learning* (Ann Arbor, Michigan)
LT	*Language Teaching* (Cambridge: Cambridge University Press); formerly *LTLA*
LTLA	*Language Teaching and Linguistics: Abstracts* (Cambridge: Cambridge University Press)
MLA	Modern Language Association (New York)
MLJ	*Modern Language Journal* (Madison: University of Wisconsin Press)
NEC	Northeast Conference on the Teaching of Foreign Languages (Middlebury, Vermont)
OISE	Ontario Institute for Studies in Education (Toronto)
TESOL	Teachers of English to Speakers of Other Languages (Washington, D.C.)
TQ	*TESOL Quarterly* (Washington, D.C.)

Notes

Preface

1   Alfred, Lord Tennyson, "Ulysses" (1842).

1. Linguistics, psychology, and language teaching

1   L. Bloomfield, in *Language* (London: Allen & Unwin, 1933), speaks of "three successive events in an act of speech: A, the speaker's situation; B, his utterance of speech-sound and its impingement on the hearer's eardrums; and C, the hearer's response. Of these three types of events, A and C include all the situations that may prompt a person to speak and all the actions which a hearer may perform in response; in sum, A and C make up the world in which we live....In principle, the student of language is concerned only with the actual speech (B); the study of speakers' situations and hearers' responses (A and C) is equivalent to the sum total of human knowledge....These two facts [are] the *meaning* (A-C) of any given speech-utterance (B)....Language, on this ideal plane, would consist of...*phonetics* in which we studied the speech-event without reference to its meaning,...and *semantics*, in which we studied the relation of these features to the features of meaning....Actually, however, our knowledge of the world in which we live is so imperfect that we can rarely make accurate statements about the meaning of a speech-form....The study of language can be conducted without special assumptions so long as we pay no attention to the meaning of what is spoken" (pp. 74–5).

2   Bloomfield, *Language*, p. 21.

3   The term "audiolingual" was proposed by Nelson Brooks of Yale University in the late fifties. Earlier the term "aural-oral" had been used.

4   For a thorough discussion of types of drills and their features, see W. M. Rivers, *Teaching Foreign-Language Skills*, 2d ed. (Chicago: University of Chicago Press, 1981), chap. 4: "Structural Practice"; and Rivers and Temperley, *A Practical Guide to the Teaching of English: As a Second or Foreign Language* (New York: Oxford University Press, 1978), chap. 4: "Oral Practice in the Learning of Grammar."

5   For a more detailed account of audiolingual techniques, see Rivers, *Teaching Foreign-Language Skills*, 2d ed., chap. 2.

6   For an early evaluation and critique, see W. M. Rivers, *The Psychologist and the Foreign-Language Teacher* (Chicago: University of Chicago Press, 1964).

194

7   See N. Chomsky, *Aspects of the Theory of Syntax* (Cambridge, Mass.: MIT Press, 1965), pp. 25–6; and "Linguistic Theory," in *Language Teaching: Broader Contexts*, ed. R. G. Mead, Jr. (Middlebury, Vt.: NEC, 1966), pp. 43–9. For a more detailed discussion, see "Rules, patterns, and creativity," chap. 2 of this book. For the present status of this theory, see "The Second-Language Teacher and Cognitive Psychology," chap. 7 of this book.

8   K. Chastain, *The Development of Modern-Language Skills: Theory to Practice* (Philadelphia: Center for Curriculum Development, 1971), p. 48.

9   K. Chastain, *Developing Second-Language Skills: Theory to Practice*, 2d ed. (Chicago: Rand McNally, 1976), pp. 156–7.

10 N. Chomsky, *Topics in the Theory of Generative Grammar* (The Hague: Mouton, 1966), p. 10. For a more detailed discussion of Chomsky's viewpoint, see "Rules, Patterns, and Creativity," chap. 2 of this book.

11 J. B. Carroll, "The Contributions of Psychological Theory and Educational Research to the Teaching of Foreign Languages," *MLJ* 49 (1965): 273–81.

12 J. B. Carroll, "Current Issues in Psycholinguistics and Second Language Teaching," *TQ* 5 (1971): 103–4. For full quotation, see chap. 2, n. 19.

13 G. A. Miller, "The Psycholinguists," in *The Psychology of Communication: Seven Essays* (New York: Basic Books, 1967), pp. 79–80.

14 Many creative activities are proposed in S. A. Sadow, *Idea Bank: Creative Activities for the Language Class* (Rowley, Mass.: Newbury House, 1982).

15 R. Brown, *A First Language: The Early Stages* (Cambridge, Mass.: Harvard University Press, 1973), p. 274. See also Jill G. and Peter A. de Villiers, *Language Acquisition* (Cambridge, Mass.: Harvard University Press, 1978), pp. 86–92.

16 J. H. Porter, "A Cross-Sectional Study of Morpheme Acquisition in First Language Learners," *LL* 27 (1977): 59. The measuring instrument was the Bilingual Syntax Measure, designed by M. K. Burt and H. C. Dulay. G. P. Sampson, "Converging Evidence for a Dialectical Model of Function and Form in Second Language Learning," *AL* 3 (1982): 20, suggests that uniformity of functions in tasks inevitably produces similar language forms and that this explains the uniformity of the morpheme acquisition studies. The particular morphemes involved in these studies are listed in N. Bailey, C. Madden, and S. D. Krashen, "Is There a 'Natural Sequence' in Adult Second Language Learning?" *LL* 24 (1974): 236.

17 E. L. Newport, H. Gleitman, and L. R. Gleitman, "Mother, I'd Rather Do It Myself: Some Effects and Non-effects of Maternal Speech Style," in *Talking to Children: Language Input and Acquisition*, ed. C. E. Snow and C. A. Ferguson (Cambridge: Cambridge University Press, 1977), pp. 109–49.

18 L. Selinker, "Interlanguage," *IRAL* 10 (1972): 209–301.

19 For a useful summary and assessment of research in this area, see K. Hakuta and H. Cancino, "Trends in Second-Language Acquisition Research," *Harvard Educational Review* 47 (1977): 294–316.

20 S. P. Corder, "The Significance of Learners' Errors," in *Error Analysis: Perspectives on Second Language Acquisition*, ed. J. C. Richards (London: Longman, 1974), pp. 19–27. Originally published in *IRAL 5* (1967): 161–70.

21 S. P. Corder, *Introducing Applied Linguistics* (Harmondsworth: Penguin Education, 1973), p. 133. See also discussion of Bruner's three systems of "knowing" in chap. 4 of this book. For a discussion of psychological factors hindering the acquisition of a near-native accent in a second language, see Rivers, *Teaching Foreign Language Skills*, pp. 450–51.

22 For a description of this approach to natural language learning, see T. D. Terrell, "A Natural Approach to Second Language Acquisition and Learning," *MLJ* 61 (1977): 325–37; and "The Natural Approach to Language Teaching: An Update," *MLJ* 66 (1982): 121–32.

23 For a fuller account of Krashen's hypotheses, see S. D. Krashen, *Second Language Acquisition and Second Language Learning* (Oxford: Pergamon Press, 1981); and "The Monitor Model for Second-Language Acquisition," in *Second-Language Acquisition and Foreign Language Teaching*, ed. R. C. Gingras (Arlington, Va.: CAL, 1978). For a critique of Krashen's position, see chap. 12 of this book.

24 For TPR, see James J. Asher, "The Learning Strategy of the Total Physical Response: A Review," *MLJ* 50 (1966): 79–84; "The Total Physical Response Approach to Second Language Learning," *MLJ* 53 (1969): 3–7; and "Children's First Language as a Model for Second Language Learning," *MLJ* 56 (1972): 133–9.

25 Terrell, "Natural Approach to Language Teaching," p. 126.

26 Ibid., p. 127.

27 J. J. Gumperz and D. Hymes, eds., *Directions in Sociolinguistics: The Ethnography of Communication* (New York: Holt, Rinehart & Winston, 1972), p. vii; and D. Hymes, "The Ethnography of Speaking," in *Readings in the Sociology of Language*, ed. J. A. Fishman (The Hague: Mouton, 1968), pp. 99–138.

28 D. Hymes, *Foundations in Sociolinguistics: An Ethnographic Approach* (Philadelphia: University of Pennsylvania Press, 1974), p. 75.

29 Ibid.

30 D. Hymes, "Competence and Performance in Linguistic Theory," in *Language Acquisition: Models and Methods,* ed. R. Huxley and E. Ingram (New York: Academic Press, 1971), p. 12. For an excellent discussion of the competence-performance controversy and sociolinguistic models of communicative competence and language use, see J. Munby, *Communicative Syllabus Design* (Cambridge: Cambridge University Press, 1978).

31 For a thorough analysis of gambits, moves, and negotiating meaning, with practical proposals for teaching these to nonnative speakers, see C. J. Kramsch, *Discourse Analysis and Second Language Teaching* (Washington, D.C.: CAL, 1981); idem, "Teaching Discussion Skills: A Pragmatic Approach," in *FLA* 14 (April, 1981): 93–104; M. Coulthard, *An Introduction to Discourse Analysis* (London: Longman, 1977); and J. C. Richards, "Conversation," *TQ* 14 (1980): 413–32.

32 Many of these aspects of communicative behavior were first studied by E. T. Hall in *The Silent Language* (Garden City, N.Y.: Doubleday, 1959) and *The Hidden Dimension* (Garden City, N.Y.: Doubleday, 1966).

33 P. J. Dragonas, *The High School Goes Abroad: International Home-Stay Exchange Programs* (Arlington, Va.: CAL, forthcoming).

34 C. J. Fillmore, "The Case for Case," in *Universals in Linguistic Theory*, ed. E. Bach and R. T. Harms (New York: Holt, Rinehart & Winston, 1968), pp. 1–88.

35 See G. Lakoff, "On Generative Semantics," in *Semantics: An Interdisciplinary Reader in Philosophy, Linguistics, and Psychology*, ed. L. A. Jakobovits and D. Steinberg (Cambridge: Cambridge University Press, 1971), pp. 232–96.

36 W. L. Chafe, *Meaning and the Structure of Language* (Chicago: University of Chicago Press, 1970).

37 We have now covered the whole gamut of the speech act, arriving at this point at the A and C of Bloomfield's analysis (see n. 1, this chap.). It is not surprising then that artificial intelligence researchers are now preoccupied with "our knowledge of the world" (Bloomfield, *Language*, p. 74). See R. C. Schank and R. P. Abelson, *Scripts, Plans, Goals and Understanding: An Inquiry into Human Knowledge Structures* (Hillsdale, N.J.: Erlbaum, 1977).

38 For a fuller discussion of these developments, see "Foreign-Language Acquisition: Where the Real Problems Lie," chap. 12 of this book.

39 Brown, *A First Language.*

40 I. M. Schlesinger, *Production and Comprehension of Utterances* (Hillsdale, N.J.: Erlbaum, 1977).

41 J. S. Bruner, "From Communication to Language: A Psychological Perspective," *Cognition* 3 (1974–5): 283.

42 M. A. K. Halliday, *Learning How to Mean: Explorations in the Development of Language* (London: Edward Arnold, 1975; New York: Elsevier-North Holland, 1977).

43 J. Tough, *Listening to Children Talking: A Guide to the Appraisal of Children's Use of Language* (London: Ward Lock, 1976). Tough's chart of language functions, with strategies employed, is reproduced in Sampson, "Converging Evidence...," p. 10.

44 For an application of Halliday's functions to language teaching, see "The Natural and the Normal in Language Learning," chap. 8 of this book.

45 See "Talking Off the Tops of Their Heads," chap. 3 of this book; and Rivers and Temperley, *A Practical Guide.*

46 For useful suggestions for realistic tasks, see P. Ur, *Discussions that Work: Task-Centred Fluency Practice* (Cambridge: Cambridge University Press, 1981).

47 D. A. Wilkins, *Notional Syllabuses* (Oxford: Oxford University Press, 1976), p. 13.

48 Ibid., p. 19.

49 D. A. Wilkins, "Notional Syllabuses Revisited," *AL* 2 (1981), p. 83.

50 Ibid., p. 84.
51 Ibid., p. 85.
52 See J. L. M. Trim, R. Richterich, J. A. van Ek, and D. A. Wilkins, *Systems Development in Adult Language Learning: A Unit-Credit System for Modern Language Learning by Adults* (Strasbourg: Council of Europe, 1973); J. A. van Ek, *The Threshold Level in a European Unit/Credit System for Modern Language Learning for Adults* (Strasbourg: Council of Europe, 1975); and R. Richterich and J-L. Chancerel, *Identifying the Needs of Adults Learning a Foreign Language* (Strasbourg: Council of Europe, 1977). These three books were republished in 1980 by Pergamon Press.
53 For minicourses, see F. M. Grittner, *Teaching Foreign Languages*, 2d ed. (New York: Harper & Row, 1977), pp. 197–201, 279–83.
54 N. Chomsky, *Generative Grammar*, p. 10.
55 For a description of these early experiments, see D. I. Slobin, *Psycholinguistics* (Glenview, Ill.: Scott, Foresman, 1971), chap. 2. Later experiments are described in the second edition of his book (1979). N. Chomsky did express belief in the psychological reality of aspects of his model, stating that "the transformational operations relating deep and surface structure are actual mental operations, performed by the mind when a sentence is produced or understood." See *Language and Mind*, enlarged ed. (New York: Harcourt Brace Jovanovich, 1972). More recently attempts have been made to bring together psychologists and transformational-generative linguists to explore differences and similarities in findings about the human capacity for language. See M. Halle, J. Bresnan, and G. A. Miller, eds., *Linguistic Theory and Psychological Reality* (Cambridge, Mass.: MIT Press, 1978).
56 Slobin's term. See Slobin, *Psycholinguistics*, p. 24.
57 T. G. Bever, "The Cognitive Basis for Linguistic Structures," in J. R. Hayes, ed., *Cognition and the Development of Language* (New York: Wiley, 1970), p. 350. Strategies A–D are described in detail in Rivers et al., *Practical Guides*, chap. 3.
58 See T. G. Bever, "Psychologically Real Grammar Emerges Because of Its Role in Language Acquisition," in D. P. Dato, ed., *Developmental Psycholinguistics: Theory and Applications*, GURT 1975 (Washington, D.C.: Georgetown University Press, 1977), pp. 63–75.
59 I. M. Schlesinger, *Production and Comprehension of Utterances*.
60 Research in these areas is discussed with applications to language teaching in chaps. 7 and 9 of this book, and in chaps. 4 and 5 of Rivers, *Speaking in Many Tongues: Essays in Foreign-Language Teaching*, 3rd ed. (Cambridge: Cambridge University Press, 1983).
61 Valerian A. Postovsky, "Effects of Delay in Oral Practice at the Beginning of Second Language Learning," *MLJ* 58 (1974): 229–39; "Why Not Start Speaking Later?" in *Viewpoints on English as a Second Language*, ed. M. K. Burt, H. C. Dulay, and M. Finocchiaro (New York: Regents, 1977), pp. 17–26; and "The Priority of Aural Comprehension in the Language Acquisition Process," in *The Comprehension Approach*

to Foreign Language Instruction, ed. H. Winitz (Rowley, Mass.: Newbury House, 1981), pp. 170–86.

62 H. Winitz and J. A. Reeds, "Rapid Acquisition of a Foreign Language (German) by the Avoidance of Speaking," *IRAL* 11 (1973): 295–317.

63 J. Olmsted Gary, "Delayed Oral Practice in Initial Stages of Second Language Learning," in *On TESOL '75: New Directions in Second Language Learning, Teaching and Bilingual Education*, ed. M. K. Burt and H. C. Dulay (Washington, D.C.: TESOL, 1975), pp. 89–95; and "Why Speak If You Don't Need to? The Case for a Listening Approach to Beginning Foreign Language Learning," in *Second Language Acquisition Research: Issues and Implications*, ed. W. C. Ritchie, (New York: Academic Press, 1978), pp. 185–99.

64 K. S. Goodman, "Reading: A Psycholinguistic Guessing Game," *Journal of the Reading Specialist* (1967): 126–35; and *Psycholinguistics and Reading*, ed. F. Smith (New York: Holt, Rinehart & Winston, 1973).

65 This approach to reading is discussed in detail in "Reading Fluently," chap. 6 of Rivers, *Speaking in Many Tongues*, 3rd ed.

66 B. Inhelder and J. Piaget, *The Growth of Logical Thinking from Childhood to Adolescence* (New York: Basic Books, 1958).

67 E. J. Rosansky, "The Critical Period for the Acquisition of Language: Some Cognitive Developmental Considerations," *Working Papers in Bilingualism* 6 (1975): 93–100 (Toronto: OISE); and S. D. Krashen, "The Critical Period for Language Acquisition and Its Possible Bases," in ed. D. Aaronson and R. W. Rieber, *Developmental Psycholinguistics and Communicative Disorders* (New York: New York Academy of Sciences, 1975), pp. 445–52.

68 J. Schachter, "An Error in Error Analysis," *LL* 24 (1974): 205–14; and S. D. Krashen and H. W. Seliger, "The Essential Contributions of Formal Instruction in Adult Second Language Learning," *TQ* 9 (1975): 173–83, are examples.

69 See C. Gattegno, *Teaching Foreign Languages in Schools: The Silent Way*, 2d ed. (New York: Educational Solutions, 1972); and E. W. Stevick, *Teaching Languages: A Way and Ways* (Rowley, Mass.: Newbury House, 1980), pp. 37–82. For a further discussion of the Silent Way, see "Student-Centered Trends," chap. 6 of this book.

70 For an assessment of brain research in relation to second-language acquisition, see "Neurolinguistics and Second Language Acquisition," A. D. Cohen, Coordinator, *TQ* 16 (1982): 305–31, containing the following papers: H. W. Seliger, "On the Possible Role of the Right Hemisphere in Second Language Acquisition" (pp. 307–14); F. Genesee, "Experimental Neuropsychological Research on Second Language Processing" (pp. 315–22); T. Scovel, "Questions concerning the Application of Neurolinguistic Research to Second Language Learning/Teaching" (pp. 323–28).

71 For forgetting, see R. D. Lambert and B. F. Freed, eds., *The Loss of Language Skills* (Rowley, Mass.: Newbury House, 1982).

72 For applications of this research, see "Apples of Gold," chap. 9 of this book.

73 See A. H. Maslow, *Motivation and Personality*, 2d ed. (New York: Harper & Row, 1970); C. H. Rogers, *Freedom to Learn* (Columbus, Oh.: Merrill, 1969); G. I. Brown, *Human Teaching for Human Learning: An Introduction to Confluent Education* (New York: Viking, 1971); and C. A. Curran, *Counseling-Learning: A Whole-Person Model for Education* (New York: Grune & Stratton, 1972).

74 Maslow's hierarchy of needs is discussed in detail in "Motivation in Bilingual Programs," chap. 11 of this book.

75 For a detailed discussion of motivation, see "Motivating through Classroom Techniques," chap. 7 of Rivers, *Speaking in Many Tongues*, 3rd ed.; and "Motivation in bilingual programs," chap. 11 of this book.

76 G. Moskowitz, *Caring and Sharing in the Foreign Language Class: A Sourcebook on Humanistic Techniques* (Rowley, Mass.: Newbury House, 1978), contains details of many activities to meet this need.

77 For the philosophy of individualized instruction, see chap. 5 of this book.

78 B. Galyean, "A Confluent Design for Language Teaching," *TQ* 11 (1977): 143–56 (italics in the original); and "Humanistic Education: A Mosaic Just Begun," in *An Integrative Approach to Foreign Language Teaching: Choosing among the Options*, ed. G. A. Jarvis, ACTFL Foreign Language Education Series 8 (Skokie, Ill.: National Textbook Co., 1976), pp. 201–43.

79 Galyean, "A Confluent Design…," p. 151.

80 C. A. Curran, *Counseling-Learning in Second Languages* (Apple River, Ill.: Apple River Press, 1976); E. W. Stevick, *Memory, Meaning and Method: Some Psychological Perspectives on Language Learning* (Rowley, Mass.: Newbury House, 1976), pp. 125–33; and Stevick, *Teaching Languages*, pp. 86–212.

81 Curran, *Counseling-Learning in Second Languages*, p. 19.

82 Ibid., p. 37.

83 Ibid., p. 39. For a further discussion of C-L/CLL, see "Student-Centered Trends," chap. 6 of this book.

84 For Lozanov's Suggestopaedia, see G. Lozanov, *Suggestology and Outlines of Suggestopedy* (New York: Gordon & Breach, 1978); and Stevick, *Teaching Languages*, pp. 229–59. For a further discussion of Suggestopaedia, see "Student-Centered Trends," chap. 6 of this book.

85 R. A. Via, "English through Drama," in *The Art of TESOL*, ed. A. C. Newton, *ETF* 13, 1–2 (1975): 158–62. Quotation from p. 159. Italics not in the original.

86 Ibid., p. 161.

87 Ibid.

88 R. J. Di Pietro, "Discourse and Real-Life Roles in the ESL Classroom," *TQ* 15 (1981): 27–33.

89 R. J. Di Pietro, "The Open-Ended Scenario: A New Approach to Conversation," *TQ* 16 (1982): 15–20.

90 R. C. Scarcella, "Socio-Drama for Social Interaction," *TQ* 12 (1978): 41–6. Quotation from p. 45.

91 R. A. Via, "TESL and Creative Drama," in *The Art of TESOL*, ed. A. C. Newton, *ETF* 13, 1–2 (1975): 172–3.
92 S. Luxenberg, "All the Class a Stage," *Change* 10, 1 (Jan. 1978): 30–3. Quotation from p. 30.
93 Ibid., p. 30.
94 A. Maley and A. Duff, *Drama Techniques in Language Learning* (Cambridge: Cambridge University Press, 1978), pp. 3–4.

2. Rules, patterns, and creativity

1   N. Chomsky, "Linguistic Theory," in *Language Teaching: Broader Contexts*, ed. R. G. Mead, Jr., NEC 1966 (New York: MLA Materials Center, 1966), p. 43. This article should be read in its entirety.
2   Ibid., p. 45.
3   Namely, the audiolingual approach (see chap. 1). For a detailed description and critique, see Rivers, *The Psychologist and the Foreign-Language Teacher* (Chicago: University of Chicago Press, 1964), or Rivers, *Teaching Foreign-Language Skills*, 2d ed. (Chicago: University of Chicago Press, 1981), chap. 2.
4   Chomsky, "Linguistic Theory," p. 44.
5   Ibid.
6   Ibid.
7   S. Saporta uses this term in "Applied Linguistics and Generative Grammar," in *Trends in Language Teaching*, ed. A. Valdman (New York: McGraw-Hill, 1966), p. 86.
8   W. G. Moulton, "Linguistics and Language Teaching in the United States 1940–1960," in *Trends in European and American Linguistics*, ed. C. Mohrmann, A. Sommerfelt, and J. Whatmough (Utrecht: Spectrum, 1961), p. 87; Rivers, *The Psychologist*, gives a critique of this position (pp. 31–42).
9   For a scientific use of this term, see G. A. Miller, "Some Preliminaries to Psycholinguistics," *American Psychologist*, 20 (1965): 15–20. Reprinted in *Readings in the Psychology of Language*, ed. L. A. Jakobovits and M. S. Miron (Englewood Cliffs, N.J.: Prentice-Hall, 1967), pp. 172–9; see especially p. 175.
10 N. Chomsky, *Topics in the Theory of Generative Grammar* (The Hague: Mouton, 1966), p. 10.
11 Ibid., p. 16.
12 Ibid., p. 10.
13 N. Chomsky, "Linguistic Theory," p. 44.
14 Ibid., p. 46.
15 Since 1966, the role of "situational context" has been of paramount concern to more performance-oriented linguists, like Halliday. See "Apples of Gold," chap. 9 of this book.
16 N. Chomsky, "Linguistic Theory," p. 44.
17 Motivation must be aroused and channeled. See "Motivating through Classroom Techniques," chap. 7 in Rivers, *Speaking in Many Tongues:*

Essays in Foreign-Language Teaching, 3rd ed. (Cambridge: Cambridge University Press, 1983).

18 Chomsky, quoting Humboldt, in *Aspects of the Theory of Syntax* (Cambridge, Mass.: MIT Press, 1965), p. 8.

19 J. B. Carroll, in "Current Issues in Psycholinguistics and Second Language Teaching," *TQ* 5 (1971): 103, comments on Chomsky's position as follows: "I do not find any basic opposition between conceiving of language behavior as resulting from the operation of 'habits' and conceiving of it as 'rule-governed'. . . I would define a habit as any learned disposition to perceive, behave, or perform in a certain manner under specified circumstances. To the extent that an individual's language behavior conforms to the habits of the speech community of which he is a member, we can say that his behavior is 'rule-governed.' "

20 This subject is discussed in relation to all four fundamental language skills in Rivers, *Teaching Foreign-Language Skills*, 2d ed.

21 It is interesting to note that many of these features, particularly the morphological ones, are excluded by Chomsky from his system of rewrite rules and are included in the lexicon as parts of complex symbols. See *Aspects*, pp. 82–8.

22 Rivers, *Teaching Foreign-Language Skills*, 2d ed., chap. 7, gives five inductive options and three deductive options for presenting grammar.

23 Ways of providing such practice are described in "Talking Off the Tops of Their Heads," chap. 3 of this book.

24 A directional framework is provided unobtrusively when a discussion is set in motion that requires, for instance, conditional statements: "If you were (the Mayor), what would you (do?)" or past tense situations such as, "When I (came in), were you (talking)?" or "When you were (a baby), did you (cry) often?"

25 For a more detailed discussion of conceptual distinctions, see "Foreign-Language Acquisition," chap. 12 of this book.

26 The importance of understanding the operation of the target language as a system is discussed at greater length in "Contrastive Linguistics in Textbook and Classroom," GURT 1968: 151–8, *ETF* 8, 4 (1970), pp. 1–10; and Rivers, *Speaking in Many Tongues*, exp. 2d ed. (Rowley, Mass.: Newbury House, 1976), pp. 64–72, or 1st ed., pp. 36–44.

3. Talking off the tops of their heads

1 *The Advisor* [Teacher-Course Evaluation, University of Illinois, 1970–1], p. 122.

2 F. Agard and H. Dunkel, *An Investigation of Second-Language Teaching* (Lexington, Mass.: Ginn, 1948), p. 288.

3 L. Kelly, *25 Centuries of Language Teaching* (Rowley, Mass.: Newbury House, 1969).

4 I have borrowed the division into skill-getting and skill-using from Don H. Parker, "When Should I Individualize Instruction?" in *Individualization of Instruction: A Teaching Strategy*, ed. Virgil M. Howes (New York: Macmillan, 1970), p. 176.

5   D. L. Wolfe, "Some Theoretical Aspects of Language Learning and Language Teaching," *LL* 17 (1967): 175.

6   M. Benamou and E. Ionesco, *Mise en Train* (New York: Macmillan, 1969): "Le professeur est dans la poche du gilet de la montre," p. 44; "Le crocodile est plus beau que Marie-Jeanne," p. 114; "Il dit que ses parents sont aussi grands que la Tour Eiffel," p. 141.

7   "From Skill Acquisition to Language Control," chap. 3 of Rivers, *Speaking in Many Tongues: Essays in Foreign-Language Teaching*, 3rd ed. (Cambridge: Cambridge University Press, 1983); or *TQ* 3 (1969): 12.

8   *Teaching Foreign-Language Skills*, 2d ed. (Chicago: University of Chicago Press, 1981), p. 110. See also 1st ed., p. 109. Italics not in the original.

9   C. B. Paulston, "Structural Pattern Drills: A Classification," *FLA* 4 (1970): 187–93.

10 Adrian Palmer, "Teaching Communication," *LL* 20 (1970): 55–68.

11 S. Savignon used this technique in her "Study of the Effect of Training in Communicative Skills as Part of a Beginning College French Course on Student Attitude and Achievement in Linguistic and Communicative Competence," unpublished Ph.D. dissertation, University of Illinois at Champaign-Urbana, 1971, since published as *Communicative Competence: An Experiment in Foreign-Language Teaching* (Philadelphia: Center for Curriculum Development, 1972).

12 Rivers, *Teaching Foreign-Language Skills*, 2d ed., pp. 110–11. See also 1st ed., p. 109.

13 *The Psychologist and the Foreign-Language Teacher* (Chicago: University of Chicago Press, 1964), p. 78. Italics not in the original.

14 *Teaching Foreign-Language Skills*, 1st ed., p. 201. Italics not in the original.

15 Savignon, *Communicative Competence*, p. 25. On pp. 28 and 29 are listed a variety of communicative tasks used during the practice sessions. Savignon acknowledges her indebtedness to L. A. Jakobovits, *Foreign Language Learning: A Linguistic Analysis of the Issues* (Rowley, Mass.: Newbury House, 1970), chap. 3, for guidelines in defining these tasks. Jakobovits was the director of Savignon's study.

16 Savignon, *Communicative Competence*, p. 30.

17 J. B. Carroll, "Conscious and Automatic Processes in Language Learning," *CMLR* 37 (1981): 471.

18 These activities are described in greater detail in Rivers et al., the *Practical Guides*, chap. 2, with many suggestions for their implementation. Many of the activities listed in the Index of these books under *Games* are also appropriate.

19 J. B. Carroll, *The Study of Language* (Cambridge, Mass.: Harvard University Press, 1953), p. 188. Italics in the original.

20 This is one of the techniques employed in Curran's Counseling-Learning/Community Language Learning approach.

21 Otto Jespersen, *How to Teach a Foreign Language* (London: Allen & Unwin, 1961), p. 48. Originally published in English translation in 1904.

4 Bridging the gap to autonomous interaction

1 The perceived goal may, of course, be listening comprehension or reading, in which case a different design will be indicated. Here I am concerned with programs for which facility in oral communication is the goal. I have made some methodological suggestions for listening and reading programs in "Linguistic and Psychological Factors in Speech Perception and Their Implications for Listening and Reading Materials," and "Reading Fluently," chaps. 5 and 6 of Rivers, *Speaking in Many Tongues: Essays in Foreign-Language Teaching*, 3rd ed. (Cambridge: Cambridge University Press, 1983).

2 These systems are described and discussed by Bruner in considerable detail in J. S. Bruner, *Toward a Theory of Instruction* (Cambridge, Mass.: Harvard University Press, 1966), pp. 10–14; and in J. S. Bruner et al., *Studies in Cognitive Growth* (New York: Wiley, 1966), pp. 6–48.

3 Bruner et al., *Studies in Cognitive Growth*, p. 6.

4 In "The second-language teacher and cognitive psychology," chap. 7 of this book, I quote a number of cognitive psychologists and certain linguists of the generative semantics group who consider that the acquisition of language draws on the general cognitive processes basic to other learning. See also "Foreign-Language Acquisition," chap. 12 of this book.

5 In Bruner, *Theory of Instruction*, this is spelled "ikonic."

6 Bruner, *Theory of Instruction*, pp. 5–6.

7 It is at this point that much of value can be drawn from Fillmore's linguistic theory of Case Grammar, which shows how the new language expresses universal relations within its own system. See B. L. Pearson, *Introduction to Linguistic Concepts* (New York: Knopf, 1977), pp. 174–82; and C. J. Fillmore, "The Case for Case," in *Universals in Linguistic Theory*, ed. E. Bach and R. T. Harms (New York: Holt, Rinehart & Winston, 1968), pp. 1–88.

8 For a more detailed discussion of this subject, see "Contrastive Linguistics in Textbook and Classroom," GURT 1968: 151–8, *ETF* 8, 4 (1970); and Rivers, *Speaking in Many Tongues*, exp. 2d ed. (Rowley, Mass.: Newbury House, 1976), pp. 64–72, or 1st ed., pp. 36–44.

9 A. R. Luria and F. I. Yudovich, *Speech and the Development of Mental Processes in the Child: An Experimental Investigation*, ed. J. Simon (London: Staples Press, 1959), pp. 28–64.

10 Type A and Type B exercises are applied to French, German, Spanish, English, and Hebrew, in Rivers et al., the *Practical Guides*, chap. 4.

11 Natural uses of language and normal purposes of language are distinguished and discussed in "The Natural and the Normal . . .," chap. 8 of this book.

5. Individualized instruction and cooperative learning

1 R. F. Butts and L. A. Cremin, *A History of Education in American Culture* (New York: Henry Holt & Co., 1953), pp. 218–21, 329–31.

2   A. Clegg, "Why Did We Change?" Selections from *Revolution in the British Primary Schools* (Washington, D.C.: NAESP, NEA, 1971), in *The Open Classroom Reader*, ed. C. E. Silberman (New York: Random House, 1973), p. 82.

3   R. S. Barth, *Open Education and the American School* (New York: Agathon Press, 1972), pp. 34–6, and L. Weber, in *Open Classroom Reader*, pp. 150–4, extracted from *The English Infant School and Informal Education* (Englewood Cliffs, N.J.: Prentice-Hall, 1971).

4   Silberman, *Open Classroom Reader*, pp. 36–42.

5   Weber in *Open Classroom Reader*, pp. 150–66.

6   In foreign-language teaching in the United States, an early exposition and advocacy of individualized instruction in its present cycle appeared in *Individualization of Instruction*, ed. D. L. Lange. Britannica Review of Foreign Language Education, vol. 2 (Chicago: Encyclopedia Britannica, 1970). The series has now become the *ACTFL Review of Foreign Language Education* (Skokie, Ill.: National Textbook Co.). Volume 2 contains a comprehensive "Rationale for the Individualization and Personalization of Foreign-Language Instruction," by Lorraine A. Strasheim.

7   Butts and Cremin, *History of Education*, p. 590.

8   Butts and Cremin, *History of Education*, p. 589. In the Dalton Schools in New York, while Helen Parkhurst was headmistress (1916–42), pupils studied in "laboratory brigades," without tests or examinations, with the aim of having the more capable students raise the standards of the backward ones. The students were also self-disciplined. As a further demonstration of the cross-Atlantic influence, Parkhurst drew her inspiration from Maria Montessori. Crossing the Pacific, we find a similar implementation of individualizing principles described in K. S. Cunningham and D. J. Ross, *An Australian School at Work* (Hawthorn, Victoria: Australian Council for Educational Research, 1967), an account of the educational program at the Melbourne Church of England Girls' Grammar School from 1939–55, in which the author participated. See also J. Epstein, *A Golden String: The Story of Dorothy J. Ross* (Collingwood, Victoria: Greenhouse Publications, 1981).

9   F. M. Grittner and F. H. LaLeike, in *Individualized Foreign Language Instruction* (Skokie, Ill.: National Textbook Co., 1973), use the term "unipac"; LAPs are discussed by J. K. Phillips in "Individualization and Personalization," chap. 8 of *Responding to New Realities*, ed. G. A. Jarvis, ACTFL Review of Foreign Language Education, vol. 5 (Skokie, Ill.: National Textbook Co., 1974), pp. 233–4, along with FLAPs (Foreign Language Activity Packets) and DISKs (Dewey Independent Study Kits). The latter, appropriately enough in the light of our discussion in the introductory paragraph, are used at the John Dewey High School in Brooklyn, which has conducted an individualized foreign language program since 1969; see S. L. Levy, "Foreign Languages in John Dewey High School, New York City: An Individualized Approach," in *Individualization of Instruction in Foreign Languages: A Practical Guide*, ed. R. L. Gougher (Philadelphia: Center for Curriculum Development, 1972). G. E. Logan, whose pioneering work at Live Oak High School in Cali-

fornia dates from 1967, still uses the term "assignment"; see G. E. Logan, *Individualized Foreign Language Learning: An Organic Process* (Rowley, Mass.: Newbury House, 1973). For a discussion of the organization of an individualized classroom, see G. E. Logan, "Individualized Foreign-Language Instruction: American Patterns for Accommodating Learner Differences in the Classroom," in *Foreign Language Teaching: Meeting Individual Needs*, ed. H. B. Altman and C. V. James (Oxford: Pergamon, 1980), pp. 94–110.

10 L. Weber in *Open Classroom Reader*, pp. 152–3. She is summarizing Nathan Isaac's explication of Piaget's views.

11 Grittner and LaLeike, *Individualized Foreign Language Instruction*, p. 92, discuss the dangers of this approach.

12 G. M. Green, *Semantics and Syntactic Regularity* (Bloomington: Indiana University Press, 1974), pp. 156–67: "The *Teach* Conspiracy." Green points out that this distinction is basically that between *apprendre* and *enseigner* in French. It is interesting that *apprendre* can be used for both the teacher's and Jane's part in the interaction. *Apprendre* is like the piece of paper in the Saussurean metaphor: If you cut into one side, you cut into the other. This concept of interwoven learning and teaching is basic to the discussion in this chapter.

13 These terms are used by A. H. Maslow in his hierarchy of basic needs, set out in *Motivation and Personality*, 2d ed. (New York: Harper & Row, 1970), chap. 4. For a more detailed application of this theory in second-language teaching, see W. M. Rivers, "Motivation in Bilingual Programs," chap. 11 of this book. E. W. Stevick also applies it to language instruction in "Before Linguistics and Beneath Method," in *Language and International Studies*, ed. K. Jankowsky (Washington, D.C.: Georgetown University Press, 1973), pp. 99–106. See also the discussion of "defensive" and "receptive" learning in E. W. Stevick, "Language Instruction Must Do an About-Face," *MLJ* 58 (1974): 379–84.

14 See E. Hatch, ed., *Second Language Acquisition: A Book of Readings* (Rowley, Mass.: Newbury House, 1977).

15 The observations in this paragraph are from E. Hatch, "Second Language-Learning – Universals?" *Working Papers on Bilingualism* 3 (1974): 1–17. Toronto: Ontario Institute for Studies in Education.

16 G. Butterworth and E. Hatch, "A Spanish-speaking Adolescent's Acquisition of English Syntax," in Hatch, *Second Language Acquisition*, pp. 231–45.

17 For a lengthy discussion of autonomous interaction, with many suggestions for its implementation, see Rivers et al., *Practical Guides*, chap. 2.

18 The author remembers vividly an Australian "slow learner" of French who found it difficult to put two sentences together to express meaning but who, having married a Frenchman, is now happily bringing up a family in Paris and "talking a stream" quite effortlessly.

19 For a useful discussion of three modes of individualized instruction, see V. M. Howes, "Individualized Instruction: Form and Structure," in *Individualization of Instruction: A Teaching Strategy*, ed. V. M. Howes (New York: Macmillan, 1970), pp. 69–81.

20 See references in n. 9, this chapter.
21 For a flexible system of computer-assisted instruction, see the description of PLATO (Programmed Logic for Automated Teaching Operations) at the University of Illinois, in R. T. Scanlan, "The Application of Technology to the Teaching of Foreign Languages," in *Changing Patterns in Foreign Language Programs*, ed. W. M. Rivers et al. (Rowley, Mass.: Newbury House, 1972). Despite the sophisticated potential of modern computer languages, computer programs for second-language learning are still dependent on the programmer. Until some second-language materials writers begin to utilize fully the innovative possibilities of the technological developments, even computer-assisted instruction will remain basically similar to classical programming.
22 Programming in theory and practice is discussed at length in W. M. Rivers, *Teaching Foreign-Language Skills*, 2d ed. (Chicago: University of Chicago Press, 1981), pp. 111–23.
23 J. B. Carroll, "Psychological Aspects of Programmed Learning in Foreign Languages," in *Proceedings of the Seminar on Programmed Learning*, ed. T. H. Mueller (New York: Appleton-Century-Crofts, 1968), p. 63.
24 See T. H. Mueller, "The Development of Curricular Materials (Including Programmed Materials) for Individualized Foreign Language Instruction," in *Individualizing Foreign Language Instruction*, ed. H. B. Altman and R. L. Politzer (Rowley, Mass.: Newbury House, 1971), pp. 148–55; and J. Ornstein, R. W. Ewton, Jr., and T. H. Mueller, *Programmed Instruction and Educational Technology in the Language Teaching Field* (Philadelphia: Center for Curriculum Development, 1971). For a rounded statement of Skinner's views, see B. F. Skinner, *The Technology of Teaching* (New York: Appleton-Century-Crofts, 1968). Skinner does not pass all teaching over to the program. "The contact between teacher and student characteristic of classroom teaching is particularly important when the contingencies are social. In exposition, discussion, and argumentation (written or spoken), in productive interchange, in the exploration of new areas, in ethical behavior, in the common enjoyment of literature, music, and art – here the teacher is important, and he is important as a human being" (p. 254).
25 This definition of a performance objective and the description of an objective that follows are taken from R. M. Valette and R. S. Disick, *Modern Language Performance Objectives and Individualization: A Handbook* (New York: Harcourt Brace Jovanovich, 1972), pp. 17–18.
26 The concepts "micro-language learning" and "macro-language use" (used later in this chapter) are explained and applied in Rivers et al., the *Practical Guides*, chap. 3.
27 For the distinction between skill-getting and skill-using, see chap. 3 of this book.
28 From E. B. and P. J. Hartley, "Teach Yourself to Write Behavioral Objectives: An Exercise for Foreign Language Teachers," in *American Foreign Language Teacher* 3, 2 (1972): 17. The behaviorist ancestry of the objectives is clearly demonstrated in this article by the sentence:

"Remember that a *behavioral* objective is some activity that is *observable* and *measurable*" (p. 18, italics in the original).
29 From F. Steiner, *Performing with Objectives* (Rowley, Mass.: Newbury House, 1975), p. 78.
30 Hartley and Hartley, "Teach Yourself. . .," p. 17.
31 Ibid., p. 18. Italics in the original.
32 J. B. Carroll, "A Model of School Learning," *Teachers College Record* 64 (1963): 723–33.
33 L. A. Jakobovits, *Foreign Language Learning: A Psycholinguistic Analysis of the Issues* (Rowley, Mass.: Newbury House, 1970), p. 95.
34 For two sides of the debate on behavioral or performance objectives, see F. M. Grittner, "Behavioral Objectives, Skinnerian Rats, and Trojan Horses," *FLA* 6 (1972): 52–60; and Steiner, *Performing with Objectives.*
35 This subject is discussed at length in W. M. Rivers, "The Non-Major: Tailoring the Course to Fit the Person – Not the Image," in Rivers, *Speaking in Many Tongues: Essays in Foreign-Language Teaching*, 2d ed. (Rowley, Mass.: Newbury House, 1976).
36 A. N. Whitehead, *The Aims of Education* (New York: New American Library, 1949), p. 13. Original copyright: Macmillan, 1929.
37 J. Dewey, "The Need for a Philosophy of Education," in R. D. Archambault, *John Dewey on Education* (New York: Random House, 1964), p. 11. Originally published 1934. Italics not in the original.
38 I. H. Buchen, "Humanism and Futurism: Enemies or Allies?" in *Learning for Tomorrow: The Role of the Future in Education*, ed. A. Toffler (New York: Random House, 1974), p. 139.
39 R. S. Barth, *Open Education*, p. 28.
40 J. Dewey in Archambault, *John Dewey on Education*, p. 4. Italics in the original.

6. Student-centered trends

1 W. M. Rivers, *Teaching Foreign-Language Skills* (Chicago: University of Chicago Press, 1968), pp. 1–7; 2d ed. (1981), pp. 1–7. The four classrooms were representative of the grammar-translation (A), direct (B), audiolingual (C), and reading (D) methods.
2 See C. Gattegno, *Teaching Foreign Languages in Schools: The Silent Way* (Reading: Educational Explorers Ltd., 1963). Gattegno uses rods of different colors and lengths as a means of eliciting utterances from students.
3 C. A. Curran, "Counseling Skills Adapted to the Learning of Foreign Languages," *Bulletin of the Menninger Clinic* 25, 2 (1961): 78–93. This is discussed in detail in W. M. Rivers, *The Psychologist and the Foreign-Language Teacher* (Chicago: University of Chicago Press, 1964), pp. 96–7. See also C. A. Curran, *Counseling-Learning in Second Languages* (Apple River, Ill.: Apple River Press, 1976).
4 S. Ostrander and L. Schroeder, *Psychic Discoveries behind the Iron Curtain* (Englewood Cliffs, N.J.: Prentice-Hall, 1970). For more infor-

mation on Suggestopaedia, see G. Lozanov, *Suggestology and Outlines of Suggestopedy* (New York: Gordon and Breach, 1978).

5 G. L. Trager, "The Field of Linguistics," *SIL Occasional Papers*, vol. 1 (Oklahoma City: Summer Institute of Linguistics, 1949), p. 4.

6 See "Rules, Patterns, and Creativity," chap. 2 of this book.

7 K. Chastain, *Developing Second-Language Skills: Theory to Practice*, 2d ed. (Chicago: Rand McNally, 1976), pp. 156–7.

8 C. Gattegno, *Teaching Foreign Languages in Schools: The Silent Way*, 2d ed. (New York: Educational Solutions, 1972), p. xii.

9 Ibid., p. ix.

10 C. A. Curran, *Counseling-Learning: A Whole-Person Model for Education* (New York: Grune & Stratton, 1972).

11 G. L. Racle, "Can Suggestopaedia Revolutionize Language Teaching," *FLA* 12 (1979): 39–49. Quotation from p. 40.

12 Curran, *Counseling-Learning in Second Languages*, p. 41.

13 Gattegno, *Silent Way*, 2d ed., p. xii.

14 Ibid., p. 8.

15 Ibid., p. 31.

16 Curran, *Counseling-Learning in Second Languages*, p. 33.

17 Racle, "Can Suggestopaedia...," p. 44.

18 Ibid., p. 46.

19 Curran, *Counseling-Learning in Second Languages*, pp. 1, 7.

20 For a full discussion of the Silent Way, Counseling-Learning–Community Language Learning, and Suggestopaedia, see E. W. Stevick, *Memory, Meaning and Method: Some Psychological Perspectives on Language Learning* (Rowley, Mass.: Newbury House, 1976), chaps. 8–11; and *Teaching Languages: A Way and Ways* (Rowley, Mass.: Newbury House, 1980).

7. The second-language teacher and cognitive psychology

1 M. D. S. Braine, "On Two Types of Models of the Internalization of Grammars," in *The Ontogenesis of Grammar*, ed. D. I. Slobin (New York: Academic Press, 1971), pp. 160–1.

2 Example cited in S. Ervin-Tripp, "Structure and Process in Language Acquisition," in *Bilingualism and Language Contact: Anthropological, Linguistic, Psychological, and Sociological Aspects*, ed. J. E. Alatis, GURT 1970 (Washington, D.C.: Georgetown University Press, 1970), p. 340.

3 R. L. Cooper, "What Do We Learn when We Learn a Language?" *TQ* 4 (1970): 312. Italics in the original. In this article Cooper has provided us with a number of interesting insights into language learning. I have extracted from it the particular sections quoted because in them Cooper has described succinctly a particular viewpoint I wished to analyze and discuss.

4 Notably in *Aspects of the Theory of Syntax* (Cambridge, Mass.: MIT Press, 1965); *Cartesian Linguistics* (New York: Harper & Row, 1966); and *Language and Mind* (New York: Harcourt, Brace & World, 1968).

5 "Possible" in the sense that it is congruent with the particular form of innate equipment with which each human being is endowed and is, therefore, a language of a type that a human being can learn naturally.

6 Chomsky, *Theory of Syntax*, p. 25.

7 Ibid.

8 For a full description of LAD, see D. McNeill, *The Acquisition of Language: The Study of Developmental Psycholinguistics* (New York: Harper & Row, 1970), pp. 70–1.

9 Chomsky, *Language and Mind*, p. 76.

10 Chomsky, *Aspects*, p. 30.

11 V. J. Cook, "The Analogy between First and Second Language Learning," *IRAL* 7 (1969): 216. After examining the research on first-language acquisition of the mid-1960s, Cook sets out four requirements that would need to be met by a method of teaching foreign languages claiming to be based on Chomskyan theory. The suggestion taken up by Cooper is one of these requirements. Cook concludes: "No method can at present claim to fulfill these requirements."

12 Cooper, "What Do We Learn...," pp. 312–13. Italics in the original.

13 "Talking off the tops of their heads," chap. 3 of this book.

14 Chomsky, *Aspects*, p. 53.

15 McNeill, *Acquisition of Language*, p. 36.

16 Cook, "The Analogy...," p. 216.

17 Cooper, in "What Do We Learn...," claiming that "first and second language learning are analogous" and that a second language is not "learned in any fundamentally different way than a first language," nevertheless lists some of the "cognitive differences" in the two situations. "In spite of these differences," he says, "there seems to be little evidence that the actual language-learning *processes* differ for the child and the adult," this despite the abundant research on the cognitive development of the maturing human being. (See J. Bruner et al., *Studies in Cognitive Growth*. New York: Wiley, 1966.) It is essential also to distinguish between informal and formal language-learning contexts (the former being the situation for native-language learners and the latter being more common for older learners). See also "Foreign-Language Acquisition," chap. 12 of this book; and "Reading Fluently," chap. 6 of Rivers, *Speaking in Many Tongues: Essays in Foreign-Language Teaching*, 3rd ed. (Cambridge: Cambridge University Press, 1983).

18 See "Learning a Sixth Language," chap. 13 of this book.

19 In "The Arbitrary Basis of Transformational Grammar," *Language* 48 (1972): 76–87, G. Lakoff says: "The theory of generative semantics claims that the linguistic elements used in grammar have an independent natural basis in the human conceptual system....In generative semantics, possible grammars are limited by the requirement that the non-phonological elements used have a natural semantic basis, independent of the grammar of any particular natural language" (pp. 77–8).

20 R. Ravem, "Language Acquisition in a Second Language Environment," *IRAL* (1968): 175–85, and "Two Norwegian Children's Acquisition of English Syntax," in *Second Language Acquisition: A Book of Readings*,

ed. E. Hatch (Rowley, Mass.: Newbury House, 1978), pp. 149–54. Also in Hatch, see articles by N. Imedaze and D. Uznadze; H. Wode; K. Hakuta; A. Chamot; and G. Butterworth and E. Hatch.

21 J. C. Richards, "Error Analysis and Second Language Strategies," in *Language Sciences* no. 17 (1971): 12–22.

22 H. H. Stern, "First and Second Language Acquisition," in *Perspectives on Second Language Teaching*, Modern Language Center Publications no. 1 (Toronto: OISE, 1970), p. 64.

23 As an example, see E. Pulgram, Review Essay on N. Chomsky, "Language and Mind," in *MLJ* 55 (1971): 474–80.

24 See N. Goodman, "The Emperor's New Ideas," in *Language and Philosophy*, ed. S. Hook (New York: New York University Press, 1969), pp. 138–42.

25 I. M. Schlesinger, "Production of Utterances and Language Acquisition," in Slobin, *Ontogenesis of Grammar*, p. 100.

26 J. Bruner, "On Cognitive Growth," in Bruner et al., *Studies in Cognitive Growth*, p. 43.

27 Braine, "On Two Types of Models...," p. 171.

28 Ervin-Tripp, "Structure and Process...," p. 335.

29 T. G. Bever, "The Cognitive Basis for Linguistic Structures," in *Cognition and the Development of Language*, ed. J. R. Hayes (New York: Wiley, 1970), p. 352.

30 McNeill, *Acquisition of Language*, pp. 70–1.

31 Braine, "On Two Types of Models...," pp. 155–68.

32 E. Lenneberg says that even "children suffering from gross and criminal parental neglect" learn to speak the language of their community, in "A Biological Perspective of Language," in *New Directions in the Study of Language*, ed. E. Lenneberg (Cambridge, Mass.: MIT Press, 1964), p. 67.

33 R. Brown, C. Cazden, and U. Bellugi, "The Child's Grammar from I to III," in *Studies in Child Language Development*, ed. C. A. Ferguson and D. I. Slobin (New York: Holt, Rinehart & Winston, 1973), p. 330.

34 For a similar example, see D. McNeill, "Developmental Psycholinguistics," in *The Genesis of Language*, ed. F. Smith and G. A. Miller (Cambridge, Mass.: MIT Press, 1966), p. 69.

35 See L. A. Jakobovits, "Psychological Perspectives on Individualized Foreign Language Instruction," in *Individualizing Foreign Language Instruction*, ed. H. B. Altman and R. L. Politzer (Rowley, Mass.: Newbury House, 1971), p. 94.

36 See L. A. Jakobovits, *Foreign Language Learning: A Psycholinguistic Analysis of the Issues* (Rowley, Mass.: Newbury House, 1970), p. 25.

37 S. Ervin-Tripp, "An Overview of Theories of Grammatical Development," in Slobin, *Ontogenesis of Grammar*, p. 194.

38 Ibid.

39 R. Weir, "Some Questions on the Child's Learning of Phonology," in Smith and Miller, *Genesis of Language*, p. 162.

40 I. M. Schlesinger, "Production of Utterances...," p. 100. In fact, Chomsky is now up to his third model, Extended Standard Theory.

41 Here I am referring to the active controversy in the 1970s between "classical" transformational-generative grammarians who were further developing Chomsky's system into Extended Standard Theory and the generative semanticists, like Lakoff and McCawley. Lakoff tended to the view that what was innate and universal was an apprehension of logical categories and meaningful relations rather than abstract syntactic principles of a potential language. By 1980, it was estimated that there were at least fifteen vigorously promoted linguistic theories providing models for syntax. The various linguistic schools of thought have provided interesting (and often unexpected) insights into the way language operates. We should draw on these in constructing teaching materials and in helping students learn language, but we should use caution in making definitive statements about language learning based on one particular theory rather than another.

42 J. T. Lamendella, "On the Irrelevance of Transformational Grammar to Second Language Pedagogy," *LL* 19 (1969): 270.

43 Bever, "The Cognitive Basis...," p. 350.

44 For a discussion of the induction-deduction controversy down the ages, see L. Kelly, *25 Centuries of Language Teaching* (Rowley, Mass.: Newbury House, 1969), pp. 34–43. The Lubinus quotation is on p. 37.

45 Ervin-Tripp, in "Structure and Process...," p. 316, states that "at a minimum, it can be shown that imitation requires perception, storage, organization of output, and motor output. In addition, before the storage phase there will be interpretation if the material is interpretable." See also D. O. Hebb, W. E. Lambert, and G. R. Tucker, "Language, Thought, and Experience," *MLJ* 55 (1971): 218.

46 Ervin-Tripp, "Structure and Process...," p. 317.

47 For a more detailed discussion of Piaget's system, particularly as it applies to adolescent and adult learners, see "Reading Fluently," chap. 6 of Rivers, *Speaking in Many Tongues*, 3rd ed.

48 This subject is discussed in detail in R. L. Browne, "Aural and Visual Recognition of Cognates and Their Implications for the Teaching of Cognate Languages," Ph.D. dissertation, Harvard University, 1982; publication no. 8222599 (Ann Arbor, Mich.: University Microfilms).

49 U. Neisser, *Cognitive Psychology* (New York: Appleton-Century-Crofts, 1967), p. 4.

50 Discussed in Ervin-Tripp, "Structure and Process...," p. 317.

51 See "The 'Tip of the Tongue' Phenomenon" in R. Brown, *Psycholinguistics* (New York: Free Press/Macmillan, 1970), pp. 274–301. Discussed with example in chap. 9.

52 For further information on this phenomenon see "Linguistic and Psychological Factors in Speech Perception and Their Implications for Listening and Reading Materials," chap. 5 of Rivers, *Speaking in Many Tongues*, 3rd ed.

53 This remark indicates that listener and speaker both possess the same script (in the sense in which this term is used later in this chapter). Consequently, much detail can be omitted. See "The 'Click of Comprehension Presumes Knowledge of the Script,' " in W. Rivers, *Teaching*

Foreign-Language Skills, 2d ed. (Chicago: University of Chicago Press, 1981), pp. 162–4.

54 Both listening and reading are discussed at length in Rivers, *Speaking in Many Tongues*, 3rd ed., chaps. 5 and 6.

55 Practical exercises for the three stages discussed here are described in chap. 3 of the *Practical Guides*.

56 The "chunking" process is discussed in G. A. Miller, "The Magical Number Seven, Plus or Minus Two: Some Limits on Our Capacity for Processing Information," *Psychological Review* 63 (1956): 81–96.

57 J. M. Keenan, B. MacWhinney, and D. Mayhew, "Pragmatics in Memory: A Study of Natural Conversation," *Journal of Verbal Learning and Verbal Behavior* 16 (1977): 549–60.

58 R. C. Schank and R. P. Abelson, "Scripts, Plans, and Knowledge," in *Thinking: Readings in Cognitive Science*, ed. P. N. Johnson-Laird and P. C. Wason (Cambridge: Cambridge University Press, 1977), pp. 421–32. More fully expounded in R. C. Schank and R. P. Abelson, *Scripts, Plans, Goals and Understanding: An Inquiry into Human Knowledge Structures* (Hillsdale, N.J.: Erlbaum, 1977).

59 As well as the processes outlined in note 45 for imitation, the student's own production of sounds when speaking is dependent on articulatory skill and kinesthetic feedback, which vary from individual to individual, so that the student's internal representation of the sound may not be reflected accurately in production. Students also vary in their inhibitions about making "strange" sounds or in adopting these sounds as a permanent form of expression, since the way we sound is part of our feeling of identity. See Rivers, *Teaching Foreign-Language Skills*, 2d ed., pp. 450–1. Also, during production other factors are competing for the limited processing capacity of the individual. For a full discussion, see Ervin-Tripp, "Structure and Process...," pp. 316–26.

60 See Ervin-Tripp, "Structure and Process...," p. 323.

61 Alexander Pope, *Essay on Criticism* III.

62 Reprinted in J. C. Richards, ed. (1974), pp. 31–54.

8. The natural and the normal in language learning

1 "Macro-language use" is discussed in "Testing and Student Learning," chap. 10 of W. Rivers, *Speaking in Many Tongues: Essays in Foreign-Language Teaching*, 3rd ed. (Cambridge: Cambridge University Press, 1983).

2 "Talking off the Tops of Their Heads," originally published in *TQ* 6 (1972): 71–81. Reprinted in revised version as chap. 3 of this book.

3 Ibid.

4 C. B. Paulston, "Linguistic and Communicative Competence," *TQ* 8 (1974): 347–62.

5 M. A. K. Halliday, *Explorations in the Functions of Language* (London: Edward Arnold, 1973), chap. 1.

6 Ibid., p. 34.

7 Ibid., chap. 2, "The Functional Basis of Language."

8 "Testing and Student Learning," chap. 10 of Rivers, *Speaking in Many Tongues*, 3rd ed. Micro-language learning and macro-language use are also discussed in Rivers et al., *Practical Guides*, chap. 3.
9 See W. M. Rivers and M. S. Temperley (1978), *Practical Guides*, pp. 187–8, 260, and 318–20, for normal purposes of reading and writing. How to relate language-teaching activities to normal purposes of language is one of the major emphases of the *Practical Guides*.
10 R. C. Gardner, "Motivational Variables in Second Language Learning," Research Bulletin No. 298 of the Department of Psychology. (London: University of Western Ontario, 1974), p. 11.
11 L. J. Guidry and C. J. Jones, "What Comes out of the Cowboy's Pen? Tailoring the Course to the Student," *American Vocational Journal*, vol. 49 (1974): 34–5.

9. Apples of gold in pictures of silver

1 From *The Great Didactic of John Amos Comenius*, tr. and ed. by M. W. Keatinge (New York: Russell and Russell, 1896), p. 204. Reproduced in *Approaches to Teaching Foreign Languages*, ed. M. G. Hesse (Amsterdam: North Holland; New York: American Elsevier, 1975), p. 116. First published in 1657.
2 J. A. Comenius, *Orbis Sensualium Pictus* (1658), p. 286. Reproduced in L. G. Kelly, *25 Centuries of Language Teaching* (Rowley, Mass.: Newbury House, 1969), p. 19, from copy in Widener Library, Harvard University (an appropriate repository, as Comenius was invited to be the first president of Harvard College but had to decline).
3 J. H. Pestalozzi, quoted from L. F. Anderson, *Pestalozzi* (New York: McGraw Hill, 1931), reproduced in Hesse, ed., *Teaching Foreign Languages*, p. 250. Italics not in the original. See also D. Jedan, *Johann Heinrich Pestalozzi and the Pestalozzian Method of Language Teaching*, Stanford German Studies, vol. 16 (Bern: Langverlag, 1981).
4 M. D. Berlitz, *Berlitz Method of Teaching Modern Languages*, Illustrated Edition for Children, English Part (New York: M. D. Berlitz, 1907), p. 5. Reproduced in Hesse, ed., *Teaching Foreign Languages*, p. 317. Italics not in the original.
5 Hesse, ed., *Teaching Foreign Languages*, p. 321, reproduces the Fourth Lesson of Berlitz (1907), which uses labeled pictures of parts of the body.
6 R. Meadmore, *The Object-Lesson Handbook: A Companion to 34 Object-Lessons in Pictures without Words* (Paris: Fernand Nathan, 1905), p. 3.
7 Ibid., p. 12.
8 Comenius, *Orbis Sensualium Pictus*, in Hesse, ed., *Teaching Foreign Languages*, pp. 132–3.
9 Meadmore, *Object-Lesson Handbook*, p. 3.
10 For examples from Gouin, see R. Titone, *Teaching Foreign Languages: An Historical Sketch* (Washington, D.C.: Georgetown University Press, 1968), pp. 35–6; Rivers (1975), *Practical Guides*, p. 19; and Rivers and Temperley (1978), *Practical Guides*, p. 21.

11 F. Gouin, *The Art of Teaching and Studying Languages.* Tr. H. Swan and V. Bétis (London: George Philip & Son; New York: Scribner's, 1892), pp. 76–7.

12 H. Sweet, *The Practical Study of Languages* (London: Dent, 1899; rpt. ed., London: Oxford University Press, 1964), p. 73.

13 For a full discussion of frequency counts for English as a second or foreign language, see Rivers and Temperley (1978), *Practical Guides,* pp. 204–12; for French, Rivers (1975), *Practical Guides,* pp. 183–90; for German, Rivers et al. (1975), *Practical Guides,* pp. 180–7; and for Spanish, Rivers et al. (1976), *Practical Guides,* pp. 182–8.

14 The complete list of 850 words for Basic English is given in I. A. Richards and C. Gibson, *Techniques in Language Control* (Rowley, Mass.: Newbury House, 1974), pp. 27–9.

15 Ibid., p. 26.

16 G. Gougenheim, R. Michéa, P. Rivenc, and A. Sauvageot, *L'Elaboration du français fondamental (1er degré). Etude sur l'établissement d'un vocabulaire et d'une grammaire de base,* nouvelle édition refondue et augmentée (Paris: Didier, 1964), p. 151. Italics in the original. For more details about *le français fondamental,* see Kelly, *25 Centuries,* pp. 184–207; Rivers (1975), *Practical Guides,* pp. 183–8; and W. F. Mackey, *Language Teaching Analysis* (London: Longman, 1965), pp. 176–90.

17 J. A. van Ek and L. G. Alexander, *Threshold Level English* (Oxford: Pergamon Press, 1980; originally published Strasbourg: Council of Europe, 1975).

18 J. A. van Ek, *The Threshold Level for Modern Language Learning in Schools* (London: Longman, 1977; originally published Strasbourg: Council of Europe, 1976).

19 D. Coste et al., *Un niveau-seuil* (Strasbourg: Council of Europe, 1976).

20 Ibid., p. 36.

21 See G. L. Racle, "Can Suggestopaedia Revolutionize Language Teaching," *FLA* 12 (1979): 39–49.

22 T. D. Terrell, "A Natural Approach to Second Language Acquisition and Learning," *MLJ* 61 (1977): 325–37; and "The Natural Approach to Language Teaching: An Update," *MLJ* 66 (1982): 121–32.

23 D. H. Hymes, "On Communicative Competence," in *The Communicative Approach to Language Teaching,* ed. C. J. Brumfit and K. Johnson (Oxford: Oxford University Press, 1979), p. 8.

24 R. G. Shapiro, "The Non-learning of English: Case Study of an Adult," in *Second Language Acquisition: A Book of Readings,* ed. E. Hatch (Rowley, Mass.: Newbury House, 1978), p. 253.

25 Ibid., p. 254.

26 *Good News Bible: The Bible in Today's English Version* (New York: American Bible Society, 1976), p. 717.

27 L. A. Vygotsky, *Thought and Language,* trans. E. Hanfmann and G. Vakar (Cambridge, Mass.: MIT Press, 1962), p. 150.

28 Ibid.

29 F. de Saussure, *Course in General Linguistics,* ed. C. Bally and A. Sechehaye, trans. W. Baskin (New York: Philosophical Library, 1959), p. 117.

30 A. M. Collins and M. R. Quillian, "How to Make a Language User," in *Organization of Memory*, ed. E. Tulving and W. Donaldson (New York: Academic Press, 1972), pp. 313–14. Italics not in the original.

31 Saussure, *General Linguistics*, p. 115.

32 L. Wittgenstein, *Schriften* (Frankfurt am Main: Suhrkamp Verlag, 1960), pp. 324–5, quoted by D. I. Slobin in *Psycholinguistics*, 2d ed. (Glenview, Ill.: Scott, Foresman, 1979), p. 195, and in translation on p. 151.

33 G. A. Miller and P. N. Johnson-Laird, *Language and Perception* (Cambridge, Mass.: Belknap Press/Harvard University Press, 1976), p. 704.

34 M. A. K. Halliday, *Explorations in the Functions of Language* (London: Edward Arnold, 1973), p. 72.

35 B. Malinowski, "The Problem of Meaning in Primitive Languages," in *The Meaning of Meaning*, ed. C. K. Ogden and I. A. Richards (New York: Harcourt, Brace, 1946).

36 Halliday, *Functions of Language*, pp. 76–83.

37 T. G. Bever, "Perceptions, Thought, and Language," in *Language Comprehension and the Acquisition of Knowledge*, ed. J. B. Carroll and R. O. Freedle (Washington, D.C.: Winston, 1972), p. 101.

38 Ibid.

39 J. Lyons, *Semantics*, vol. 1 (Cambridge: Cambridge University Press, 1977), p. 238.

40 K. Johnson, "Communicative Approaches and Communicative Processes," in Brumfit and Johnson, eds., *Communicative Approach*, p. 193.

41 G. L. N. Robinson, *Issues in Second Language and Crosscultural Education: The Forest Through the Trees* (Boston: Heinle & Heinle, 1981), p. 28.

42 H. G. Widdowson, "The Teaching of English as Communication," in Brumfit and Johnson, eds., *Communicative Approach*, p. 118.

43 H. G. Widdowson, *Teaching Language as Communication* (Oxford: Oxford University Press, 1978), p. 13.

44 Widdowson, *Teaching Language*, p. 3.

45 W. M. Rivers, "The Natural and the Normal . . .," chap. 8 of this book.

46 This is demonstrated in examples R21 and R23 in chap. 6 of the *Practical Guides*.

47 E. Tulving, "Episodic and Semantic Memory," in Tulving and Donaldson, *Organization of Memory*, p. 386.

48 See also W. M. Rivers and B. S. Melvin, "If Only I Could Remember It All! Facts and Fiction about Memory in Language Learning," chap. 4 of Rivers, *Speaking in Many Tongues: Essays in Foreign-Language Teaching*, 3rd ed. (Cambridge: Cambridge University Press, 1983).

49 Collins and Quillian, "How to Make a Language User," p. 324.

50 J. A. Jenkins, "Language and Memory," in *Communication, Language, and Meaning: Psychological Perspectives*, ed. G. A. Miller (New York: Basic Books, 1973), p. 170. Italics in the original.

51 C. W. Morris, *Foundations of the Theory of Signs* (Chicago: University of Chicago Press, 1960), p. 44.

52 C. S. Hardwick, *Language Learning in Wittgenstein's Later Philosophy* (The Hague: Mouton, 1971), p. 107.

53 J. H. Schumann, "Social Distance as a Factor in Second Language Acquisition," *LL* 26: 135–43; and *The Pidginization Process: A Model for Second Language Acquisition* (Rowley, Mass.: Newbury House, 1978), pp. 69–100.
54 G. A. Miller, "The Magical Number 7 Plus or Minus 2: Some Limits on Our Capacity for Processing Information," *Psychological Review* 63 (1956): 81–96. Reprinted in G. A. Miller, *The Psychology of Communication: Seven Essays* (New York: Basic Books, 1967).
55 R. Brown, *Psycholinguistics* (New York: Free Press/Macmillan, 1970), pp. 274–301.
56 Collins and Quillian, "How to Make a Language User," p. 324.
57 As I wrote this section, I tried free association for a moment and wrote: "Chantal Linda hair color red black eye open door burglar shut-in ill vomiting flu Veronica elevator floor carpet rug clean cleaners house tax Champaign...," a series containing associations of parent, proximity, part, similarity, attribute, consequence, precedence, proximity, superordinate, precedence, and occupation, among others, with many idiosyncratic associations that will be a mystery to my readers.
58 See also Rivers, *Teaching Foreign-Language Skills*, 2d ed. (Chicago: Chicago University Press, 1981), pp. 469–70.
59 W. Kintsch, "Notes on the Structure of Semantic Memory," in Tulving and Donaldson, eds., *Organization of Memory*, p. 302.
60 For techniques for augmenting aural recognition vocabulary, see Rivers et al. (1975, 1976, 1978), *Practical Guides*, chap. 3.
61 This section on learning how to learn vocabulary is more fully developed in Rivers, *Teaching Foreign-Language Skills*, 2d ed., pp. 464–7.
62 Naiman and colleagues list a number of strategies for acquiring vocabulary cited by their thirty-four adult interviewees in N. Naiman et al., *The Good Language Learner*. Research in Education Series, vol. 7 (Toronto: OISE, 1978), pp. 15–16.
63 Jenkins, "Language and Memory," p. 163.
64 Vygotsky, *Thought and Language*, p. 153.

10. Language learners as individuals

1 R. Llewellyn, *At Sunrise, the Rough Music* (Garden City, N.Y.: Doubleday, 1976), p. 202.
2 The National Council on Foreign Language and International Studies has received financial support from the Exxon Educational Foundation; the Ford, Rockefeller, and Hewlett Foundations; and the U.S. International Communication Agency. A further indication of the political and social factors determining the direction language learning and teaching will follow is the bill for an American Defense Education Act introduced in the U.S. Congress in 1982. The act proposes that the federal government provide incentives to local school districts "to improve the quality of instruction in the fields of mathematics, the sciences, the communication skills, foreign languages, technology, and guidance and counseling,

in addition to reaffirming equality of access to education for all." See *ACTFL Public Awareness Network Newsletter* 1, 3 (Sept. 1982).

3 The Group of Experts consisted primarily of René Richterich of Eurocentres, Neuchâtel; John L. M. Trim of Cambridge University; Jan A. van Ek of the University of Utrecht; and David A. Wilkins of the University of Reading.

4 J. L. M. Trim, R. Richterich, J. A. van Ek, and D. A. Wilkins, *Systems Development in Adult Language Learning: A Unit-Credit System for Modern Language Learning by Adults* (Oxford: Pergamon, 1980; originally published 1973, Council of Europe, Strasbourg), p. 1. Italics not in the original.

5 Quoted from Recommendation 814 (1977) on modern languages in Europe, Twenty-ninth Ordinary Session of the Parliamentary Assembly of the Council of Europe.

6 See D. A. Wilkins, *Notional Syllabuses* (Oxford: Oxford University Press, 1976); R. Richterich and J.-L. Chancerel, *Identifying the Needs of Adults Learning a Foreign Language* (Oxford: Pergamon Press, originally published 1975, Council of Europe, Strasbourg); M. Oskarsson, *Approaches to Self-Assessment in Foreign Language Learning* (Strasbourg: Council of Europe, 1978); H. Holec, *Autonomy and Foreign Language Learning* (Oxford: Pergamon Press, for the Council of Europe, 1981); W. M. Rivers and M. S. Temperley (1978), *Practical Guides*, pp. 56–7; and Rivers, *Teaching Foreign-Language Skills*, 2d ed. (Chicago: University of Chicago Press, 1981), chap. 8, pp. 232–6.

7 For a full account of Manpower ESL, see Alicia D. Ramirez and Victoria L. Spandel, "Occupational English as a Second Language," *FLA* 13, 3 (1980): 169–77.

8 "Second language" is the term commonly used for a language, not the native language, that is in general use in the community in which the learner lives and works. In actuality, this may, of course, be a third or fourth language for the learner.

9 For original questionnaire, see Rivers, *Speaking in Many Tongues: Essays in Foreign-Language Teaching*, 3rd ed. (Cambridge: Cambridge University Press, 1983), chap. 2.

10 For a full report of the results of the 1978 survey of Foreign Language Learners' Goals, see Rivers, "Educational Goals," chap. 2 of *Speaking in Many Tongues*, 3rd ed.; and the statements of goals from different countries appended to this chapter. A short report of the 1978 survey is given in the Appendix to this book.

11 For a detailed plan of actions that can be taken to find out the type of program the situation demands, see Rivers, *Speaking in Many Tongues*, 3rd ed., chap. 2.

12 This is the approach of the New York State curriculum guide, *Modern Languages for Everyone* (Albany, N.Y.: Bureau of General Education Curriculum Development, State Education Department, 1978).

13 Rivers, *Speaking in Many Tongues*, 3rd ed., chap. 2.

14 See also note 10, this chapter. Altogether, 581 responses to this questionnaire were received from the fifty states of the United States and

from Algeria, Argentina, Australia, Belgium, Brazil, Canada, Chile, Cuba, Denmark, Egypt, Finland, France, Guatemala, Hong Kong, India, Iran, Iraq, Israel, Italy, Japan, Jordan, Kuwait, Libya, Mexico, Morocco, Netherlands, New Zealand, Nigeria, Norway, Peru, Poland, Portugal, Rumania, Saudi Arabia, Singapore, South Korea, Sudan, Sweden, Switzerland, Syria, Taiwan, Thailand, Tunisia, Turkey, the United Kingdom, USSR, Venezuela, West Germany, and Yugoslavia.

11. Motivation in bilingual programs

1 Bilingual programs in this chapter refer to educational programs for students whose home language is not that of the larger community and the school system (the latter being termed the *majority language*). These programs may be *transitional*: providing instruction in the native (minority) language and in the majority language until the student is able to move over into the regular majority-language classes; *two-way*: with parallel instruction provided in both the home and the majority languages, or with some subjects taught in one language and some in another; *maintenance*: with instruction in the home language continuing in some subjects (often music, art, or ethnic studies) after the student has moved into the regular school classes in the majority language; or *immersion*: where a home-school language switch provides instruction in all school subjects in a minority language for majority language speakers. Where minority language speakers experience a home-school language switch (providing instruction in all subjects in the majority language, often, but not always with an hour or two per day of instruction in the majority language itself as a second langue), the program is usually referred to as a *submersion* program. The types of programs to which this chapter addresses itself are transitional, two-way, and maintenance programs, with some reference to immersion experiments. The type of program and the length of time it is permitted to continue depend on community convictions, which determine funding by a local, provincial, or national agency.
Useful readings are: C. B. Paulston, *Bilingual Education: Theories and Issues* (Rowley, Mass.: Newbury House, 1980); B. Spolsky and R. L. Cooper, eds., *Frontiers of Bilingual Education* (Rowley, Mass.: Newbury House, 1977); B. Spolsky and R. L. Cooper, eds., *Case Studies in Bilingual Education* (Rowley, Mass.: Newbury House, 1978); M. Garner, ed., *Community Languages: Their Role in Education* (Melbourne: River Seine Publications; and Sidney: Applied Linguistics Association of Australia, 1981); Arturo Tosi, "Mother-Tongue Teaching for the Children of Migrants," Survey Article in *LTLA* 12, 4 (1979): 213–31; and Merrill Swain, "Home-School Language Switching," in *Understanding Second and Foreign Language Learning: Issues and Approaches*, ed. J. C. Richards (Rowley, Mass.: Newbury House, 1978), pp. 238–50.

2 I have examined the question of motivation in depth, relating various psychological theories to practical teaching situations in chap. 9 of Rivers, *The Psychologist and the Foreign-Language Teacher* (Chicago: Chicago

University Press, 1964), and in "Motivating through Classroom Techniques," chap. 7 of Rivers, *Speaking in Many Tongues: Essays in Foreign-Language Teaching*, 3rd ed. (Cambridge: Cambridge University Press, 1983).

3 Maslow's hierarchy of basic needs passes from physiological needs through the needs for safety, belongingness and love, esteem, and self-actualization, the hierarchy being based on relative potency. See A. H. Maslow, *Motivation and Personality*, 2d ed. (New York: Harper & Row, 1970), chap. 4.

4 Anomie is a concept first developed by Emile Durkheim, the French sociologist, in *Le Suicide* (Paris: F. Alcan, 1897). For a readily available description of the concept, see quotation from W. E. Lambert in L. A. Jakobovits, *Foreign Language Learning: A Psycholinguistic Analysis of the Issues* (Rowley, Mass.: Newbury House, 1970), pp. 62–3.

5 R. C. Gardner and W. E. Lambert, *Attitudes and Motivation in Second-Language Learning* (Rowley, Mass.: Newbury House, 1972), pp. 11–16.

6 Ibid., p. 132. Gardner and Lambert state: "Thus the development of skill in the language could lead the language learner ever closer to a point where adjustments in allegiances would be called for."

7 One overseas student in the United States, on coming into contact for the first time with the notion that cultural values and attitudes are interwoven with language and must be understood and appreciated if the language is to be used as a native speaker would use it, wrote: "We learn these words without their connotations of the culture in English-speaking countries. It is not debated whether or not we need to learn language in relation to its culture. We are trying hard to get ourselves unshackled from the chains of this colonial gift – the language itself. But we have still to learn it – out of desperate need. Shouldn't we rather stop resisting, and start learning it in a more fruitful way? I have no answer to this question: I would be burnt alive if I said 'yes.'"

8 A. S. Alschuler, D. Tabor, and J. McIntyre, *Teaching Achievement Motivation* (Middletown, Conn.: Educational Ventures, Inc., 1971), p. 60.

9 For a detailed discussion of this subject, see "Individualized Instruction and Cooperative Learning," chap. 5 of this book.

10 Maslow, *Motivation and Personality*, p. 73. Maslow defines self-actualization as "the desire to become more and more what one idiosyncratically is, to become everything that one is capable of becoming" (p. 46).

11 Alschuler et al., *Teaching Achievement Motivation*, p. xviii. Italics not in the original.

12 Described in W. E. Lambert and G. R. Tucker, *Bilingual Education of Children* (Rowley, Mass.: Newbury House, 1972).

13 Normal purposes of language in oral interaction are listed in "Talking Off the Tops of Their Heads," chap. 3 of this book. These categories are expanded and described in more detail, along with normal uses of listening, reading and writing, in the *Practical Guides*. See also chap. 3, n. 11.

14 See the account of Guidry and Jones's experience at East Texas State University in "The Natural and the Normal in Language Learning," chap. 8 of this book.

15 E. Birkmaier, "The Meaning of Creativity in Foreign Language Teaching," *MLJ* 55 (1971): 345–52.

12. Foreign-language acquisition

1 A. W. Staats, "Linguistic-Mentalistic Theory versus an Explanatory S-R Learning Theory of Language Development," in Slobin, *Psycholinguistics* (Glenview, Ill.: Scott, Foresman, 1971), pp. 103–50.

2 T. G. Bever, "The Cognitive Basis for Linguistic Structures," in *Cognition and the Development of Language*, ed. J. R. Hayes (New York: Wiley, 1970), pp. 279–362.

3 L. Bloom, *Language Development: Form and Function in Emerging Grammars* (Cambridge, Mass.: MIT Press, 1970), pp. 232–3.

4 For Halliday's functions applied to language learning, see "The Natural and the Normal in Language Learning," chap. 8 of this book.

5 J. S. Bruner, "From Communication to Language: A Psychological Perspective," *Cognition* 3, 3 (1974–5): 283.

6 Ibid., p. 261.

7 Ibid., p. 271.

8 C. J. Fillmore, "The Case for Case," in *Universals in Linguistic Theory*, ed. E. Bach and R. T. Harms (New York: Holt, Rinehart & Winston, 1968).

9 Inhelder and Piaget postulate three stages of cognitive development: sensory-motor operations (the first 18 months); concrete thinking operations (from 18 months to the 11th or 12th year); and formal thinking operations (from 11 or 12 years, stabilizing at 14 or 15 years). See also H. G. Furth, *Piaget and Knowledge: Theoretical Foundations* (Englewood Cliffs, N.J.: Prentice-Hall, 1969), pp. 29–32. For details of the formal operations stage, see "Reading Fluently," chap. 6 of Rivers, *Speaking in Many Tongues: Essays in Foreign-Language Teaching*, 3rd ed. (Cambridge: Cambridge University Press, 1983).

10 Furth, *Piaget and Knowledge*, pp. 99–105.

11 For a thorough evaluative review of contrastive analysis, error analysis, and second-language acquisition studies in the 1970s, see K. Hakuta and H. Cancino, "Trends in Second-Language Acquisition Research," *Harvard Educational Review* 47 (1977): 294–316.

12 J. Schachter, "An Error in Error Analysis," *LL* 24 (1974): 205–14.

13 This hypothesis is discussed in H. C. Dulay and M. K. Burt, "Creative Construction in Second Language Learning and Teaching," in *On TESOL: New Directions in Second Language Learning, Teaching and Bilingual Education*, ed. M. K. Burt and H. C. Dulay (Washington, D.C.: TESOL, 1975), pp. 24–5.

14 S. P. Corder, "The Significance of Learners' Errors," *IRAL* 5 (1967): 161–70. Reprinted in *Error Analysis: Perspectives on Second Lan-*

221

guage Acquisition, ed. J. C. Richards (London: Longman, 1974), pp. 19–27.

15 N. Chomsky, *Aspects of the Theory of Syntax* (Cambridge, Mass.: MIT Press, 1965), p. 30.

16 S. D. Krashen, "The Monitor Model for Second-Language Acquisition," in *Second-Language Acquisition and Foreign Language Teaching*, ed. R. C. Gingras (Arlington, Va.: CAL, 1978), pp. 1–26.

17 Ibid., p. 2.

18 See Dulay and Burt, "Creative Construction...."

19 S. D. Krashen, J. Butler, R. Birnbaum, and J. Robertson, "Two Studies in Language Acquisition and Language Learning," *ITL: Review of Applied Linguistics* 39–40 (1978): 73–92.

20 B. McLaughlin, "The Monitor Model: Some Methodological Considerations," *LL* 28 (1978): 309–32.

21 J. B. Carroll, "Current Issues in Psycholinguistics and Second Language Teaching," *TQ* 5 (1971): 103–4.

22 Krashen, "The Monitor Model...," says: "Conscious learning is quite different from acquisition and may be a totally independent system.... Conscious learning does not initiate utterances or produce fluency. It also does not contribute directly to acquisition" (pp. 22–3). In S. D. Krashen, *Second Language Acquisition and Second Language Learning* (Oxford: Pergamon Press, 1981), we read that "adults have two independent systems for developing ability in second languages, subconscious language *acquisition* and conscious language *learning*, and that these systems are interrelated in a definite way: subconscious acquisition appears to be far more important" (p. 1). However, Krashen does not spell out in any explicit fashion what this relationship may be and continues to speak of the acquisition and learning systems in the same terms as in the 1978 article. (See n. 16, this chapter.)

23 For a model based on much of the same data as Krashen's, which, however, emphasizes the importance of learning and the teachability of a second language, see G. P. Sampson, "Converging Evidence for a Dialectal Model of Function and Form in Second Language Learning," *AL* 3 (1982): 1–28.

24 McLaughlin, "The Monitor Model...," p. 330.

25 J. B. Carroll, "Conscious and Automatic Processes in Language Learning," *CMLR* 37 (1981): 467, quoting W. Schneider and R. M. Shiffrin, "Controlled and Automatic Human Information Processing: I. Detection, Search, and Attention," *Psychological Review* 84 (1977): 1–66.

26 See Rivers, *The Psychologist and the Foreign-Language Teacher* (Chicago: Chicago University Press, 1964), chap. 6. The two levels of language behavior are discussed in greater detail in "Rules, Patterns, and Creativity," chap. 2 of this book.

27 N. Chomsky, *Language and Mind* (New York: Harcourt, Brace & World, 1968), p. 84.

28 For a discussion of intralingual, overgeneralization, and fossilized errors, see L. Selinker, "Interlanguage," *IRAL* 10 (1972): 219–31.

29 See W. M. Rivers, "Contrastive Linguistics in Textbook and Classroom," GURT 1968: 151–8, *ETF* 8, 4 (1970); and Rivers, *Speaking in Many Tongues*, 2d ed. (Rowley, Mass.: Newbury House, 1976), pp. 64–72; 1st ed., 1972, pp. 36–44.

30 Selinker, "Interlanguage," p. 218.

31 J. Schachter, A. F. Tyson, and F. J. Diffley, "Learner Intuitions of Grammaticality," *LL* 26 (1976): 67–76.

32 Hakuta and Cancino, "Trends...," p. 299. Italics not in the original.

33 I. M. Schlesinger, *Production and Comprehension of Utterances* (Hillsdale, N.J.: Erlbaum, 1977), p. 94.

34 Ibid., p. 96.

35 Discussed in detail in B. S. Melvin, "Recent Developments in Memory Research and their Implications for Foreign-Language Teaching," *Studies in Language Learning* (Urbana, Ill.) 2, 1 (1977): 89–110; and R. L. Klatzky, *Human Memory: Structures and Processes* (San Francisco: Freeman, 1975). For a more detailed discussion, see "Apples of Gold," chap. 10 of this book.

36 As examples, see "Learning a Sixth Language," chap. 13 of this book; and C. M. Fields, "How Berlitz Taught Me Spanish Rapidamente," *Chronicle of Higher Education*, July 17, 1978.

37 J. Schachter, "An Error in Error Analysis."

38 K. Hakuta, "Prefabricated Patterns and the Emergence of Structure in Second Language Acquisition," *LL* 24 (1974): 287–97.

39 E. M. Hatch, "Discourse Analysis and Second Language Acquisition," in *Second Language Acquisition: A Book of Readings*, ed. E. Hatch (Rowley, Mass.: Newbury House, 1978), pp. 401–35.

40 Bruner, "From Communication...," p. 283.

41 Discussed in "Reading Fluently," chap. 6 of Rivers, *Speaking in Many Tongues*, 3rd ed.

42 Quoted from Humboldt in Chomsky, *Theory of Syntax*, p. 8.

43 For a study along these lines, see C. Hosenfeld, "Cindy: A Learner in Today's Foreign Language Classroom," in *The Foreign Language Learner in Today's Classroom Environment*, ed. W. C. Born (Middlebury, Vt.: NEC, 1979), pp. 53–75.

44 U. Neisser, *Cognitive Psychology* (New York: Appleton-Century-Crofts, 1967), pp. 4–5.

Bibliography

Aaronson, Doris, and Rieber, Robert W., eds. 1975. *Developmental Psycholinguistics and Communicative Disorders*. New York: New York Academy of Sciences.

Agard, F., and Dunkel, H. 1948. *An Investigation of Second-Language Teaching*. Lexington, Mass.: Ginn.

Alatis, James E., ed. 1970. *Bilingualism and Language Contact: Anthropological, Linguistic, Psychological, and Sociological Aspects*. Washington, D.C.: Georgetown University Press.

Alatis, James E.; Altman, Howard, B.; and Alatis, Penelope M., eds. 1981. *The Second Language Classroom: Directions for the 1980's*. New York: Oxford University Press.

Alschuler, Alfred S.; Tabor, Diane; and McIntyre, James. 1971. *Teaching Achievement Motivation*. Middletown, Conn.: Educational Ventures.

Altman, Howard B., and James, C. Vaughan, eds. 1980. *Foreign Language Teaching: Meeting Individual Needs*. Oxford: Pergamon Press.

Altman, Howard B., and Politzer, Robert L., eds. 1971. *Individualizing Foreign Language Instruction*. Rowley, Mass.: Newbury House.

Anderson, L. F. 1931. *Pestalozzi*. New York: McGraw-Hill.

Archambault, R. D. 1964. *John Dewey on Education*. New York: Random House. Originally published 1934.

Bach, Emmon, and Harms, Robert T., eds. 1968. *Universals in Linguistic Theory*. New York: Holt, Rinehart & Winston.

Barth, Roland S. 1972. *Open Education and the American School*. New York: Agathon Press.

Benamou, M., and Ionesco, E. 1969. *Mise en Train*. New York: Macmillan.

Berlitz, Maximilian D. 1907. *Berlitz Method of Teaching Modern Languages*. Illustrated Edition for Children, English Part. New York: M. D. Berlitz.

Bloom, Lois. 1970. *Language Development: Form and Function in Emerging Grammars*. Cambridge, Mass.: MIT Press.

Bloomfield, Leonard. 1933. *Language*. London: Allen & Unwin.

Born, Warren C., ed. 1978. *New Contents; New Teachers; New Publics*. Middlebury, Vt.: NEC.

Brown, George Isaac. 1971. *Human Teaching for Human Learning: An Introduction to Confluent Education*. New York: Viking.

Brown, Roger. 1970. *Psycholinguistics*. New York: Free Press/Macmillan.

1973. *A First Language: The Early Stages*. Cambridge, Mass.: Harvard University Press.

224

Browne, Robin L. 1982. *Aural and Visual Recognition of Cognates and Their Implications for the Teaching of Cognate Languages*. Ph.D. dissertation, Harvard University. Ann Arbor, Mich.: University Microfilms No. 8222599.

Brumfit, Christopher J., and Johnson, Keith, eds. 1979. *The Communicative Approach to Language Teaching*. Oxford: Oxford University Press.

Bruner, Jerome S. 1966. *Toward a Theory of Instruction*. Cambridge, Mass.: Harvard University Press.

Bruner, Jerome S.; Olver, Rose R.; Greenfield, Patricia M.; et al. 1966. *Studies in Cognitive Growth*. New York: Wiley.

Burt, Marina K., and Dulay, Heidi C., eds. 1975. *On TESOL '75: New Directions in Second Language Learning, Teaching and Bilingual Education*. Washington, D.C.: TESOL.

Burt, Marina K.; Dulay, Heidi C.; and Finocchiaro, Mary, eds. 1977. *Viewpoints on English as a Second Language*. In Honor of James E. Alatis. New York: Regents.

Butts, R. Freeman, and Cremin, Lawrence A. 1953. *A History of Education in American Culture*. New York: Henry Holt & Co.

Carroll, John B. 1953. *The Study of Language*. Cambridge, Mass.: Harvard University Press.

Carroll, John B., and Freedle, Roy O. 1972. *Language Comprehension and the Acquisition of Knowledge*. Washington, D.C.: Winston.

Chafe, Wallace L. 1970. *Meaning and the Structure of Language*. Chicago: University of Chicago Press.

Chastain, Kenneth. 1971. *The Development of Modern-Language Skills: Theory to Practice*. Philadelphia: Center for Curriculum Development. 2d ed. published 1976 as *Developing Second-Language Skills: Theory to Practice*. Chicago: Rand McNally.

Chomsky, Noam. 1965. *Aspects of the Theory of Syntax*. Cambridge, Mass.: MIT Press.

1966a. *Cartesian Linguistics*. New York: Harper & Row.

1966b. *Topics in the Theory of Generative Grammar*. The Hague: Mouton.

1968. *Language and Mind*. New York: Harcourt, Brace & World. Enlarged ed., 1972.

Comenius, John Amos. 1648. *Orbis Sensualium Pictus*. Prague.

1896. *The Great Didactic of John Amos Comenius*. Tr. and ed. M. W. Keatinge. New York: Russell & Russell. Originally published as *Didactica Magna* (Prague, 1657).

Corder, S. Pit. 1973. *Introducing Applied Linguistics*. Harmondsworth: Penguin Education.

Coste, Daniel; Courtillon, Janine; Ferenczi, Victor; Martins-Baltar, Michel; and Papo, Eliane. 1976. *Un niveau-seuil*. Strasbourg: Council of Europe.

Coulthard, Malcolm. 1977. *An Introduction to Discourse Analysis*. London: Longman.

Cunningham, Kenneth S., and Ross, Dorothy J. 1967. *An Australian School at Work*. Hawthorn, Victoria: Australian Council for Educational Research.

Bibliography

Curran, Charles A. 1972. *Counseling-Learning: A Whole-Person Model for Education.* New York: Grune & Stratton.
de Villiers, Jill G., and de Villiers, Peter A. 1978. *Language Acquisition.* Cambridge, Mass.: Harvard University Press.
1976. *Counseling-Learning in Second Languages.* Apple River, Ill.: Apple River Press.
Dragonas, Phyllis J. 1983. *The High School Goes Abroad: International Home-Stay Exchange Programs.* Washington, D.C.: CAL. In press.
Durkheim, Emile. 1897. *Le Suicide.* Paris: F. Alcan.
Dworkin, M. S., ed. 1959. *Dewey on Education.* New York: Teachers College Press.
Epstein, June. 1981. *A Golden String: The Story of Dorothy J. Ross.* Collingwood, Victoria, Australia: Greenhouse Publications.
Ferguson, Charles A., and Slobin, Dan I., eds. 1973. *Studies in Child Language Development.* New York: Holt, Rinehart & Winston.
Fishman, Joshua A., ed. 1968. *Readings in the Sociology of Language.* The Hague: Mouton.
Furth, Hans G. 1969. *Piaget and Knowledge: Theoretical Foundations.* Englewood Cliffs, N.J.: Prentice-Hall.
Gardner, R. C., and Lambert, W. E. 1972. *Attitudes and Motivation in Second-Language Learning.* Rowley, Mass.: Newbury House.
Garner, Mark, ed. 1981. *Community Languages: Their Role in Education.* Melbourne: River Seine Publications; Sydney: Applied Linguistics Association of Australia.
Gattegno, C. 1963. *Teaching Foreign Languages in Schools: The Silent Way.* Reading: Educational Explorers. 2d ed. 1972, New York: Educational Solutions.
Gingras, Rosario C., ed. 1978. *Second-Language Acquisition and Foreign Language Teaching.* Arlington, Va.: CAL.
Gougenheim, G.; Michéa, R.; Rivenc, P.; and Sauvageot, A. 1964. *L'Elaboration du français fondamental (1er degré). Etude sur l'établissement d'un vocabulaire et d'une grammaire de base.* Nouvelle édition refondue et augmentée. Paris: Didier.
Gougher, Ronald L., ed. 1972. *Individualization of Instruction in Foreign Languages: A Practical Guide.* Philadelphia: Center for Curriculum Development.
Gouin, François. 1892. *The Art of Teaching and Studying Languages.* Trans. H. Swan and V. Bétis. London: George Philip & Son; New York: Scribner's.
Green, Georgia M. 1974. *Semantics and Syntactic Regularity.* Bloomington: Indiana University Press.
Grittner, Frank M. 1977. *Teaching Foreign Languages,* 2d ed. New York: Harper & Row.
Grittner, Frank M., and LaLeike, Fred H. 1973. *Individualized Foreign Language Instruction.* Skokie, Ill.: National Textbook Co.
Gumperz, John J., and Hymes, Dell, eds. 1972. *Directions in Sociolinguistics: The Ethnography of Communication.* New York: Holt, Rinehart & Winston.

Hall, Edward T. 1959. *The Silent Language.* Garden City, N.Y.: Doubleday.
1966. *The Hidden Dimension.* Garden City, N.Y.: Doubleday.

Halle, Morris; Bresnan, Joan; and Miller, George, A., eds. 1978. *Linguistic Theory and Psychological Reality.* Cambridge, Mass.: MIT Press.

Halliday, Michael A. K. 1973. *Explorations in the Functions of Language.* London: Edward Arnold. Rpt. 1977, New York: Elsevier-North Holland.
1975. *Learning How to Mean: Explorations in the Development of Language.* London: Edward Arnold.

Hardwick, Charles S. 1971. *Language Learning in Wittgenstein's Later Philosophy.* The Hague: Mouton.

Hatch, Evelyn, ed. 1978. *Second Language Acquisition: A Book of Readings.* Rowley, Mass.: Newbury House.

Hayes, J. R., ed. 1970. *Cognition and the Development of Language.* New York: Wiley.

Hesse, M. G., ed. 1975. *Approaches to Teaching Foreign Languages.* Amsterdam: North Holland; New York: American Elsevier.

Holec, Henri. 1981. *Autonomy and Foreign Language Learning.* Oxford: Pergamon Press for the Council of Europe.

Hook, Sidney, ed. 1969. *Language and Philosophy.* New York: New York University Press.

Howes, Virgil M., ed. 1970. *Individualization of Instruction: A Teaching Strategy.* New York: Macmillan.

Huxley, Renira, and Ingram, Elizabeth, eds. 1971. *Language Acquisition: Models and Methods.* New York: Academic Press.

Hymes, Dell. 1974. *Foundations in Sociolinguistics: An Ethnographic Approach.* Philadelphia: University of Pennsylvania Press.

Inhelder, Bärbel, and Piaget, Jean. 1958. *The Growth of Logical Thinking from Childhood to Adolescence.* New York: Basic Books.

Jakobovits, Leon A. 1970. *Foreign Language Learning: A Psycholinguistic Analysis of the Issues.* Rowley, Mass.: Newbury House.

Jakobovits, Leon A., and Miron, Murray S., eds. 1967. *Readings in the Psychology of Language.* Englewood Cliffs, N.J.: Prentice-Hall.

Jakobovits, Leon A., and Steinberg, Danny, eds. 1971. *Semantics: An Interdisciplinary Reader in Philosophy, Linguistics, and Psychology.* Cambridge: Cambridge University Press.

Jankowsky, Kurt, ed. 1973. *Language and International Studies.* Washington, D.C.: Georgetown University Press.

Jarvis, Gilbert A., ed. 1974. *Responding to New Realities.* ACTFL Review of Foreign Language Education, vol. 5. Skokie, Ill.: National Textbook Co.

Jarvis, Gilbert A., ed. 1976. *An Integrative Approach to Foreign Language Teaching: Choosing among the Options.* ACTFL Foreign Language Education Series, vol. 8. Skokie, Ill.: National Textbook Company.

Jedan, Dieter. 1981. *Johann Heinrich Pestalozzi and the Pestalozzian Method of Language Teaching.* Stanford German Studies, vol. 16. Bern: Langverlag.

Jespersen, Otto. 1961. *How to Teach a Foreign Language.* London: Allen & Unwin. Originally published in English translation 1904.

Johnson-Laird, Philip N., and Wason, P. C., eds. 1977. *Thinking: Readings in Cognitive Science.* Cambridge: Cambridge University Press.

Kelly, Louis. 1969. *25 Centuries of Language Teaching.* Rowley, Mass.: Newbury House.

Kramsch, Claire J. 1981. *Discourse Analysis and Second Language Teaching.* Washington, D.C.: Center for Applied Linguistics.

Krashen, Stephen D. 1981. *Second Language Acquisition and Second Language Learning.* Oxford: Pergamon Press.

Krashen, Stephen D.; Scarcella, Robin C.; and Long, Michael H. 1982. *Child-Adult Differences in Second Language Acquisition.* Rowley, Mass.: Newbury House.

Lambert, Richard D., and Freed, Barbara F., eds. 1982. *The Loss of Language Skills.* Rowley, Mass.: Newbury House.

Lambert, William E., and Tucker, G. Richard. 1972. *Bilingual Education of Children.* Rowley, Mass.: Newbury House.

Lange, Dale L., ed. 1970. *Individualization of Instruction.* Britannica Review of Foreign Language Education, vol. 2. Chicago: Encyclopedia Britannica.

Lenneberg, Eric, ed. 1964. *New Directions in the Study of Language.* Cambridge, Mass.: MIT Press.

Levin, H., and Williams, J., eds. 1970. *Basic Studies on Reading.* New York: Basic Books.

Littlewood, William. 1981. *Communicative Language Teaching: An Introduction.* Cambridge: Cambridge University Press.

Llewellyn, R. 1976. *At Sunrise, the Rough Music.* Garden City, N.Y.: Doubleday.

Logan, Gerald E. 1973. *Individualized Foreign Language Learning: An Organic Process.* Rowley, Mass.: Newbury House.

Lozanov, Georgi. 1978. *Suggestology and Outlines of Suggestopedy.* New York: Gordon & Breach.

Luria, A. R., and Yudovich, F. I. 1959. *Speech and the Development of Mental Processes in the Child: An Experimental Investigation.* Ed. J. Simon. London: Staples Press.

Lyons, John. 1977. *Semantics,* vols. 1 and 2. Cambridge: Cambridge University Press.

Mackey, William F. 1965. *Language Teaching Analysis.* London: Longman.

McNeill, David. 1970. *The Acquisition of Language: The Study of Developmental Psycholinguistics.* New York: Harper & Row.

Maley, Alan, and Duff, Alan. 1978. *Drama Techniques in Language Learning.* Cambridge: Cambridge University Press.

Maslow, A. H. 1970. *Motivation and Personality,* 2d ed. New York: Harper & Row.

Mead, Robert, G., Jr. 1966. *Language Teaching: Broader Contexts.* NEC 1966. New York: MLA Materials Center.

Meadmore, R. 1905. *The Object-Lesson Handbook: A Companion to 34 Object-Lessons in Pictures without Words.* Paris: Fernand Nathan.

228

Miller, George A. 1967. *The Psychology of Communication: Seven Essays.* New York: Basic Books. Republished 1969, Baltimore, Md.: Penguin.

——— ed. 1973. *Communication, Language, and Meaning: Psychological Perspectives.* New York: Basic Books.

Miller, George A., and Johnson-Laird, Philip N. 1976. *Language and Perception.* Cambridge, Mass.: Belknap Press/Harvard University Press.

Modern Languages for Everyone. 1978. Albany, N.Y.: Bureau of General Education Curriculum Development, State Education Department.

Mohrmann, Christine; Sommerfelt, A.; and Whatmough, Joshua, eds. 1961. *Trends in European and American Linguistics, 1930–1960.* Utrecht: Spectrum.

Morris, Charles W. 1960. *Foundations of the Theory of Signs.* Chicago: University of Chicago Press.

Moskowitz, Gertrude. 1978. *Caring and Sharing in the Foreign Language Class: A Sourcebook on Humanistic Techniques.* Rowley, Mass.: Newbury House.

Mowrer, O. Hobart. 1960. *Learning Theory and the Symbolic Processes.* New York: Wiley.

Mueller, Theodore H., ed. 1968. *Proceedings of the Seminar on Programmed Learning.* New York: Appleton-Century-Crofts.

Munby, John. 1978. *Communicative Syllabus Design.* Cambridge: Cambridge University Press.

Naiman, N.; Fröhlich, M.; Stern, H. H.; and Todesco, A. 1978. *The Good Language Learner.* Research in Education Series, vol. 7. Toronto: OISE.

Neisser, Ulrich. 1967. *Cognitive Psychology.* New York: Appleton-Century-Crofts.

Ogden, C. K. 1930. *Basic English: A General Introduction with Rules and Grammar.* London: Kegan Paul.

Ogden, C. K., and Richards, Ira A. 1946. *The Meaning of Meaning.* New York: Harcourt, Brace.

Ornstein, Jacob; Ewton, Ralph W., Jr.; and Mueller, Theodore H. 1971. *Programmed Instruction and Educational Technology in the Language Teaching Field.* Philadelphia: Center for Curriculum Development.

Oskarsson, Mats. 1978. *Approaches to Self-Assessment in Foreign Language Learning.* Strasbourg: Council of Europe.

Ostrander, S., and Schroeder, L. 1970. *Psychic Discoveries behind the Iron Curtain.* Englewood Cliffs, N.J.: Prentice-Hall.

Paulston, C. B. 1980. *Bilingual Education: Theories and Issues.* Rowley, Mass.: Newbury House.

Pearson, Bruce L. 1977. *Introduction to Linguistic Concepts.* New York: Knopf.

Richards, Ira A. 1943. *Basic English and Its Uses.* New York: Norton. 1944. *Learning Basic English.* New York: Norton.

Richards, Ira A., and Gibson, Christine. 1974. *Techniques in Language Control.* Rowley, Mass.: Newbury House.

Richards, Jack C., ed. 1974. *Error Analysis: Perspectives on Second Language Acquisition.* London: Longman.

ed. 1978. *Understanding Second and Foreign Language Learning: Issues and Approaches.* Rowley, Mass.: Newbury House.

Richterich, René, and Chancerel, Jean-Louis. 1980. *Identifying the Needs of Adults Learning a Foreign Language.* Oxford: Pergamon Press. Originally published 1975, Strasbourg: Council of Europe.

Ritchie, W. C., ed. 1978. *Second Language Acquisition Research: Issues and Implications.* New York: Academic Press.

Rivers, Wilga M. 1964. *The Psychologist and the Foreign-Language Teacher.* Chicago: University of Chicago Press.

1968. *Teaching Foreign-Language Skills.* Chicago: University of Chicago Press. 2d ed., 1981.

1972. *Speaking in Many Tongues: Essays in Foreign-Language Teaching.* Rowley, Mass.: Newbury House. 2d ed., 1976. 3rd ed., 1983, Cambridge: Cambridge University Press.

1975. *A Practical Guide to the Teaching of French.* New York: Oxford University Press.

Rivers, Wilga M.; Allen, Louise H.; Savignon, Sandra J.; and Scanlan, Richard J., eds. 1972. *Changing Patterns in Foreign Language Programs.* Rowley, Mass.: Newbury House.

Rivers, Wilga M.; Azevedo, Milton M.; Heflin, William H., Jr.; and Hyman-Opler, Ruth. 1976. *A Practical Guide to the Teaching of Spanish.* New York: Oxford University Press.

Rivers, Wilga M.; Dell'Orto, Kathleen A.; and Dell'Orto, Vincent J. 1975. *A Practical Guide to the Teaching of German.* New York: Oxford University Press.

Rivers, Wilga M., and Temperley, Mary S. 1978. *A Practical Guide to the Teaching of English: As a Second or Foreign Language.* New York: Oxford University Press.

Rivers, Wilga M., and Nahir, Moshe. *A Practical Guide to the Teaching of Hebrew.* In preparation.

Robinson, Gail L. Nemetz. 1981. *Issues in Second Language and Cross-cultural Education: The Forest through the Trees.* Boston: Heinle & Heinle.

Rogers, Carl R. 1969. *Freedom to Learn.* Columbus, Oh.: Merrill.

Sadow, Stephen A. 1982. *Idea Bank: Creative Activities for the Language Class.* Rowley, Mass.: Newbury House.

Saussure, Ferdinand de. 1959. *Course in General Linguistics.* Ed. C. Bally and A. Sechehaye, trans. W. Baskin. New York: Philosophical Library.

Savignon, Sandra J. 1972. *Communicative Competence: An Experiment in Foreign-Language Teaching.* Philadelphia: Center for Curriculum Development.

Schank, Roger C., and Abelson, Robert P. 1977. *Scripts, Plans, Goals and Understanding: An Inquiry into Human Knowledge Structures.* Hillsdale, N.J.: Erlbaum.

Schlesinger, I.M. 1977. *Production and Comprehension of Utterances.* Hillsdale, N.J.: Erlbaum.

Schumann, John H. 1978. *The Pidginization Process: A Model for Second Language Acquisition.* Rowley, Mass.: Newbury House.

Silberman, Charles E., ed. 1973. *The Open Classroom Reader.* New York: Random House.

Simon, Paul. 1980. *The Tongue-Tied American: Confronting the Foreign Language Crisis.* New York: Continuum.

Skinner, Burrhus F. 1957. *Verbal Behavior.* New York: Appleton-Century-Crofts.

Slobin, Dan I. 1971a. *Psycholinguistics.* Glenview, Ill.: Scott, Foresman. 2d ed., 1979.

ed. 1971b. *The Ontogenesis of Grammar.* New York: Academic Press.

Smith, Frank, ed. 1973. *Psycholinguistics and Reading.* New York: Holt, Rinehart & Winston.

Smith, Frank, and Miller, George A., eds. 1966. *Genesis of Language.* Cambridge, Mass.: MIT Press.

Snow, Catherine E., and Ferguson, Charles A. 1977. *Talking to Children: Language Input and Acquisition.* Cambridge: Cambridge University Press.

Spolsky, Bernard, and Cooper, Robert L., eds. 1977. *Frontiers of Bilingual Education.* Rowley, Mass.: Newbury House.

eds. 1978. *Case Studies in Bilingual Education.* Rowley, Mass.: Newbury House.

Steiner, Florence. 1975. *Performing with Objectives.* Rowley, Mass.: Newbury House.

Stern, H. H., ed. 1970. *Perspectives on Second Language Teaching.* Modern Language Center Publication No. 1. Toronto: OISE.

Stevick, Earl W. 1976. *Memory, Meaning and Method: Some Psychological Perspectives on Language Learning.* Rowley, Mass.: Newbury House.

1980. *Teaching Languages: A Way and Ways.* Rowley, Mass.: Newbury House.

1982. *Teaching and Learning Languages.* Cambridge: Cambridge University Press.

Sweet, Henry. 1899. *The Practical Study of Languages.* London: Dent. Reprint ed., 1964, London: Oxford University Press.

Titone, Renzo. 1968. *Teaching Foreign Languages: An Historical Sketch.* Washington, D.C.: Georgetown University Press.

Toffler, Alvin, ed. 1974. *Learning for Tomorrow: The Role of the Future in Education.* New York: Random House.

Tough, Joan. 1976. *Listening to Children Talking: A Guide to the Appraisal of Children's Use of Language.* London: Ward Lock.

Trim, John L. M. 1980. *Developing a Unit/Credit Scheme of Adult Language Learning.* Oxford: Pergamon Press.

Trim, John L. M.; Richterich, René; van Ek, Jan A.; and Wilkins, David A. 1980. *Systems Development in Adult Language Learning: A Unit-*

Credit System for Modern Language Learning by Adults. Oxford: Pergamon. Originally published 1973, Strasbourg: Council of Europe.

Tulving, Edel, and Donaldson, Wayne, eds. 1972. *Organization of Memory.* New York: Academic Press.

Ur, Penny. 1981. *Discussions that Work: Task-Centred Fluency Practice.* Cambridge: Cambridge University Press.

Valdman, Albert, ed. 1966. *Trends in Language Teaching.* New York: McGraw-Hill.

Valette, Rebecca M., and Disick, Renee S. 1972. *Modern Language Performance Objectives and Individualization: A Handbook.* New York: Harcourt Brace Jovanovich.

van Ek, Jan A. 1977. *The Threshold Level for Modern Language Learning in Schools.* London: Longman. Originally published 1976, Strasbourg: Council of Europe.

van Ek, Jan A., and Alexander, L. G. 1980. *Threshold Level English.* Oxford: Pergamon Press. Originally published 1975 in a preliminary edition as *The Threshold Level in a European Unit-Credit System for Modern Language Learning for Adults.* Strasbourg: Council of Europe.

van Ek, Jan A.; Alexander, L. G.; and Fitzpatrick, M. A. 1977. *Waystage English.* Oxford: Pergamon Press. Originally published 1977 in a preliminary edition as *Waystage.* Strasbourg: Council of Europe.

Vygotsky, L. A. 1962. *Thought and Language.* Trans. E. Hanfmann and G. Vakar. Cambridge, Mass.: MIT Press.

Whitehead, Alfred N. 1949. *The Aims of Education.* New York: New American Library. Original copyright 1929, Macmillan.

Widdowson, Henry G. 1978. *Teaching Language as Communication.* Oxford: Oxford University Press.

Wilkins, David A. 1976. *Notional Syllabuses.* Oxford: Oxford University Press.

Winitz, Harris, ed. 1981. *The Comprehension Approach to Foreign Language Instruction.* Rowley, Mass.: Newbury House.

Wittgenstein, L. 1960. *Schriften.* Frankfurt am Main: Suhrkamp Verlag.

Wright, Andrew; Betteridge, David; and Buckby, Michael. 1979. *Games for Language Learning.* Cambridge: Cambridge University Press.

Yorio, Carlos A.; Perkins, Kyle; and Schachter, Jacquelyn; eds. 1979. *On TESOL '79. The Learner in Focus.* Washington, D.C.: TESOL.

Index

233

errors, correction of, (*cont.*)
159–160, 173; *see also* error
analysis; fossilization of errors;
hypothesis testing; overcompensation; overgeneralization
Ervin-Tripp, S., 91, 92, 93
evaluation, 49
exchange and study-abroad
programs, 15
exercises for intensive practice, 34,
35, 37, 43, 59, 60–4, 174, 176,
184; *see also* drills; pseudo-
communication
expectations, 99, 100
explanation, 4, 5, 7, 35, 37, 58,
83, 90, 124, 165, 174

festivals, *see* camps, clubs, and
festivals
Fillmore, C. J., 156; *see also* case
grammar
films, 127
first-language (L_1) acquisition, 19,
20, 83, 86, 90–1, 95, 105–6,
155–8; behaviorist theory of,
2–3; Brown's research in, 9–10;
functions in, 16, 156–7;
Halliday's theory of, 106–8; and
hypothesis testing, 92; input
for, 93–4; logical relations in,
89–90, 91–2; Schlesinger's
theory of, 164; semantics in, 16,
155, 164; sociolinguistic view
of, 14; *see also* Brown, R. W.;
Bruner, J. S.; functions of
language; $L_1 = L_2$ acquisition
controversy; language acquisition device (LAD); morphemes,
order of acquisition of; Piaget,
J.; Schlesinger, I. M.
foreign-language learning, 161–7;
see also second-language (L_2)
acquisition
forgetting, 99; *see also* language
loss
fossilization of errors, 11, 159, 222
n28; *see also* error analysis;
errors, correction of

français fondamental, le, 115, 118
frequency counts, 117–18, 124,
215 n13
Froebel, F., 65
functionalism, 16, 106–8
functional-notional approach, 119,
135; see also *niveau-seuil*;
notional syllabuses; threshold
level; Wilkins, D. A.
functions of language: in learning,
106–7, 108; in teaching, 10,
16–17

Galyean, B., 23–4
gambits, communicative, 196 n31
games and competitions, 13, 37,
50–1, 61–2, 128; with words,
52, 107, 114
Gardner, R. C., 109, 149, 154
Gary, J. Olmsted, 19
Gattegno, C., *see* Silent
Way
generative semantics, 16, 21, 210
n19, 212 n41
gestures, *see* body language and
gestures
gist, reduction to, 98
global education, 136
Goodman, K. S., 20
Gouin, F., 115, 116, 118
grammar: linguistic, 31; pedagogic,
31, 32–3; *see also* grammar
learning
grammar learning, 8, 30–1, 34,
57–9, 162–3, 165, 172, 181,
183–5; in audiolingual approach, 4, 118; in cognitive
approach, 7, 82; in grammar-
translation approach, 81, 117; in
natural language learning, 12;
in notional syllabus, 17, 119; *see
also* drills; exercises for
intensive practice; grammar;
grammatical system; rule-
governed behavior
grammar-translation approach, 81,
117
grammatical system, 32, 34–9